Reading Matters

What the Research Reveals about Reading, Libraries, and Community

Catherine Sheldrick Ross,
Lynne (E.F.) McKechnie, and
Paulette M. Rothbauer

LIBRARIES
UNLIMITED
A Member of the Greenwood Publishing Group

Westport, Connecticut • London

Library of Congress Cataloging-in-Publication Data

Ross, Catherine Sheldrick.
  Reading matters : what the research reveals about reading, libraries, and community /
    by Catherine Sheldrick Ross, Lynne E.F. McKechnie, and Paulette M. Rothbauer.
      p. cm.
  Includes bibliographical references and index.
  ISBN 1-59158-066-8 (pbk. : alk. paper)
  1. Books and reading. 2. Reading promotion. 3. Reading interests. 4. Reading—
Social aspects. 5. Public services (Libraries) 6. Libraries and community. I.
McKechnie, Lynne. II. Rothbauer, Paulette M. III. Title.
  Z1003.R75 2006
  028'.9—dc22   2005030839

British Library Cataloguing in Publication Data is available.

Library of Congress Catalog Card Number: 2005030839
ISBN: 1-59158-066-8

First published in 2006

Libraries Unlimited, 88 Post Road West, Westport, CT 06881
A Member of the Greenwood Publishing Group, Inc.
www.lu.com

Printed in the United States of America

The paper used in this book complies with the
Permanent Paper Standard issued by the National
Information Standards Organization (Z39.48–1984).

10   9   8   7   6   5   4   3

To Margaret Meek

Contents

Preface

This book was written for people who are interested in reading and in the role that reading plays in people's lives. Because our focus is on the intersection of reading, libraries, and communities, we anticipate that our primary audience will be library staff, library trustees, and students in library information science programs who are interested in libraries, together with parents, teachers, and community members who are interested in reading. Library staff, in particular, have a gut feeling that reading is a Good Thing and that libraries should play—and do play—a vital role in promoting it. But library staff members often find it hard to explain *why*. This book helps them know why and will help them articulate the why to others—such as to board members and trustees who mistakenly think that libraries are improved when popular materials, including series books and romance titles, are weeded out. Teachers and parents sometimes need to be reassured of the value of pleasure reading, a domain in which libraries have taken a lead role. What the research shows is that people become readers by doing lots of reading of extended text; that what motivates novice readers is the pleasure of the reading experience itself; and that libraries, schools, and communities need to support pleasure reading by making the books accessible, by helping readers choose books, by celebrating and modeling the love of reading, and by creating communities of readers—either face-to-face or in an electronic environment—who share the excitement of books.

In the past fifteen years or so, a great deal of research has been published about reading, reader response, audiences, genres, the value of popular culture, book clubs, communities of readers who meet face-to-face or virtually to talk about books, and the role of libraries in promoting literacy and reading. The literature is scattered and fragmentary, however, published variously in scholarly journals and monographs in education, cultural studies, media studies, and library and information science. Library-oriented readers would benefit from having a single accessible source that draws together the scattered findings that relate to reading and the library's role in fostering reading. The goal of this book is to provide a map to the research findings, organized according to themes that are central to people interested in the intersection of reading, readers, and libraries. Although there is a growing body of useful books and Web sites on leisure reading, most focus on one or another specialized aspect of reading—for example, guides to genre fiction, handbooks for reading groups, or guides to collection development or readers' advisory. Or they focus on one segment of the reading public—romance readers or YA (young adult) readers or children. This book takes a synoptic approach to pleasure reading and will include the entire life span of the reader from childhood through adolescence to adulthood.

To illustrate various themes in the book, we have drawn on the extensive empirical data on reading for pleasure that we have gathered in our own research. Lynne McKechnie is engaged in a longitudinal, ethnographic study of the role of the public library in the life of thirty girls. The children were four years old at the beginning of the study, which involved three kinds of data: observations and tape recordings of each child's visit to the library; diaries kept by mothers of the uses made of the library materials in the week following the library visit; and interviews with mothers. Lynne studied the children again when they were seven and plans to follow up when they are ten. Paulette Rothbauer's interest is in young adult readers, especially the role of pleasure reading in the discovery of identity. She has interviewed seventeen readers between the ages of sixteen and twenty-four to find out about their reading interests and experiences. Catherine Ross is engaged in an ongoing research study of adult readers who read for pleasure and at last count had more than 220 open-ended interviews with avid readers. In this book, we use of some of the data from our own research so that the voices of real readers can be heard.

This book has been designed with the expectation that some readers will have a particular interest in a particular aspect of reading or in a particular age of reader. With this in mind, each section is more or less self-contained, with selected suggestions for further reading. You can start at the beginning or dip into it at whatever section most engages your interest.

Chapter 1

The Company of Readers

Catherine Ross

1.1. Henny Penny and the Case for Reading

A lot of experts have been saying glumly that reading is a dying art, being killed off apparently by the competition of television, film, video, and the Internet. People in general—taxi drivers, talk-show hosts, and your next door neighbor—have horror stories to tell about children who can't read or *won't* read or can't spell or can't identify a noun when they see it. Sounding the alarm, books such as Jane Healy's *Endangered Minds* (1990) and Sven Birkerts's *Gutenberg Elegies* (1994) argue that the capacity for reading sustained text is being threatened by competition from the visual media and by the fragmentary nature of the discontinuous hypertext read on screens. Healy claims that what we now call thinking—the ability to pursue the development of an idea, step by step in a logical chain of reasoning, through sentences and paragraphs—is an outgrowth of the linearity of

1

print and is endangered by the shift from reading print to watching screens. Other titles of books on reading and literacy also sound an elegiac note. In some, such as Leslie Fiedler's *What Was Literature?* (1982) and Alvin Kernan's *The Death of Literature* (1990), the losses referred to have to do with the ability to read and write literary texts at the highest levels. Kernan blames television, claiming that "reading of all kinds is becoming a lost skill in a time when more and more information is available on the electronic screen." He claims, "At the deepest level the worldview of television is fundamentally at odds with the worldview of literature based on the printed book" (147).

Other titles such as Jonathan Kozol's *Illiterate America* (1985) and *A Nation at Risk* (National Commission 1983) refer to basic literacy skills that are thought to be disappearing. Newspaper headlines talk about a "literacy crisis," "plummeting" test scores, and "skills gaps" and connect these perceived literacy deficits to social problems such as unemployment, poverty, and crime. In 2004, the National Endowment for the Arts (NEA) released a major study, *Reading at Risk: A Survey of Literary Reading in America*, with a preface by the NEA Chair Dana Gioia (see section 1.3 for more discussion of this study). Gioia warned that "the news in the report is dire" and predicted "an imminent cultural crisis." His summary of the report is the following: "literary reading in America is not only declining rapidly among all groups, but the rate of decline has accelerated, especially among the young" (NEA 2004, vii). Even worse, "at the current rate of loss, literary reading as a leisure activity will virtually disappear in half a century" (xiii).

In the meantime, countering this worried talk about plummeting test scores among the young and weakening literacy skills in the general population is other compelling evidence that literacy is holding its own or improving. Studies show that 95 percent of people in nationwide North American surveys say that they read *something* in the past week; that North Americans spend on average 7 to 10 hours a week of leisure time on reading and say that reading is their second most popular leisure activity after television watching; that book production and book sales are at an all time high; and that, in fact, younger readers are on average more proficient than older ones (Statistics Canada 1996). Over the last hundred years, the literacy rates in North America and elsewhere have steadily gone up (Stedman and Kaestle 1991). The 1983 Consumer Research Study on Reading and Book Purchasing sponsored by the Book Industry Study Group (BISG 1984, 13) starts off with "America is overwhelmingly a nation of readers." A national poll commissioned by the National Education Association was reported in *Reading Today* (June 2001) in an article headed, "Reading remains popular among youth." This article quotes the association's president, Bob Chase, as saying that "the poll shows a strong foundation for sustaining a nation of readers, but indicates the need for continuing attention." Even *Reading at Risk*, which put a heavy emphasis on the predicted imminent cultural crisis, reported on the enormous expansion in book publishing and book sales over the past quarter century: "Books are big business in the United States. In 2000, the book industry published 122,000 new titles and sold a total of 2.5 billion books, a number that has tripled over the past 25 years" (National Education Association 2004, 1).

So what should we believe? Is there a crisis or isn't there? Is reading dying out, or is literacy expanding triumphantly? Is on-screen reading killing off the physical book, reading, and all the values, practices, and social relations associated with print culture, or is it enhancing literacy? After all, the interactive electronic screen culture of Web pages, online discussion groups, blogs, fanzines, and e-mail provide new opportunities for writing as well as reading. The real story turns out to be more complex than a simple either-or account of "national crisis" or "nation of readers." A so-called literacy crisis occurs and the news media carry stories of "declining standards," not when fewer people learn to read but when what counts as literacy changes. Whereas in the nineteenth century, the measure of literacy was being able to sign one's name instead of an X on a document, expectations are now far higher. To be literate in a modern society means not only being able to read documents but being able to use them effectively in everyday life contexts. Literate people make reading and writing work for them.

The concept of literacy has quite clearly evolved beyond the ability to meet some arbitrarily fixed standard such as being able to sign one's name on a marriage license or answering "Yes" to a census survey question, "Can you read and write?" or having completed eight years of schooling. Literacy is now viewed as a continuum of skills from very basic to proficient to the most advanced. As Margaret Meek (1991, 8) pointed out in *On Being Literate,* "There are different versions of literacy, some much fuller than others, some much more powerful than others." The National Assessment of Educational Progress, which tracks literacy in America, has concluded that by yesterday's standards, the news is good: 95 percent of the population *can* read and understand the printed word. However, only a small percentage can understand and use texts at the most complex levels (Kirsch and Jungeblut 1986, iii). Similarly, a Statistics Canada study, *Reading the Future,* found that 22 percent of adult Canadians sixteen years and older fall into the lowest levels of literacy, which means they have serious difficulty reading printed materials. Even so, Level 1 skills "does not mean the absence of literacy, but a lower level of it" (Statistics Canada 1996, 9). Another 25 percent read—but not well: they can manage with printed material that is clearly laid out and where the tasks involved are not too complex (Statistics Canada 1996, 2). So the real problem is that levels of literacy achievement are going up, but they are not going up fast enough. The literacy demands of a complex, modern society are going up even faster.

The public concern about literacy is justified because so much is at stake. To be literate is to be at home in a world that is thoroughly permeated by texts: job application forms, customs declaration forms, bus schedules, driving tests, operator's manuals, maps, restaurant menus, "best before" dates on perishable food, ingredient labels on packaged food, hurricane warnings running along the bottom of the television screen, birthday cards, advertising, and so on. To lack literacy skills means being shut out of jobs and opportunities; conversely, being able to read and write is a ticket to ride. Parents know this and view literacy as an entitlement that schools are expected to deliver. However, literacy is not something that is acquired once and for all in school and then, like an inoculation, lasts a lifetime. Practice is continually required. Those individuals who are the most successful in school have the credentials to pursue jobs where they practice their literacy skills and put an even greater distance between themselves and people who are struggling to read basic texts.

It doesn't usually work for parents to say to their six-year-old, "Learn to read or you won't get into law school"—especially if the child comes from a background where getting into a professional job is not the norm. A shorter-term motivation is needed, and this is where the pleasure of the reading experience itself becomes important. Stephen Krashen (2004) has argued persuasively that the remedy for low literacy skills is what he calls "free voluntary reading" or FVR, which means reading because you want to. Free voluntary reading is what avid readers do every time they pick up a book to read for pleasure. The connection between voluntary reading and powerful literacy is that people learn to read by reading.

What keeps readers reading for the thousands and thousands of hours necessary to produce the bulk of reading experience that creates confident readers? Research suggests that a key factor in motivating readers is pleasure in the reading experience itself. This connection between reading for pleasure and proficiency in reading has been known for a long time. The report *Reading in America* noted that a number of findings "underscore the importance of pleasure as the reason for a higher incidence of book reading and more sustained reading in general" (Cole and Gold 1979, 61). People who do not find reading pleasurable tend to view book reading the way most people view preparing an income tax return: it is hard to do, done under compulsion, and requires long blocks of uninterrupted time. Confident readers, in contrast, find reading effortless. They say that they pick up a book whenever they have a few spare minutes and frequently carry books with them in case they have to wait in line. Because literacy is a skill requiring practice, this means that those who are already good at reading end up getting the most additional practice. As noted in *Reading the Future* (Statistics Canada 1996, 9), "Whether literacy skills are practised in or out of the workplace, individuals with higher literacy skills engage in literacy-related activities more frequently and in greater depth." Hence Krashen's conclusion that "those who do not develop the pleasure reading habit simply don't have a chance—they will have a very difficult time reading and writing at a level high enough to deal with the demands of today's world" (Krashen 2004, x).

In this book, we examine some of the contending arguments about reading, in an attempt to see where libraries and communities fit in and how they contribute to the dialogue on reading. We don't think it is helpful to take a Henny Penny—the sky-is-falling—approach to the research findings on reading. We argue for an expanded definition of reading and readers, generous enough to include both Montaigne studying leather-bound books in his tower and the preschool child chiming in on *Rosie's Walk*. The most common image of the reader is the solitary person—intent scholar or entranced novel reader—who is "lost in a book." But reading is also a social activity, as we discuss in section 4.9. It turns out that reading is a remarkably complex and variable behavior, as is evident from the number of words we use to refer to the act of reading—browsing, scanning, skimming, consulting, studying, immersed or lost in a book, reading for pleasure, reading for information.

The company of readers includes a motley group: the commuter scanning the headlines of the newspaper, the serious scholar, the six-year old reading a primer, the video game player looking at an on-screen help file, the Web surfer using Google to find information about hotel accommodation in New York City, the Harlequin Romance reader, the reader of Booker-Mann prize-winning fiction, and the adolescent reading graphic novels. Clearly reading is not a single activity, but many, with different kinds of purposes, satisfactions, and required skills. There is professional reading, reading for pleasure, skimming to find some small usable fact or quotation, immersion in the text to the point of forgetting your physical surroundings, reading for the first time, rereading, silent reading, reading aloud in a shared reading experience, reading alone with the intention of sharing the reading experience with others in a reading group, and no doubt many other kinds of reading.

Librarians need to be aware of this variety and recognize the role of the library in supporting these different styles and purposes of reading. Reading is woven into a majority of the activities that libraries consider foundational: reference, collection building, the provision of leisure materials, readers' advisory services, storytelling programs, adult literacy programs, and the like. Similarly parents and family members need to be aware of the crucial importance of family literacy practices in the making of avid readers. In a large proportion of cases, people who grow up to be enthusiastic and powerful readers come from families where the bedtime story is a crucial part of the nightly ritual of getting ready for bed and where parents themselves read for pleasure and have books and magazines in the house. In other cases, however, where parents may not be readers, it is an aunt or uncle, a neighbor, a teacher, or a librarian who provides the supportive environment for reading by giving books as gifts or by talking about a favorite book.

There is growing evidence suggesting that an important factor in encouraging reading in children is the presence in the child's life of an adult who helps the child make connections between text and life—in other words, who helps the child see books as sources of knowledge relevant in many situations in the real world (Heath 1983; Cochran-Smith 1984, 21). Nadine Rosenthal's book *Speaking of Reading* (1995), which summarizes interviews with various readers, contains a chapter on "Reading Mentorship," which demonstrates that many adults can also benefit from having a reading mentor. She says, "If you are an avid reader who has seen your own reflection somewhere among these pages, it is now your turn to come to the aid of an infrequent reader" (203).

≻like Brandt's Sponsorship

You will notice that we put special emphasis on the phenomenon of reading for pleasure, because this aspect of reading tends to be downplayed in comparison with the importance given to reading for information or literacy as a life skill. In public libraries, the role of providing leisure reading materials has historically been a source of embarrassment and regret, as if public libraries are at their most respectable when providing utilitarian facts and information. We argue that public libraries are selling themselves short when they downplay leisure reading and apologize for circulating fiction. After all, what do people use libraries, especially public libraries, for? Certainly library users do come to the library to consult electronic resources, check their e-mail, and get answers to their reference questions. But book lending, according to a recent major study by Toyne and Usherwood (2001, 5), "is still perceived to be the major function of the public library, and libraries are seen as natural places for those who wish to develop as readers." Consistently studies have found that people think of the public library as the place, par excellence, to get books— in 1950 the Public Library Inquiry found that 25 percent of books read come from public libraries (Leigh 1950, 31). Thirty years later the Book Industry Study Group's study estimated that one-fifth of all books read come from the public library (BISG 1984, 199).

A large percentage of these books are borrowed for leisure reading, especially fiction—this despite strong efforts by librarians to reduce fiction reading and emphasize the information aspects of library service. In *Hints for Home Reading,* a certain M. F. Sweetser noted with regret in 1880 that "a recent tabulation of the reports of more than a score of public libraries . . . showed that sixty-eight percent, or a little more than two thirds of the books taken out, were novels." He added, "The great Public Library of Boston, with its 370,000 volumes, also reports that fully two-thirds of its issues are of this class, although the consoling statement is added that the ratio is much less than a few years ago, before the attractive catalogues of history, biography and travel were published" (Sweetser 1880, 7).

In 1950, the Public Library Inquiry found that in U.S. public libraries "fiction constitutes 60 to 65 percent of total circulation, ranging from 50 percent or a little less in the largest libraries to 75 percent in the smallest ones" (Leigh 1950, 92). Thirty years later in the United Kingdom, the ratio of two-thirds fiction was unchanged. A British sociologist of reading, Peter Mann, reported on the circulation of books issued in 134 British library authorities in 1979–80 as follows: adult fiction accounted for 59.9 percent of all books circulated; adult nonfiction— 22 percent; children's books—18.1 percent. In summary, he says, "The rough figure of two-thirds of borrowing or borrowers for leisure or relaxation seems to come up time and again in surveys" (Mann 1982, 137). At the end of the twentieth century, Kenneth Shearer (2001, xiii) analyzed circulation statistics in Kentucky, New York, and North Carolina—the only states that separate fiction and nonfiction in their circulation data—and found that fiction accounted for 60 to 70 percent of public library circulation. In Australia, the pattern is similar. Of the total number of books borrowed by respondents in a household survey, 58 percent were fiction, 30 percent nonfiction, and 12 percent children's books (Guldberg 1990, 5). That is, 66 percent of the adult books borrowed were fiction.

In short, a major function of public libraries is the circulation of books for leisure reading, and it always has been. Instead of treating this fact as a shameful secret, we need to celebrate it. The research reviewed in this book indicates that pleasure and free choice are both key elements in the making of readers. Educational researchers are finding that best practices in the teaching of reading in elementary school include encouraging students to choose their own reading materials as well as grouping students by their reading interests and book choices into "literature circles" rather than by reading levels. With their large collections of books and magazines and newspapers that are free to all, promoting leisure reading for all ages is a role that public libraries are ideally suited to fill. It's time for public libraries to stop feeling apologetic and begin to celebrate one of their most important functions: the support of pleasure reading. This is starting to happen as public libraries across North American have revived the readers' advisor and woken up to the fact that people have a deep need not just for facts, but for story.

Case 1: What Does an Avid Reader Look and Sound Like?

Jean (teacher librarian, age forty-four) is one of the some 220 readers interviewed for Ross's study of avid readers who read for pleasure. Here's what Jean said in answer to the question, "Can you come up with a summary of the importance of reading in your life?"

I hate to say that reading is everything, but I think sometimes it's more important than people, and that scares me. It is; it's everything. If I don't have a book, I'm bare. I feel like there's something lacking in my life. I cannot be without something to read; and if it's not a book—if I don't have access to a book (which is fairly rare)—then I'll buy a good magazine. But I have to have something. If I have three or four at one time, that's all the better. I remember when I was in school in a guidance class and one of the girls said to the guidance teacher, "I want to become an artist, and my parents won't let me draw. What do I do?" And the teacher said, "If you are going to be an artist, you will draw. Nobody can stop you from drawing." And that's what it's like being a reader. If you're going to be a reader, nobody can stop you. You are going to be that. That's what reading is to me. I just am. It's part of me.

Comments

Although obviously at the upper end of the scale in terms of committed reading, Jean was not untypical. Like addicts, avid readers in Ross's study talked about laying in supplies, to make sure that they wouldn't be stuck without something to read. They described in compelling terms the way the act of reading itself was an important part of their identity and the way they thought of themselves. For more discussion of this theme, see section 4.3.

What Libraries and Community Members Can Do

1. Be aware that there are a large number of people in your community who are passionate about books and who value access to books of all kinds. Make the library a place that celebrates booklovers. In turn, they will become the library's most vocal supporters in times when advocates are needed for investment in libraries.

2. Resist the view that there is something inherently better about providing facts and information over fiction and stories. If a board member or library trustee wants you to reduce fiction circulation or get rid of series books, point to research findings included in this book that demonstrate the value of pleasure reading in the making of readers.

3. If you are an avid reader, take up Rosenthal's challenge of becoming a reading mentor for an infrequent reader who expresses an interest in reading more. But as Rosenthal (1995, 204) warns, "Tread softly. Don't be overzealous."

To Read More

Krashen, Stephen. 2004. *The Power of Reading. Insights from the Research.* 2nd ed. Westport, CT: Libraries Unlimited.

Krashen reviews the reading literature conducted in education to make the case that what he calls "free voluntary reading" is the best way for children, less literate adults, and second-language readers to become better readers. He argues that direct instruction can never give novice readers enough exposure to language for them to learn to read and spell and develop a rich vocabulary. Rather novices learn to read through exposure to lots of print, which happens most readily when they are reading materials they have chosen and enjoy.

Toyne, Jackie, and Bob Usherwood. 2001. *Checking the Books: The Value and Impact of Public Library Book Reading.* Centre for the Public Library and Information in

Society, University of Sheffield. Available at http://cplis.shef.ac.uk/ checkingthebooks.pdf (accessed January 5, 2005).

Researchers in the Department of Information Studies at the University of Sheffield combined several qualitative approaches—a social process audit, uses and gratification theory, and reader response theory—to figure out the value to society of the reading that is supported by public libraries. They found that the library's provision of "free access to reading material and a wide range of stock . . . were shown as being imperative for establishing and maintaining the reading habit."

References

Birkerts, Sven. 1994. *The Gutenberg Elegies: The Fate of Reading in an Electronic Age.* Boston and London: Faber and Faber.

Book Industry Study Group. 1984. *1983 Consumer Research Study on Reading and Book Purchasing.* New York: Book Industry Study Group.

Cochran-Smith, Marilyn. 1984. *The Making of a Reader.* Norwood, NJ: Ablex.

Cole, John Y., and Carol S. Gold, eds. 1979. *Reading in America: Selected Findings of the Book Industry Study Group's 1978 Study.* Washington, D.C.: Library of Congress.

Fiedler, Leslie. 1982. *What Was Literature?* New York: Simon & Schuster.

Guldberg, Hans Hoegh. 1990. *Books—Who Reads Them? A Study of Borrowing and Buying in Australia.* Sydney: Australia Council for the Arts.

Healy, J. M. 1990. *Endangered Minds: Why Our Children Don't Think.* New York: Simon & Shuster.

Heath, Shirley Brice. 1983. *Ways with Words: Language, Life and Work in Communities and Classrooms.* New York: Cambridge University Press.

Kernan, Alvin. 1990. *The Death of Literature.* New Haven, CT: Yale University Press.

Kirsch, Irwin S., and Ann Jungeblut. 1986. *Literacy: Profiles of America's Young Adults.* ETS Report no. 16-PL-02. Princeton, NJ: National Assessment of Educational Progress.

Kozol, Jonathan. 1985. *Illiterate America.* Garden City, NY: Anchor Press.

Krashen, Stephen. 2004. *The Power of Reading. Insights from the Research.* 2nd ed. Westport, CT: Libraries Unlimited.

Leigh, Robert D. 1950. *The Public Library in the United States.* The General Report of the Public Library Inquiry. New York: Columbia University Press.

Mann, Peter. 1982. *From Author to Reader: A Social Study of Books.* London and Boston: Routledge and Kegan Paul.

Meek, Margaret. 1991. *On Being Literate.* London: The Bodley Head.

National Commission on Excellence in Education. 1983. *A Nation at Risk: The Imperative for Educational Reform.* Available at http://www.ed.gov/pubs/ NatAtRisk/ title.html (accessed January 4, 2005).

National Endowment for the Arts. 2004. *Reading at Risk: A Survey of Literary Reading in America.* Research Division Report #46. Washington, DC. Available at http://www.nea.gov/pub/ReadingAtRisk.pdf (accessed December 16, 2004).

Rosenthal, Nadine. 1995. *Speaking of Reading.* Portsmouth, NH: Heinemann.

Shearer, Kenneth. 2001. Preface to *The Readers' Advisor's Companion.* Edited by Kenneth D. Shearer and Robert Burgin. Englewood, CO: Libraries Unlimited.

Statistics Canada. 1996. *Reading the Future: A Portrait of Literacy in Canada.* The Canadian Report of the International Adult Literacy Survey. Available at http://www.statscan.ca/english/freepub/89F0093XIE/free.htm (accessed January 4, 2005).

Stedman, Lawrence C., and Carl F. Kaestle. 1991. "Literacy and Reading Performance in the United States from 1880 to the Present." Edited by Carl F. Kaestle et al., *Literacy in the United States: Readers and Reading since 1880.* New Haven, CT, and London: Yale University Press.

Sweetser, M. F. 1880. "What the People Read." In *Hints for Home Reading: Putnam's Handy Book Series of Things Worth Knowing,* 5–14. Edited by Lyman Abbott. New York: G. P. Putnam's Sons.

Toyne, Jackie, and Bob Usherwood. 2001. *Checking the Books: The Value and Impact of Public Library Book Reading.* Centre for the Public Library and Information in Society, University of Sheffield. Available at http://cplis.shef.ac.uk/checkingthebooks.pdf (accessed January 5, 2005).

1.2. The "Fiction Problem"

Reading for pleasure has had a checkered history in libraries. Herbert Putnam (1890, 263–4), who later became the president of the American Library Association, expressed the view that public libraries were open to criticism in one area: that they supplied material that was merely recreational:

> I do *feel* emphatically (1) that a public library is justifiable only as a part of our educational system; (2) that it is no part of our educational system to provide people with flabby mental nutriment; and (3) that unless our public libraries draw the line absolutely at what they believe to be of educational value they will forfeit the confidence of the better minds in the community. . . . I do mean to exclude merely flabby literature. The flabby is a step removed from the vicious; but logically it is as alien to the purpose for which a library is established to admit the one as the other. Of course flabby books are admitted of a supposed necessity—to attract the reader who has not read at all, or who has formed a taste for only that class of literature and must be tolled by it in order to be wheedled into something better. Our American public hardly needs to be wheedled into the reading habit; it reads too many books, not too few.

Librarians who wanted to make a case for fiction in public library collections argued that novel reading was a stepping stone that helped beginning readers until they were ready to move on to higher grade materials. At the Lake Placid Conference of 1894, George Watson Cole (1894, 20) told participants at a session on "the ruck of common novels" that the public library had an obligation to cater to the tastes of the whole community. The masses want fiction and should be provided with fiction. But fortunately, he said quoting another contemporary librarian F. B. Perkins, "Readers improve; if it were not so, reading would not be a particularly useful practice." Readers "who begin with dime novels and story weeklies may be expected to grow into a liking for a better sort of stories, then for the truer narrative of travels, of biography and history, then for essays and popular science, and so on upward." In other words, if librarians do their jobs properly, readers might start with popular fiction and story, but that's OK because eventually they would climb the reading ladder to nonfiction. It had to be admitted, however, that backsliding was often observed. Just when the librarian thought that the reader had graduated to philosophical essays and sermons, he, or often she, would be found reading a novel.

Circulation figures told the tale. In the 1880s and 1890s, *Library Journal* from time to time printed columns titled "Fiction in Libraries," in which panels of leading librarians were invited to weigh in on the fiction problem with opinions and best practices. Circulation figures were apologetically discussed: fiction was frequently reported as making up 25 to 30 percent of the collection but accounting for 70 to 80 percent of the circulation. Libraries across the continent worked valiantly to reduce the proportion of fiction circulation but to little effect. According to Dee Garrison (1979, 68), "In 1878 the Mercantile Public Library in San Francisco reported 71.4 per cent of its circulation was fiction, while .6 per cent was religious works. In the same year the Indianapolis library crowed that its fiction circulation had dropped from 80 to 72 per cent, after heroic efforts had been made by the librarian to reduce fiction reading."

What to do? Esther Jane Carrier's book *Fiction in Public Libraries 1876–1900* (1965) provides a well-documented account of the steps that some librarians took to address the "fiction problem." William Kite, librarian of the Friends' Free Library of Germantown, Pennsylvania, banned *all* works of fiction on the grounds that it was the responsibility of the librarian to protect impressionable readers, especially children, women, and the working classes: "A very considerable number of the frequenters of our library are factory girls, the class most disposed to seek amusement in novels and peculiarly liable to be injured by their false pictures of life" (quoted in Carrier 1965, 32–34).

Less drastic than banning *all* fiction, the solution practiced by William M. Stevenson was to remove from the shelves only the most popular fiction books. He reported a limited success in reducing fiction circulation when he removed books by Horatio Alger, Bertha M. Clay, May Agnes Fleming, Martha Finley (the Elsie Books), E. P. Roe, Mrs. E.D.E.N. Southworth, and others who catered to a taste for "recreation and entertainment only." In his 1896 annual report of the Carnegie Free Library of Allegheny, Pennsylvania, he said that because "devotees of this class of literature will read nothing else," it was inevitable that overall library circulation figures would drop. His weeding program which increased the proportion of "solid and substantial" reading was justified on the grounds that "It is certainly not the function of the public library to foster the mind-weakening habit of novel-reading among the very classes—the uneducated, busy or idle—whom it is the duty of the public library to lift to a higher plane of thinking" (Stevenson 1896, 9–10).

Contrary to the notion that people's reading tastes eventually improved if they kept on reading long enough, Stevenson (1897) reported that he had taken pains to follow the reading of certain "fiction fiends" and had found that "Once the [novel reading] habit is formed, it seems as difficult to throw off as the opium habit." Mellen Chamberlain, Librarian of the Boston Public Library, agreed. He started off his 1883 "Report of Fiction in Public Libraries" by comparing fiction reading with the cholera epidemic and reported glumly, "All attempts to stamp out the evil have proved vain; nor has its virulence been sensibly diminished" (Chamberlain 1883, 208).

The problem seemed intractable, although a variety of ingenious methods to decrease fiction circulation were attempted, such as the "two-book system" and the "six-months rule." With the former, readers were allowed to withdraw two books, but the second book had to be nonfiction and usually not a recently acquired work (Carrier 1965, 172–3). The purpose of the six-month rule was to stifle the demand for the latest new novel by delaying buying a work of fiction until it is six months old (Putnam 1890, 264). Other librarians made a point of always recommending nonfiction to fiction readers in the hope of improving reading tastes. The Toronto Public Library's Annual Report of 1906 claimed that "our able chief librarian, by tactful and courageous selection, endeavors to see to it that only the best class of fiction is placed on our shelves and he is proud to point to the fact that day by day and year by year there is a strong gain and increase in the percentage of solid works as against books of fiction. I am quite free to confess that there is an indulgence in the reading of trashy novels which is destructive to the mind."

The article "The Question of Fiction Reading," published in *The Library Journal* in January 1902, summarized a symposium on fiction reading published in the *New York Times Saturday Review*, with contributions from Herbert Putnam, A. E. Bostwick, F. M. Crunden, W. E. Foster, and Miss C. M. Hewins, among others. According to the *Library Journal* summary,

> Suggestions from others as to ways and means of reducing fiction reading include references to the "duplicate collections" of new books for which a small fee is charged; calling attention to generous supplies of interesting works of travel, biography, history, science etc.; issue of special reading lists; the two-book method; and the sifting out of novels of inferior quality. Mr. Crunden says: "Keep novels in the background. Advertise and push other books. . . . We reduced the demand for Mrs. Southworth about 75% in five or six months by placing in every volume of hers issued a call slip containing 20 titles of a little better novels."

In the mid–twentieth century, the Public Library Inquiry did a major stock-taking of the role of the public library in American society and discovered that things hadn't changed much: fiction still accounted for 60 to 65 percent of library circulation (Leigh 1950, 93). More generally the Public Library Inquiry found that although 85 to 90 percent of the adult population read newspapers and about two-thirds of adults read magazines, only about 50 percent read books; people got about one-quarter of the books they read from public libraries; and about 25 percent of all adults were library cardholders (28–31).

The Public Library Inquiry threw into sharp relief the contrast between what public libraries were actually doing and the then-current American Library Association objectives for what public libraries *should* be doing. The objectives emphasized the public library's role as an educational institution primarily, but the research showed that public libraries were in the entertainment business. Bernard Berelson's conclusion was that the public library should relinquish the entertainment function to others and refocus its efforts on providing high quality materials to the "serious" and "culturally alert" minority who are the core of library users (Berelson 1949, 130). While the majority of librarians surveyed in the Public Library Inquiry agreed with the ALA objectives and presumably with Berelson, there were "dissenters" who pointed out that "recreation comprises a large part of present-day library service to its patrons":

> The dissenters really challenge the whole tendency of the document
> [ALA objectives for public libraries] to limit library materials to those
> dealing with serious and significant personal and social interests. As
> opposed to this limitation, they say that the public library's function is
> to give the people what they want whatever the nature and quality of the
> demand may be. (Leigh 1950, 22)

Now, more than fifty years after the Public Library Inquiry, it is clear that the dissenters have gained ground and the public library objective of providing recreational materials has been thoroughly recognized. However, the same arguments that used to be made against fiction get redeployed in attacks on other kinds of marginalized materials that appeal to readers with the lowest status: the romance genre, the western, series books, video games, graphic novels, and so on. It is still alleged that series books and Harlequin Romances ruin readers by being *too* interesting and *too* easy to read—in short "flabby mental nutriment." In many quarters, it is still the case that reading gets official approval only to the extent that it can be shown to contribute to performance and productivity in the classroom or workplace. When reading is done in solitude and for pleasure, the suspicion arises that it may be unproductive and involve an escape from, or even a substitute for, life itself (see section 4.4, "Better than Life") .

Attitudes are changing as research accumulates that demonstrates the value of pleasure reading in the making of confident readers—but not quite fast enough, as one of us discovered in an encounter with a teacher who dismissed a ninth-grade student's request to read *The Fellowship of the Ring* for a book report, claiming that Tolkien's book is "a trivial story written at the grade five or six level." The residue of guilt associated with pleasure reading is a legacy of an earlier era when fiction was a "problem." With her path-breaking book *Genreflecting* (1982), Betty Rosenberg did more than anyone else to legitimize the place of fiction reading and especially genre fiction in libraries. Rosenberg's First Law of Reading, "Never apologize for your reading tastes," has with good reason been included in all six editions of *Genreflecting* and can't be repeated too often.

Case 2: The Inveterate Novel Reader

Here's how Noah Porter described the fiction reader in an influential book on books and reading published in the late nineteenth century:

> The *spell*-bound reader soon discovers, however, that this *appetite,* like that for confectionery and other sweets, is the soonest cloyed, and that if pampered too long it *enfeebles* the appetite for all other food. The reader of novels only, especially if he reads many, becomes very soon an intellectual *voluptuary*, with feeble judgment, a vague memory, and an incessant *craving* for some new excitement. It is rare that a reader of this class studies the novels which he seems to read. . . . He reads for the story as he says, and it usually happens that the sensational and extravagant, the piquant and equivocal stories are those which please him best. Exclusive and excessive novel reading is to the mind as a kind of *intellectual opium eating*, in its stimulant effects upon the phantasy and its stupefying and bewildering influence, on the judgment. An inveterate novel-reader speedily becomes a *literary roué*, and this is possible at a very early period of life. It now and then happens that a youth of seventeen becomes almost an intellectual idiot or an *effeminate weakling* by living exclusively upon the *enfeebling swash* or the *poisoned stimulants* that are sold so readily under the title of tales and novels. An *apprenticeship at a reform school* in literature, with a spare diet of statistics and a hard bed of mathematical problems, and the simple beverage of plain narrative, is much needed for the recovery of such inane and half-demented mortals. (Porter 1877, 231–2, emphasis added)

Comments

In the late nineteenth century, certain beliefs about reading were sufficiently familiar that they could simply be stated as a given: that reading is like eating, with classes of books that range from drugs, poisons, pabulums, and candy to strong meats and beefsteak; that books are arranged in order of value from dime novels and trashy fiction at the bottom to nonfictional, nonnarrative forms such as sermons and philosophy at the top; that librarians have an educational duty to help readers climb the reading ladder from the poorer to the better work; that fiction must be justified in the public library for its educational value, not simply as a source of pleasure; that intensive reading of a few nonfiction books such as the Bible is much better than extensive reading of a lot of popular fiction; that fiction is potentially dangerous as an agent that instills "false views of life," especially in impressionable women, children, and working-class readers.

What Libraries Can Do

1. Be on the watch for practices that are taken for granted but that reflect an earlier era of suspicion toward popular fiction. Take steps to eradicate such practices. Resist the view that there is something magic about a particular format or genre, making it inherently better to read a book rather than a magazine article, or to read one kind of book rather than another.

2. Provide series entries in the catalogue so that readers can find other books in the series and read the series in order, if desired.

3. Look at book budgets and how the money is allocated. Is it relatively easy to make the case for a $200 art book on Persian carpets but a battle royal to get money for duplicate copies of the latest Harry Potter book?

To Read More on the "Fiction Problem"

Carrier, Esther Jane. 1965. *Fiction in Public Libraries 1876–1900*. New York and London: Scarecrow Press.

> With generous quotes from her nineteenth-century sources, Carrier provides a thorough look at what eminent librarians said at the time on such topics as "What is trash?" "High Quality," and "Reading Improvement." She concludes by noting that the "fiction problem" remained unsolved for some considerable time. According to Bernard Berelson's *Public Library Inquiry*, conducted at the midpoint of the twentieth century, "at least half the public library's circulation seemed to be composed of 'poor' fiction."

Golden, Catherine J. 2003. *Images of the Woman Reader in Victorian British and American Fiction*. Gainesville: University Press of Florida.

> This book is an engaging reflection on both fictional representations and pictorial representations of the female reader in the late nineteenth century, including such famous readers as Charlotte Bronte's Jane Eyre "shrined in double retirement" reading in a secluded window seat behind red moreen curtains and Flaubert's Emma Bovary married to boring Charles and reading about "rapture,"

"passion," and "bliss." Golden summarizes then-current biological, medical, and moral arguments about why reading, and especially sensationalistic novel reading, was more damaging to women than to men, inducing a drug-like dependence, threatening women's reproductive health, making them inattentive mothers, and sometimes leading to sexual scandal, ruin, and suicide.

Ross, Catherine Sheldrick. 1987. "Metaphors of Reading." *The Journal of Library History, Philosophy, and Comparative Librarianship* 22, no. 2 (spring): 147–63. Reprinted in Katz, Bill, ed. 1988. *Library Literature: The Best of 1987,* 190–206. Metuchen, NJ: Scarecrow Press.

Ross examines the metaphors that the library profession has used to talk about and think about reading—"Reading Is Eating" and "Reading Is a Ladder"— and argues that these metaphors have entailments that have affected the treatment of fiction in public libraries.

References

Berelson, Bernard. 1949. *The Library's Public: A Report of the Public Library Inquiry.* New York: Columbia University Press.

Carrier, Esther Jane. 1965. *Fiction in Public Libraries 1876–1900.* New York and London: Scarecrow Press.

Chamberlain, Mellen. 1883. "Report of Fiction in Public Libraries." *Library Journal* 8 (September/October): 208.

Cole, George Watson. 1894. "Fiction in Libraries: A Plea for the Masses." *Library Journal* 19 (January): 18–21.

Garrison, Dee. 1979. *Apostles of Culture: The Public Librarian and American Society, 1876–1920.* New York: Collier Macmillan.

Leigh, Robert D. 1950. *The Public Library in the United States.* The General Report of the Public Library Inquiry. New York: Columbia University Press.

Porter, Noah. 1877. *Books and Reading: or, What Books Shall I Read and How Shall I Read Them?,* 231–2. 4th ed. New York: Scribner, Armstrong.

Putnam, Herbert. 1890. "Fiction in Libraries: Minneapolis (Minn.) Public Library." *Library Journal* 15, no. 9 (September): 263–4.

Rosenberg, Betty. 1982. *Genreflecting: A Guide to Reading Interests in Genre Fiction.* Englewood, CO: Libraries Unlimited.

[Stevenson, William M.] *Sixth Annual Report of the Librarian . . . for the year ending 28 February 1896.* Allegheny, PA: Carnegie Free Library, pp. 9–10. Quoted in Carrier 1965, p. 258.

Stevenson, William M. 1897. "Weeding Out Fiction in the Carnegie Free Library of Allegheny, Pa." *Library Journal* 22 (March): 133–5.

"The Question of Fiction Reading." 1902. *Library Journal* 27, no. 1 (January): 18.

1.3. Myths about Reading

Which of the following statements about reading do you think are true?

- Books and reading are being killed off by television and film and the Internet.

- People don't read *as much* as they used to.

- Young people don't have the reading skills of previous generations.

- The quality of materials that people read is sinking. Where formerly people read Milton and Shakespeare and the King James Bible, now they are reading mostly trashy novels and self-help books.

- The surfeit of junk reading, too much television watching, and too much Internet surfing and video-game playing is killing off people's ability to read higher-quality books.

- It is the job of the librarian to steer readers away from popular magazines, series books, and genre fiction and get them to climb a reading ladder to the best books.

- Men don't read.

- Boys don't read.

- Men don't read fiction.

- Women don't read science fiction.

- Book readers are introverted bookworms who are antisocial and not very well rounded.

- Real reading is a solitary affair.

None of these claims are entirely true, and some are just plain false. It's *not* true that men don't read fiction; they *do* read fiction, but just not to the same extent as women do. Steven Tepper (2000, 269) found that male and female readers tend to make different reading choices, with men more likely to read history and current events and women more likely to read fiction. However, there is still a sizable proportion of male readers who *do* read fiction. A U.K. study on book reading, buying, and borrowing habits in Britain, *Reading the Situation* (Book Marketing Limited 2000, 10) found that 45 percent of men read fiction compared with 77 percent of women.

Nor is it true that people on average are reading less or that publishers are publishing fewer print materials than previously. Over the last hundred years, universal education together with increases in the efficiency of the distribution system for print has resulted in a dramatic expansion in reading and in the market for books. As noted in more detail in section 4.1, surveys of reading conducted in various high-income countries over the past fifty years have repeatedly found that about 80 to 90 percent of the population reads *something*; 50 to 60 percent of the population reads books as a chosen leisure activity; and 10 to 15 percent of the population are avid readers, who borrow and buy the lion's share of books, magazines, newspapers, and other media consumed.

Although some printed formats are in eclipse—for example, hard-copy newspapers are read by proportionately fewer people and especially fewer younger people than they were thirty years ago—other formats such as electronic newspapers, electronic journals, and Web sites are burgeoning. The 2004 National Endowment for the Arts study found that the number of adult Americans doing creative writing not for work or school increased between 1982 and 2002 from 11 million to almost 15 million—a rate faster than the growth in population (NEA 2004, 22). And despite gloomy prognostications, printed books are not yet an endangered species. Over the last seventy-five years, a graph showing books published or sold worldwide would show a steady increase. According to the 2004 NEA study, the American book industry published 122,000 new titles in 2000 and sold a total of 2.5 billion books (NEA 2004, 1).

Nor are readers dying out. The BISG study, *1983 Consumer Research Study on Reading and Book Purchasing,* which admittedly has a vested interest in finding book reading to be a vibrant activity, starts off its report with the claim, "America is overwhelmingly a nation of readers" (BISG 1984, 13). The survey *Reading in Canada, 1991*, based on mailed questionnaires completed by seven thousand Canadian households, reported that 94 percent of Canadians read for pleasure on a weekly basis, compared with 88 percent in 1978 (Graves 1992, 15). In this study, all formats were counted and not just books. On average, Canadians claimed to spend seven hours a week reading for pleasure, with more than half that time spent reading books and the rest spent reading newspapers and magazines. The conclusion: *"Reading in Canada, 1991* demonstrates that the overwhelming majority of Canadians enjoy reading" (Graves 1992, 11). Similarly, a study published in 2001 by the Australia Council for the Arts, *National Survey of Reading, Buying & Borrowing Books,* claims that "Australians are a nation of readers." According to this Australian survey, 72 percent of adult Australians surveyed claimed to have read for pleasure in some format in the previous week, and 47 percent said they had read a book for pleasure in the past week; the average Australian claimed to spend eight hours a week reading (Nielsen 2001, 21–25).

So a nation of readers or a nation at risk? As we shall see in section 4.1, different studies have converged on the finding that 50 percent or so of a national population in a high-income country reads books for reasons other than work or study. Is this good or bad? Authors of reading studies come to diametrically opposite conclusions depending on what they count as "real reading," whether they emphasize the glass-half-empty or the glass-half-full scenario, and whether they have an interest in using the study as a call to arms for educational reform (e.g., more testing, more phonics). As noted in section 1.1, in July 2004 the National

Endowment for the Arts (NEA) published a reading study titled *Reading at Risk* with a press release headlined, "Literary Reading in Dramatic Decline . . . Fewer than Half of Americans Now Read Literature." The study was drawn from the literature segment of a large-scale survey, Survey of Public Participation in the Arts (SPPA), conducted by the Census Bureau in 2002 with a survey sample of 17,000 adult Americans. It turned out that in 2002, 56.6 percent of respondents claimed to have read a book for leisure (not for work or study) and 46.7 percent claimed to have read literature—down 4 percent and 7 percent, respectively, from a similar SPPA study conducted in 1992.

"Literary reading" in the NEA study was defined as leisure-time reading of novels, short stories, plays, or poetry but not nonfiction such as cookbooks, travel books, self-help, biography, political analysis, history, or science. Of these literary readers, 96 percent read novels and short stories, which category includes not just literary fiction but also popular genres such as mysteries, romances, science fiction, fantasy, and westerns. (This privileging of popular fiction over nonfiction is an interesting reversal of the hierarchy examined in section 1.2 that put nonfiction at the top and associated nonfiction with the cultural and civic benefits here associated exclusively with fiction reading.) In the press release, NEA chair Dana Gioia is quoted as saying, "This report documents a national crisis. . . . The decline in reading among every segment of the adult population reflects a general collapse in advanced literacy. To lose this human capacity—and all the diverse benefits it fosters—impoverishes both cultural and civic life."

A story by Bruce Weber in the *New York Times,* "Fewer Noses Stuck in Books in America, Survey Finds" (July 8, 2004) echoed the gloomy language of the report itself: "tide of indifference," "sobering profile," "precipitous decline," "stark depiction," "erosion accelerated," and "literature's diminished importance." The *New York Times* story aims at balance by quoting two reading experts: a professor of English from Columbia who called the findings a "real cause for concern" and the librarian emeritus for the state of California who said that if almost 50 percent of Americans are reading literature, "that's not bad, actually."

Without any actual evidence, the NEA report fingered the new electronic media as the culprit behind the reading crisis. Gioia claims, "*Reading at Risk* merely documents and quantifies a huge cultural transformation that most Americans have already noted—our society's massive shift toward electronic media for entertainment and information" (NEA 2004, vii). The Executive Summary explains, "The decline in reading correlates with increased participation in a variety of electronic media, including the Internet, video games, and portable digital devices" (xii). This increased participation is presented as a bad thing because "Reading a book requires a degree of active attention and engagement" while most electronic media "often require no more than passive participation. Even interactive electronic media, such as video games and the Internet, foster shorter attention spans and accelerated gratification" (vii).

dn t agree w/ this

This explanation opposing the active book reader to the passive screen watcher and video gamer echoes the arguments made in Sven Birkerts's *The Gutenberg Elegies*. However, we seem to be expected to take on faith this technological explanation for the 7 percent decline in literary readers; it is not supported by empirical data presented in the study itself. "A national crisis" makes headlines, but the more reasoned analysis contained within the body of the report itself actually tells a different story:

> If the 2002 data represent a declining trend, it is tempting to suggest that fewer people are reading literature and now prefer visual and audio entertainment. Again, the data—both from SPPA and other sources—do not readily quantify this explanation. . . . [T]elevision does not seem to be the culprit. In 2002, those who do read and those who do not read literature watched the same amount of TV per day—three hours worth. The Internet, however, could have played a role . . . However, this pattern of falling literary reading rates timed with rising home Internet use may only be coincidental. The SPPA did not ask if people substituted Internet surfing for reading literary works. . . . Newspaper and magazine articles about post–September 11 developments and the war in Afghanistan may have hindered literary reading during the survey year. (NEA 2004, 30)

Attempts to find empirical evidence for claims that electronic media are killing off reading have generally been unsuccessful. Studies of leisure-time use indicate that the same people watch television *and* read, sometimes at the same time. Adults in high-income countries in the past seventy-five years have gained considerable additional discretionary time—time left over after paid work, family care, personal care, and so on. They have chosen to use this extra discretionary time on increased media use, especially television watching. According to Douglas Galbi, senior economist in the Federal Communications Commission, "growth in discretionary time can account for all the time currently spent watching television" (Galbi 2001). So television watching did not displace reading so much as get added onto it. The 1978 BISG study found, as have later investigations, that time spent viewing television does *not* displace time spent reading books, because both book readers and non–book readers spent about the same amount of time watching television (Cole and Gold 1979, 56). People with the lowest levels of literacy watch the most television, but the significance of this finding is contestable. The Canadian report on the findings of the International Adult Literacy Survey (IALS) said, "It is tempting to interpret television-watching as a *cause* of lower literacy skills, but it is just as plausible to argue that lower skills *lead to* more viewing time. Those with low skills may not be able to get the information they need from print, simply because of their low skills, and may turn to television instead" (Statistics Canada 1996, 9).

For all demographic groups, studies have found that television watching is far and away the most popular leisure-time activity in whatever country it is studied. Using data from television rating services, Pippa Norris summarized average weekly television viewing time for adults in OECD (Organization for Economic Cooperation and Development) countries and found a range from a low of 17 to 19 hours in Austria, Denmark, Finland, South Korea, Netherlands, Norway, Portugal, Sweden, and Switzerland to a high of 27 to 30 hours in Hungary, Japan, Mexico, Turkey, the United Kingdom, and the United States (Norris 2000, quoted in Galbi 2001, 15). To track who is watching what for how long, television rating services such as Nielsen Media Research use electronic setmeters attached to television sets in sample households that measure the times when the television set is on and to which channel the set is tuned. Setmeters don't take into account those times when the set is on but no one is watching or when television is being used as background for some other activity.

To address these problems, time-use studies have started to investigate the economy of attention. They have discovered that the hours reported spent on various leisure activities add up to a lot more hours than there are in a day. This is because, for most activities except sleeping, people are often doing two or more things at the same time. So people are eating breakfast or taking public transit to work, but they are also reading the morning paper; they are working at their desk, but they also have the radio on; they are eating dinner in a restaurant but are also socializing with friends; they are babysitting but are also reading a magazine or book; they are working out on their exercise bike while they are watching a cop show on television or listening to music. A telephone survey in 1981 of some 2,600 randomly selected Canadians were asked to recall minute by minute what they did in a twenty-four-hour period yesterday or the day before. Respondents were asked if they were doing anything else besides the first activity mentioned. Up to four activities could be recorded as occurring simultaneously, and these activities were coded as either primary or secondary. After television watching, "the second most popular cultural activity is reading, which accounts for 30 minutes of the day. An additional 17 minutes is spent reading as a secondary activity" (Kinsley and Graves 1983, 24). Table 1.1 shows the prevalence of multitasking. Reading newspapers and magazines resembled television watching in terms of occurrence with other activities. Reading books was more than 10 percent more likely to occur as a primary activity than was reading a newspaper or watching television.

Table 1.1

Distribution of percentage of episodes of an activity according to whether the activity occurs alone or with other activities

Type of Activity	One Primary	One Primary, One Secondary	One Primary, Two Secondary
Work	47	37	11
Movies	43	40	15
Books	30	38	15
Newspaper	19	44	25
Television	18	47	27
Magazines	16	43	23
Radio/records	1	54	35

From Kinsley and Graves 1983, 39.

Clearly the relationship among the various media is a complex one. Readers often report that they chose to buy or borrow particular books because their interest was whetted by seeing the film, watching a television program, reading a book review, or coming across information on the book on the Internet. In the ALA-sponsored national study called *Book Reading and Library Usage* (Gallup 1978, 17), more than one-quarter of respondents (28 percent) reported reading a book in the past year because of something they saw on television. Similarly, in the 1984 BISG study, 27 percent said that an important factor for them when choosing a book to read was that they had seen the movie or TV show based on the book (BISG 1984, 134). So, for example, many who saw the film *The Hours* were stimulated to read Michael Cunningham's novel *The Hours,* and some of those went on to read Virginia Woolf's *Mrs. Dalloway.* Publishers know this, which is why they reprint a novel with a cover showing the film characters. With its insatiable need for content, the 500-channel universe features television programs about books that reach audiences that do not read the book review section of newspapers, Oprah's Book Club being only the most famous.

In short, although electronic media obviously compete with reading for the scarce resource of attention, it is not a simple matter of one medium killing off another or television watching killing off reading. Many studies show that "heavy" or "frequent" readers tend also to be greater than average consumers of film, television, and recorded music, not to mention museum visits, concerts, and live theater. As early as the Public Library Inquiry, it was known that book readers consume more of almost every kind of communication media. Berelson notes, "In the case of every major medium of communication except radio, book readers listen and see and read more than those who do not read books. . . . The book readers in any community are prominent members of a group who are interested in communications in general" (Berelson 1949, 8–9). Hence the concept of the "communications elite," people who read more books, magazines, and newspapers; go to more films; watch more television; and are members of more community associations than the average person.

Contrary to the widely held view of the book reader as an introverted book-worm, many studies conducted over many years have arrived at a totally different image: the book reader as engaged with the world and socially involved. The report of the 1983 BISG survey of adult book reading and book purchasing concluded the following:

> Book readers are often portrayed in literature, films, or on stage as solitary, somewhat aloof, self-absorbed personalities whose devotion to their books seems to take the place of interaction with the rest of the world. This study, however, proves this stereotype to be nothing more than a myth. Far from being introverted or social outcasts, book readers emerge as well-rounded individuals active in a wide range of social and cultural activities. On the contrary, in many ways they are *more active* than non-book readers. (BISG 1984, 71)

In comparison to nonreaders, book readers report doing *everything* more—except taking naps. "Readers are highly social people, frequently engaged in the arts, sports, and community life," the 2004 NEA study reported; literary readers are three times more likely than non–book readers to attend a performing arts event, almost four times more likely to visit an art museum, more than two-and-a-half times more likely to do volunteer or charity work, and more than one-and-a-half times more likely to attend a sports event (NEA 2004, 5). Unfortunately, the 2004 NEA study doesn't report the participation in these activities by people who read nonfiction books but not fiction. However, it seems likely that patterns in 2004 are not very different from the ones reported in Zill and Winglee's *Who Reads Literature?* (1990), which analyzed comparable data from the SPPA collected twenty years earlier in 1992. From this analysis, it is apparent that the three groups—literature readers (57 percent), readers but not of literature (26 percent), and nonreaders (15 percent)—can be placed on a continuum. Literature readers do more of everything; nonreaders do the least; and "readers but not of literature" are in the middle but closer to literature readers end. Table 1.2 provides dramatic evidence of the differing rates of reporting participation among the three groups on *all* types of activities, not just cultural ones.

Table 1.2

Proportion of a readership group that has engaged in an activity in the past 12 months.

Leisure Activities	Literature Readers (%)	Readers but Not Literature (%)	Nonreaders (%)
Cards, board games	77	62	27
Attend movies	75	59	25
Attend sports events	59	43	17
Jog, exercise	65	43	18
Home/car repair	66	60	28
Gardening	69	53	34
Charity work	36	21	9
Go to a zoo	41	25	11

From Zill and Winglee 1990, 15.

Unlike the 2004 NEA study, which seems to imply that literary reading *causes* participation in other socially desirable activities ("The decline in literary reading foreshadows an erosion in cultural and civic participation," xii), many other studies have looked for an underlying factor such as level of education or of income that accounts for both reading *and* other forms of participation. For example, low income could explain why a single mother on welfare would be less likely to jog, read a book, repair a car, or go to the zoo. A. W. McClellan, professor at the College of Librarianship Wales, suggested that book readers are more active because, well, they are just smarter (McClellan 1973, 17). He claims that "each media acts as an 'energising agent' in relation to the others. In other words, the active, intelligent members of a community use all forms of communication to a much greater extent than do the less intelligent" (19). For Jan Hajda (1964), the factor that explains the inactivity of non-readers is depression and social isolation. Hajda investigated the myth of the avid reader as social misfit in a doctoral dissertation completed at the University of Chicago titled "An American Paradox: People and Books in the Metropolis." He found that the opposite is the case: book readers are more likely to be actively engaged with the community, and nonreaders are more likely to be lonely and isolated.

Research Tells Us

Large-scale surveys produce aggregate data that tell us a good deal about readers on average but can give a misleading picture if applied to any given, individual reader. For example, Michael Madden analyzed data from the national lifestyle study conducted in the United States by Leo Burnett in 1973. The data came from a stratified random sample of 7,829 respondents who completed a mail questionnaire. Leo Burnett was a market researcher who pioneered a segmentation approach to lifestyle. For the national lifestyle study, he collected data in the following areas: 1) product usage segments (nonusers, light, medium, and heavy users); 2) social class segments; and 3) demographic segments (young/ old, educated/uneducated, high income/low income, etc.).

Madden took Burnett's sample and sorted it initially by the "product usage segment" of library use. He then examined the differences in demographics, attitudes, and behaviors between non–library users and heavy library users. Compared with library users, for example, nonusers are more apt to dislike change, do not want to try new things, avoid foreign locales, and are suspicious of communists and hippies. According to Madden (1979, 37), "The values of the female nonuser are very traditional. Those activities they do have are taking naps and watching TV." Here in rank order are the activities, interests, and opinions that correlated most strongly with nonuse of the library by women:

1. All men should be clean shaven every day.

2. I get satisfaction out of cleaning.

3. TV is my primary source of entertainment.

4. I often wish for the good old days.

5. I like the look of a large lamp in a picture window.

6. I don't feel safe outside home at night.

On the basis of this analysis by library use segment, Madden concluded, likely erroneously, that female nonusers are poor bets for library outreach programs because their interests and activities are so limited.

Case 3: The So-Called Media Competition

At the 1984 International Federation of Library Associations (IFLA) conference, Heinz Steinberg, a German authority on books and reading, introduced his paper on "The Book in the So-Called Media Competition" with the following anecdote:

In the year 1953, when the film industry was in its hey-day, I was standing in a friend's book shop. The old gentleman looked sadly though the display window at the cinema opposite, where a queue had gathered in front of the box-office. Wrinkling his forehead with worry about the future of the book, he said: "That is where the people spend their money instead of buying my lovely books."

But, strangely enough, in this very year the increase in the German book selling turnover was especially high. By chance, I found the reason for this. In a small printed catalogue, entitled "From the Film to the Book," there was, for example, the world famous *Blue Angel* with Emil Jannings and Marlene Dietrich. Next to it the novel from which it was filmed: Heinrich Mann's *Professor Unrath.*

The catalogue, which the cinemas distributed at the box-offices, had an enormous success. People poured in their thousands, catalogue in hand, into the book shops and libraries. Booksellers and librarians complained because they had not sufficiently covered the demand. To me came the truth that the cinema has never robbed the book trade of customers, but has brought many to it. The cinema has also never competed with libraries, but has far more increased the use of them.

Comments

As Steinberg pointed out, each new media technology—newspapers, magazines, radio, television—has been greeted with prophesies about the death of the book, and in each case the doomsayers have been proved wrong. Steinberg concluded, "Television is today what the newspaper was in 1910, radio in 1930 and the film in 1950: the main promoter of book-reading" (1984, 6). It's not hard to guess which new technology in 2000 Steinberg would have named as the main promoter of reading. Steinberg did identify one way to reduce reading: cuts in library budgets. Libraries not only buy books themselves, they also stimulate their users to buy books. Steinberg cites Peter Mann, the English sociologist, who found out that the best places for bookshops are library buildings.

References

Berelson, Bernard. 1949. *The Library's Public: A Report of the Public Library Inquiry.* New York: Columbia University Press.

Book Industry Study Group. 1984. *1983 Consumer Research Study on Reading and Book Purchasing: Focus on Adults.* New York: Market Facts.

Book Marketing Limited. 2000. *Reading the Situation: Book Reading, Buying and Borrowing Habits in Britain.* London: Library and Information Commission.

Cole, John Y., and Carol S. Gold, eds. 1979. *Reading in America: Selected Findings of the Book Industry Study Group's 1978 Study.* Washington, DC: Library of Congress.

Galbi, Douglas A. 2001. "Communications Policy, Media Development, and Convergence." Available at http://www.galbithink.org/media2.pdf (accessed July 14, 2004).

Gallup Organization. 1978. *Book Reading and Library Usage: A Study of Habits and Perceptions.* Conducted for the American Library Association. Princeton, NJ: Gallup Organization.

Graves, Frank L. 1992. *Reading in Canada, 1991.* Ottawa, ON: Ekos Research Associates.

Hajda, Jan. 1964. "An American Paradox: People and Books in the Metropolis." Ph.D. dissertation, University of Chicago.

Kinsley, Brian L., and Frank Graves. 1983. *The Time of Our Lives: Explorations in Time Use*. Vol. 2. Ottawa, ON: Department of Communications.

Madden, Michael. 1979. *Lifestyles of Library Users and Nonusers*. Occasional Papers, No. 137, University of Illinois Graduate School of Library Science.

McClellan, A. W. 1973. *The Reader, the Library, and the Book*. London: Clive Bingley.

National Endowment for the Arts. 2004. *Reading at Risk: A Survey of Literary Reading in America*. Research Division Report #46. Washington, D.C. Available at http://www.nea.gov/news/news04/ReadingAtRisk.html (accessed December 15, 2004).

Nielsen, A. C. 2001. *National Survey of Reading, Buying & Borrowing Books*. Australia Council for the Arts. Available at http://www.oxco.gov.au/arts_ resources/publications/a_national_survey_of_reading,_buying_and_borrowing_ books/files/394/acnielsen_report.pdf (accessed January 4, 2005).

Norris, Pippa. 2000. *A Virtuous Circle: Political Communications in Post-Industrial Societies*. New York: Cambridge University Press.

Statistics Canada. 1996. *Reading the Future: A Portrait of Literacy in Canada*. The Canadian Report of the International Adult Literacy Survey (IALS). Available at http://www.statscan.ca/english/freepub/89F0093XIE/free.htm (accessed January 4, 2005).

Steinberg, Heinz. 1984. "The Book in the So-Called Media Competition." IFLA International Seminar on Role of Books and Reading in Cultural Development. Moscow, May 22–24, 1984 [typescript].

Tepper, Steven J. 2002. "Fiction Reading in America: Explaining the Gender Gap." *Poetics* 27: 255–75.

Zill, Nicholas, and Marianne Winglee. 1990. *Who Reads Literature? The Future of the United States as a Nation of Readers*. Cabin John, MD: Seven Locks Press.

1.4. Histories of Reading

Robert Darnton (1990, 187), historian of the book and of reading, has remarked that "Reading has a history. It was not always and everywhere the same." For us at the beginning of the twenty-first century, we may think of reading quintessentially as an encounter of a solitary reader with a book made of paper. But readers in ancient Greece read from scrolls made of papyrus (the dried and split stems of a reed-like plant), the codex books read by the Romans were made of parchment (animal skins), and now an increasing percentage of reading involves computer screens and e-books. The physical format of the text in all its materiality makes a big difference to the experience of readers and to their understanding of what reading is, whether they are breathing in the pungent smell of vellum and parchment or watching ephemeral letters dance on a computer screen. Clearly literacy practices change as societies change. Readers are embodied and reading is contextualized in a particular time and place. As Roger Chartier (1994, 8) points out, "Reading is not uniquely an abstract operation of the intellect: it brings the body into play, it is inscribed in a space and a relationship with oneself or with others."

A number of recently published histories of reading spell out the varieties of reading forms and practices from cuneiform tablets to hypertext. One thing is clear: reading is an activity that is deeply connected to its historical period and to the material and social conditions in which the reading occurs. Stephen Roger Fischer's *A History of Reading* (2003), for example, includes a chapter titled "The Papyrus Tongue," which describes the way that the papyrus scroll demanded to be read aloud. With no separation between words, no punctuation, and no distinction between upper and lower case, the physical act of reading aloud gives "meaning to the tongue where no meaning is evident to the eye" (47).

Although we may now think of reading as a silent and solitary activity, reading out loud and reading to an audience was the norm for centuries and continued after the codex book had replaced the papyrus scroll. Alberto Manguel's *A History of Reading* (1996) spends a chapter on "The Silent Readers," in which he tells the story of Father Ambrose, reader extraordinaire in the fourth century A.D. Father Ambrose was the first recorded instance of a silent reader. We know about him because Saint Augustine found his practice of silent reading so remarkable that he described the phenomenon in his *Confessions*. According to Augustine, "When he read, his eyes scanned the page and his heart sought out the meaning, but his voice was silent and his tongue was still. . . [O]ften when we came to visit him, we found him reading like this in silence, for he never read aloud." Eyes scanning the page and tongue held still—as Manguel points out, this is exactly how we would describe a reader today, and yet this manner of silent reading did not become usual in the west until the tenth century (Manguel 1996, 43). Chartier (1994, 8–9) says, "A history of reading must not limit itself to the genealogy of our own contemporary manner of reading, in silence and using only our eyes; it must also (and perhaps above all) take on the task of retracing the forgotten gestures and habits that have not existed for some time."

With each new technology from the introduction of the alphabet on, elegiac voices have been heard idealizing the older technology and warning of the dangers and losses attendant on the new. The classic case is Socrates, whom James O'Donnell (1998, 18) has described as standing "on the boundary between the worlds of spoken and written discourse." In the *Phaedrus,* Socrates is represented as deeply critical of writing. In the dialogue as written by Plato, Socrates tells the young man Phaedrus that written words, when queried, maintain the same majestic silence as a painting. Written words seem to talk to you as though they are intelligent, but if you want to know more, they give you the same answer over and over again, and they make no distinction between suitable and unsuitable readers.

Socrates tells Phaedrus the parable of the king of Egypt and the god Throth, who was the inventor of writing, geometry, and dice. Presenting to the Egyptian king each one of his inventions in turn, Throth says about the art of writing that this wonderful invention is a recipe for memory and wisdom. Not so, says the king of Egypt. In fact, relying on the written word will implant forgetfulness, because people will cease to exercise memory but will rely instead on external marks. "What you have discovered is a recipe not for memory, but for reminder," said the king of Egypt. The very things that Socrates objected to—the objectivity and externality of writing—are the qualities that we now value. And it is only because the Socratic dialogues were recorded by his disciple Plato that we can know about them 2,400 years later.

Gutenberg's invention of moveable type in the fifteenth century sped up the rate of change in reading practices. With the first Bible printed with movable metal type in Mainz, Germany, in 1456, readers realized at once its advantages: speed of production, relative cheapness, and the uniformity of the texts. Lucien Febvre and Henri-Jean Martin (1976) provide some astonishing details about the explosion of printed texts in Europe from 1450, when there was only one printing press operating in the whole of Europe, to 1500 by which time more than 15,000 titles had been published and around 20 million books had been printed. The story of the transformative effect of Gutenberg's invention has been told many times. Various accounts make a connection between advancing print culture and the fundamental changes that were going on in Europe at the same time: transformations in habits of thought, the secularization of society, the increasing authority of science, the expansion of universities as centers of learning, the rise of the nation state, the expansion of printing in vernacular languages, the decline of Latin, and the loss of the Roman Catholic Church's monopolistic power over salvation. For example, Marshall McLuhan and Walter Ong have examined the transition from an oral world dominated by the ear to a world of printed texts dominated by the eye (McLuhan 1962; Ong 1982). Elizabeth Eisenstein (1979) argues that it was not the capacity to read and write alone that transformed western Europe but the capacity of the printing press for mechanical reproduction that made possible widespread circulation of texts, the rise of modern criticism, and the emergence of the celebrity author.

Gutenberg's printed Bible was an attempt to imitate the handmade manuscript bibles of the time, with its vellum pages and typefaces designed to look like scribal letter shapes. But the logic of speed, cheapness, and reproducibility almost immediately required a shift from vellum and parchment to paper. Large folio Bibles, each one made from the skins of two hundred slaughtered calves, gave way to lighter bibles in quarto or octavo format made of the much cheaper paper. Within fifty years of the invention of the printing press, most of the typographic features that we expect in a book had been introduced: pages made of paper; readable type faces with spaces between words and spaces between paragraphs; the introduction of upper and lower cases of type; the use of chapters and running heads; pagination; and smaller-sized formats suitable for the hand rather than the lectern. Because of these changes, notes Fischer (2003, 212), "reading ceased being a painful process of decipherment, and became an act of pure pleasure."

With this we are well on our way to the modern image of the reader who reads for pleasure and who has access to a satisfyingly large stock of reading materials. German historian Rolf Engelsing has identified a *Leserevolution,* or reading revolution, in the second half of the eighteenth century. A new breed of avid reader emerged. According to Engelsing, from the Middle Ages until some time toward the end of the eighteenth century, people had just a few books such as the Bible and read them "intensively," over and over again, memorizing them, reciting them aloud, and transmitting them to the next generation (Chartier 1995, 17). Then there was a shift to "extensive" reading, as the presses produced an enormously expanded range and number of publications, especially periodicals and newspapers, but also novels. A number of factors converged: the enormous expansion of printing, the drop in costs, the expansion of reading societies, and the creation of lending libraries.

In the first decades of the nineteenth century in the United States and Canada, a similar transformation in reading went hand in hand with changes in the technology of printing and distribution. The power-driven cylinder press and new papermaking machinery dramatically lowered the cost of printed material and made it affordable to a much wider class of readers. Whereas reading in seventeenth- and eighteenth-century New England had largely been limited to a few religious and devotional texts, now readers had access to a wide selection of fiction and works of instruction in newspaper, magazine, and book formats. In the United States, in the period between 1840 and the 1890s, three formats developed to make fiction available cheaply to a large readership: the story paper, the dime novel, and the cheap library.

The story paper, which was published mostly in New York and Philadelphia for a national audience, was an eight-page weekly newspaper selling for five or six cents that was distributed by newsboys and financed in part by advertising. Michael Denning (1987, 11) describes how in the 1860s and 1870s story papers such as Street and Smith's *New York Weekly,* Beadle and Adams's *Saturday Journal,* or George Munro's *Fireside Companion* had circulations in the hundreds of thousands and contained "a carefully-balanced mixture of serialized adventure stories, domestic romances, western tales, and historical romances." During this period, the second main format for cheap fiction was the dime novel, a four-inch by six-inch pamphlet of about a hundred pages each, that by the 1860s had reached an unprecedented audience, swollen by the demand for cheap reading by Civil War soldiers. The slogan of dime novel publishers Beadle and Adams was "Books for the Million!" and by 1865 they had published 4 million dime novels with sales of individual titles ranging from 35,000 to 80,000 (Schick 1958, 51).

The third source of popular fiction was the cheap library, which sold fiction in various formats—often quartos of eight by eleven inches, on cheap paper two or three columns to the page. In the absence of an international copyright law until 1891, reprint libraries such as Beadle and Adams's Fireside Library, George Munro's Seaside Library, and John Lovell's Riverside Library pirated popular British books such as Dickens's novels or *Lady Audley's Secret* and sold them at a small fraction of their selling price in England. By 1890, an estimated 30 million volumes of the Seaside Library had been sold, distributed across America through the American News Company (Innis 1952, 75).

In Rolf Engelsing's account, "extensive" reading came at a high cost. According to Engelsing, in their pursuit of commodified amusement, people began to read a text only once before racing on to the latest work. They also read more critically as texts lost their privileged status of sacredness and authority. In Engelsing's anxiety about the expansion of extensive reading and the desacralization of the printed word, we can see some familiar oppositional pairs that reappear in other contexts: deep reading versus superficial reading; active engagement with a central canonical text versus passive consumption of a stream of ephemeral materials whose apparent novelty conceals the fact that they are essentially the same commodified and repeated product (e.g., newspapers, magazines, dime novels, series books, genre books such as romances or detective fiction, best sellers). There are, it seems, many accounts of the decline of reading from some golden age of the past when reading was deep, intensive, whole, and life affirming.

The exact point when the fall is alleged to have happened, however, differs in these various accounts. For some, it was the in the eighteenth century with the expansion of printing and the increase in the numbers of Grub Street authors satirized in Alexander Pope's *The Dunciad*. Others trace the problem to the nineteenth century, when the invention of the steam-powered press made cheap fiction, magazines, and newspapers available to whole classes of readers who had never before read much of anything. A system of distribution carried these publications efficiently from publishing centers in New York and Philadelphia to readers in the hinterlands. M. F. Sweetser (1880, 10–11), writing about the contemporary press in the late nineteenth century, claims: "The most serious attack of unbeneficial literature is made upon the youth of the country, and its avenue of advance is through the flash newspaper and the low grade of cheap novel. . . . [T]he flash paper penetrates to solitudes where even the circuit-rider never appears, and far beyond the blue-and-white signs of the telegraph companies."

Writing more than one hundred years later, Sven Birkerts (1994) blamed the global reach of the Internet and the introduction of hypertext that facilitates clicking and surfing through texts abbreviated to a single screen. However, as is evident from Michael Kammen's *The Lively Arts,* there are striking similarities between more recent doomsayers such as Birkerts who worry about the Web and those of an earlier age who worried about the cultural catastrophe introduced by moving pictures and radio. And after radio, television was the medium that was blamed. Writing before the popularization of the Internet, Alvin Kernan (1990, 151) argued that the transient, episodic culture of television is doing damage to a book culture that he associates with permanence and truth: "Looking backward it can be seen that literature and print both embodied in their related ways the assumptions of an earlier humanism about such matters as truth, imagination, language, and history."

Telling a completely different story about reading and literacy are cyber-theorists such as George Landow (1992), Richard Lanham (1993), James O'Donnell (1998), and Janet Murray (1998). They agree that the digital media have introduced a transformative shift in reading and in the ways in which cultural products are produced, disseminated and received. However they see exciting new potentials for cultural expression and for education, as the electronic environment opens up new spaces for reading and for writing. Janet Murray's book *Hamlet on the Holodeck* sketches out the aesthetics of a new type of narrative that has not yet been invented but can be seen in embryo in the work of videogame designers, computer programmers, and Web page designers. She looks forward to cyber storytellers' discovering new modes of representation by taking full advantage of the technology's strengths: its interactivity, non-linearity, ability to create immersive three-dimensional landscapes and machine-based fictional characters such as chatterbots, and its convergence of text and images, audio, and video. As her title suggests, Murray sees in the immersive electronic environment a powerful technology of sensory illusion that is "continuous with the larger human traditions of storytelling stretching from the heroic bards through the nineteenth-century novelists" (Murray 1999, 26).

In short, histories of reading provide us with a number of binaries: reading for the ear versus reading for the eye; elite reading versus mass reading; "intensive" reading versus "extensive reading"; solitary reading versus reading as a social activity. The binary currently provoking the most worried discussion is that of reading linear texts versus reading of nonlinear, linked texts that may also include images and sound. In his essay "Death of the Reader?" book historian Roger Chartier (2000) argues that the digitizing of texts represents "a third revolution of the book" following the earlier inventions of the codex book in the fourth century A.D. and Gutenberg's invention of the printing press in the fifteenth century.

As Chartier (2000) points out, the material form of the book—whether papyrus scroll or codex consisting of folded pages or electronic hypertext—has its own material logic and encourages its own particular relationship between readers and their books. When the codex book superseded the scroll as the bearer of culture, a new rapport was established between readers and their books. In particular, the invention of the page and the introduction of pagination and indexes allowed readers to mark and refer to particular passages, which could then be cited in new texts—a requirement for the development of the scholarly article.

Similarly the electronic text has its own material logic, based on the hyperlink that allows nonlinear connections among texts, sounds and images. Chartier (1995, 18) predicts, "The revolution of the electronic text will also be a revolution in reading. To read on a screen is not to read in a codex. The electronic representation of texts completely changes the text's status. . . . Such changes inevitably, imperatively require new ways of reading, new relationships to the written word, new intellectual techniques." Hang on to your hat.

Case 4: "These Multiplying Productions of a Degraded Press"

One of the books in the Putnam's Handy-Book Series, *Hints for Home Reading,* is a collection of essays written with the purpose of helping the average person with the problem of knowing what books to read and how best to read them. M. F. Sweetser warns against the "multiplying productions of a degraded press" and describes the harms worked on readers, especially on susceptible young readers, by serialized fiction in story papers:

> The titles of the stories are viciously sensational and the situations are of the most impossible character, with high spice of hair-breadth adventure, prurient description and scandalous suggestion. . . . The heroes are those most regardless of long-settled social and natural laws, and their most notable achievements are triumphant revolts against the very nature of things. . . . And the reader ever draws a lengthening chain, for no sooner is Chincapin Dick brought to his reward in the last chapter of one story than Deadwood Jim enters the most interesting part of his brutal career in the same paper, and Calamity Jane appears on the scene in the first chapters of another serial.

> And what is the result of all this mighty flood of unsavory literature? Evil, and evil, and evil again. . . . Appetites depraved by heredity are pampered and glutted in their unnatural tastes during the most tender and formative years, and the broad road to perdition is opened before the myriads of little feet. . . . The instructors in some of our public schools keep a watch on the reading of their pupils, and report that the most unruly and rebellious boys are those who are addicted to the study of these fictions. (Sweetser 1880, 11–13)

Comments

What about that "lengthening chain," in which one story is linked to another and the reader keeps reading? Funny how Sweetster has turned the serial reading into a fetter, so that the reader ends up enslaved.

> To bring this cultural critique up to date, would we need to do anything besides replacing references to "stories" and "unsavory literature" with references to video games?

What Libraries Can Do

1. Have a generous and inclusive view of what counts as a reader. Readers in history have read silently and read aloud; they have read intensively and extensively. The shape of books has varied from a set of three-inch-square clay tablets kept in a pouch in early Mesopotamia to the contemporary paperback to the electronic e-book.

    Librarians are familiar with a range of different formats and have experience dealing with them. They have watched formats such as the eight-track tape and the CD-ROM come into and go out of use. Librarians ought to be more able than most to avoid fetishizing a particular format as the only one to be associated with "real reading."

2. Take a second look at the less preferred element in any given binary. We tend to privilege the silent private reading of extended linear texts. When we see a girl curled up reading the *Secret Garden,* we are more apt to count it as "real reading" than when we see a group of boys reading. Be prepared to recognize as "real reading" the reading that groups of boys do when they read car magazines and instruction manuals.

3. Make use of the new possibilities for interaction created by the electronic text. The printed book narrows the reader's interaction with the text to marginalia and surreptitious inscription. With library Web pages that allow readers to post their responses to books, readers can become authors of their own texts.

To Read More on the History of Books and Reading

Altick, Richard D. 1998. *The English Common Reader: A Social History of the Mass Reading Public 1800–1900.* 2nd ed. Columbus: Ohio State University Press.

This classic book on the development of mass literacy in England, originally published by the University of Chicago Press in 1957, has been reissued with a new foreword by Jonathan Rose. Altick paints a vividly detailed picture of both the expanded production of reading matter in nineteenth century England—books, periodicals, and newspapers—and their improved distribution to the public through such institutions as mechanics' institutes and public libraries.

Cavallo, Guglielmo, and Roger Chartier, eds. 1999. *A History of Reading in the West.* Translated by Lydia G. Cochrane. Amherst: University of Massachusetts Press.

Written by thirteen scholars well known in their fields, this collection of essays reconstructs the various modes of reading that have prevailed in Western society from the ancient Greeks to the twenty-first century. The authors examine the technical innovations that have changed the physical nature of the book as well as changes in the way books are read.

Chartier, Roger. 1994. *The Order of Books*: *Readers, Authors, and Libraries in Europe between the Fourteenth and Eighteenth Centuries*. Translated by Lydia G. Cochrane. Stanford, CA: Stanford University Press.

> The organization of books has its own history. By the late Middle Ages, the expansion in book production had produced an anxiety of organization and bibliographical control as efforts were made to marshal the burgeoning profusion into some order. Chartier examines the tension familiar to librarians between the ideal of total inclusion—all the books ever published gathered in one universal library—and the constraints of necessarily incomplete collections. He says, "Inventorying titles, categorizing works, and attributing texts were all operations that made it possible to set the world of the written word in order. Our own age is the direct heir of this immense effort motivated by anxiety" (vii).

Darnton, Robert. 1982. "What Is the History of Books?" *Daedalus* (summer): 65–83.

> To map the terrain of research on reading, Darnton provides a model of the Communications Circuit, which shows the progression of a text from Author to Publisher to Shipper to Bookseller to Reader. "The reader completes the circuit, because he influences the author both before and after the act of composition" (67). Darnton illustrates his model with the example of Rigaud, a provincial bookseller in eighteenth-century France, and what was involved in Rigaud's selling Voltaire's book *Questions sur encyclopédie*, an important book of the Enlightenment that was forbidden by French authorities.

Davidson, Cathy N., ed. 1989. *Reading in America: Literature and Social History*. Baltimore: Johns Hopkins University Press.

> A useful collection of articles on reading that includes Darnton's "What Is the History of Books?" and Radway's "The Book of the Month Club and the General Reader" as well as other suggestive articles that examine specific kinds of reading delimited by geographic area or time period or genre of reading material.

Febvre, Lucien, and Henri-Jean Martin. 1958. *The Coming of the Book: The Impact of Printing, 1450–1800*. Translated by David Gerard. Reprint, London: NLB, 1976.

> Everything you've ever needed to know about know about the early history of the printed book, including the changing costs of paper, press equipment, and typecasts between the fifteenth and eighteenth centuries; the average print runs of the Church Fathers and Latin Classics; the special trade laws that governed book fairs; and the typical pay scale of journeyman printers. A foundational book.

Kaestle, Carl F., and Helen Damon-Moore, eds. 1991. *Literacy in the United States: Readers and Reading since 1880*. New Haven, CT: Yale University Press.

> Going beyond the question of how many people in a given society were nominally literate as measured by the ability to sign their name, this study examines the different levels of literacy and links the history of literacy to its broader contexts in the history of the book, education, publishing, and popular reading.

To Read More on the Future of Reading

Bloch, R. Howard, and Carla Hesse, eds. 1995. *Future Libraries*. Berkeley: University of California Press.

    This collection of articles written from the multidisciplinary perspective of computer scientists, librarians, linguists, historians, lawyers, and architects examines how libraries, faced with the job of storing texts and making them accessible, have become a test bed for new technologies of writing and reading. An especially interesting article is Geoffrey Nunberg's essay, "The Places of Books in the Age of Electronic Reproduction," with its echo of a famous essay by Walter Benjamin on "The Place of Art in an Age of Mechanical Reproduction."

O'Donnell, James. 1998. *Avatars of the Word: From Papyrus to Cyberspace*. Cambridge, MA: Harvard University Press.

    An engaging book that examines recent developments in hyperlinked text, virtual libraries, and distance education through a series of comparisons with earlier revolutions: from oral to written culture ("Hearing Socrates, Reading Plato"), from the papyrus scroll to codex, and from manuscript to print. O'Donnell argues that print will be supplemented rather than superseded by the electronic word.

References

Birkerts, Sven. 1994. *The Gutenberg Elegies: The Fate of Reading in an Electronic Age*. Boston and London: Faber and Faber.

Chartier, Roger. 1994. *The Order of Books: Readers, Authors, and Libraries in Europe Between the Fourteenth and Eighteenth Centuries*. Translated by Lydia G. Cochrane. Stanford, CA: Stanford University Press.

Chartier, Roger. 1995. *Forms and Meanings: Texts, Performances, and Audiences from Codex to Computer*. Philadelphia: University of Pennsylvania Press.

Chartier, Roger. 2000. "Death of the Reader?" 100-day dialogue. Topic 2: "What Has Happened to Reading?" Available at http://www.honco.net/100day/02/2000-0531-chartier.html (accessed June 26, 2003).

Darnton, Robert. 1990. "First Steps toward a History of Reading." *The Kiss of Lamourette: Reflections in Cultural History*. London: Faber & Faber.

Denning, Michael. 1987. *Mechanic Accents: Dime Novels and Working-Class Culture in America*. London and New York: Verso.

Eisenstein, Elizabeth L. 1979. *The Printing Press as an Agent of Change: Communications and Cultural Transformations in Early Modern Europe*. 2 vols. Cambridge, England: Cambridge University Press.

Fischer, Steven Roger. 2003. *A History of Reading*. London: Reaktion Books.

Febvre, Lucien, and Henri-Jean Martin. 1958. *The Coming of the Book: The Impact of Printing, 1450–1800*. Translated by David Gerard. Reprint, London: NLB, 1976.

Innis, Harold A. [1952]. "The Strategy of Culture." In *Contexts of Canadian Criticism*, 71–92. Edited by Eli Mandel. Reprint, Chicago and London: University of Chicago Press, 1971.

Kammen, Michael. 1996. *The Lively Arts: Gilbert Seldes & the Transformation of Cultural Criticism in the United States*. New York: Oxford University Press.

Kernan, Alvin. 1990. *The Death of Literature*. New Haven, CT, and London: Yale University Press.

Landow, George. 1992. *Hypertext: The Convergence of Technology and Contemporary Critical Theory*. Baltimore: Johns Hopkins University Press.

Lanham, Richard. 1993. *The Electronic Word: Technology, Democracy, and the Arts*. Chicago: University of Chicago Press.

Manguel, Alberto. 1996. *A History of Reading*. New York: Viking.

McLuhan, Marshall. 1962. *The Gutenberg Galaxy: The Making of Typographic Man*. Toronto: University of Toronto Press.

Murray, J. H. 1998. *Hamlet on the Holodeck: The Future of Narrative in Cyberspace*. Boston: MIT Press.

O'Donnell, James J. 1998. *Avatars of the Word: From Papyrus to Cyberspace*. Cambridge, MA: Harvard University Press.

Ong, Walter J. 1982. *Orality and Literacy: The Technologizing of the Word*. London and New York: Methuen.

Schick, Frank. 1958. *The Paperbound Book in America*. New York: R. R. Bowker.

Steinberg, Sigfrid Henry. 1974. *Five Hundred Years of Printing*. Harmondsworth, England and Baltimore: Penguin Books.

Stock, Brian. 1983. *The Implications of Literacy: Written Language and Models of Interpretation in the Eleventh and Twelfth Centuries*. Princeton, NJ: Princeton University Press.

Sweetser, M. F. 1880. "What the People Read." In *Hints for Home Reading: Putnam's Handy Book Series of Things Worth Knowing*, 5–14. Edited by Lyman Abbott. New York: G. P. Putnam's Sons.

1.5. Introduction to Reading Research

There is nothing like the threat of extinction to catch people's attention. With all the publicity given to the so-called literacy crisis and the end of reading, reading itself has become a hot topic for research. Reading has been studied from almost every possible angle. Reading researchers themselves come from a great variety of disciplines, including education, psychology, sociology, history, library and information science, and literary and cultural studies. Research into the processes of reading has been done mostly by psychologists. Research into learning how to read has been done mostly in faculties of education. And research into reading theory has been done in literature departments. The richness of the research findings is welcome, but sometimes it can seem that disciplinary boundaries have created research traditions that are hermetically sealed. An assumption taken for granted in one discipline is challenged in another; findings commonplace within one discipline are little regarded in another.

Which aspects of reading have received the most attention? Perhaps the largest body of research has focused on the teaching of reading, especially the acquisition of literacy. In the field of education, researchers ask questions about learning to read: what do children need to know to become good readers? What risk factors set a child up for reading failure? Which children are most at risk? What are the pathologies that stand in the way of fluent reading? Coming at the topic from a different perspective, psychologists have studied reading as the outcome of complex cognitive processes. Linguists have studied competencies that enable us to generate sentences and understand them when we hear or read them. Psycholinguistic research has looked at discrete variables such as the role of short-term memory, phonemic awareness, and miscue analysis. Demographic research has investigated the correlation of reading with such factors as the gender, age, level of income, level of education, and geographic location of the reader. This body of demographic research, reported in more detail in section 4.1, is typically conducted in the service of the book industry or of libraries. It answers questions such as who reads what for how many minutes a day in what part of the country. In the library field, researchers have studied both the circulation and use of library books and the nature of the users who do the using.

Some disciplines study reading by focusing on texts as autonomous objects. Within literature departments, literary critics have studied the rhetorical resources of the text itself, examining texts as sources of evidence about literary genres, about the readers implied by the texts, and about gaps in the text that invite interpretive activity from readers. Sociologists, historians, and cultural studies scholars, on the other hand, are less interested in the individual reader than in the social practices and power relations that accompany reading. They have examined the political economy of the production, distribution, and consumption of reading materials and more generally have studied the roles played by publishing houses, libraries, and booksellers. In the work of researchers such as Brian Street (1995), literacy research becomes a branch of cultural studies in which the researcher lays bare the power relations that pervade literacy practices.

Historians have studied the book as an agent of social or intellectual change and book reading as part of the history of taste. They have examined census records, library catalogs, subscription lists, and estate inventories to discover which books have been available to readers from different economic classes and in different historical periods. A valuable representative of this type of investigation is William Gilmore's *Reading Becomes a Necessity of Life* (1989), which examined transformations in reading in rural New England from 1780 to 1835. Book publishers and booksellers have studied the marketability of the book as commodity. In a classic paper titled "What Is the History of Books?" Robert Darnton mapped a new area of study called *histoire du livre,* or history of the book, which he describes as focused on understanding "how ideas were transmitted through print and how exposure to the printed word affected the thought and behavior of mankind during the last five hundred years" (Darnton 1982, 65).

By and large, historians and literary scholars have tended to focus attention on texts and deduce from the texts what they imagine the readers must experience. So one way to sort out research on reading is to distinguish between the ones that focus on real living-and-breathing readers and the ones that don't. Several important studies have tried to recover the reading experience of real readers from the past. Notable examples are Robert Darnton's study (1984) of the Rousseauistic reading of an eighteenth-century merchant based on the reader's surviving letters to a publisher and Cathy Davidson's study (1986) of nineteenth-century American novel readers based, among other sources, on the marginalia inscribed in copies of early American novels. Only a small number of book-length studies take an ethnographic approach to studying contemporary reading and readers. Some of these have examined how children become readers (e.g., Clark 1976; Heath 1983; Cochran-Smith 1984), sometimes focusing on the case study of a single child (e.g., Butler 1975; Bissex 1980; Crago and Crago 1983).

Although it is known that a key factor in reading for pleasure is that the reader is in control and can make choices, it is notable how few reading studies focus on materials chosen by the reader, preferring instead to ask readers to respond to preselected texts. Among the most interesting book-length studies that focus on voluntary reading or reading of personal significance are Donald Fry's *Children Talk about Books* (1985) that reports case studies of individual children's reading; Janice Radway's *Reading the Romance* (1984), that used a combination of individual and group interviews and questionnaires to understand readers' experience of romantic fiction; Joseph Gold's *Read for Your Life* (1990), based on his clinical work using books in family therapy; and Elizabeth Long's *Book Clubs* (2003), an ethnographic study of 77 contemporary women's reading groups in Houston, Texas.

The problem for the average person concerned about reading is not that there is too little information about reading but that there is too much, and what there is seems sometimes contradictory and difficult to synthesize. When Edmund Burke Huey (1908) wrote his celebrated review of the research literature on reading, his analysis could be comprehensive because there were fewer than forty studies for him to review. By the time Helen M. Robinson and Samuel Weintraub were compiling their annual reviews of reading research for the International Reading Association (IRA; 1980–1997), there were more than a thousand new research reports on reading each year that met the IRA criteria for inclusion. According to Briony Train (2003, 85), the U.S. National Reading Panel estimated that 100,000 research studies on reading had been published in English between 1996 and 1999.

Nevertheless, despite the fragmentary nature of some of the work, there is a sense of a growing body of work that is reaching an increasingly nuanced understanding of the complex phenomenon of reading. To deal with the flood of studies on literacy, efforts have been made to summarize and synthesize findings. In a chapter of the *Handbook of Reading Research* titled "Research Synthesis: Making Sense of the Accumulation of Knowledge in Reading," Timothy Shanahan summarizes some of the efforts at synthesis of the research on literacy. His chapter singles out some twenty-five "influential research syntheses in literacy," including Marilyn J. Adams's *Beginning to Read* (1990), Richard Anderson and colleagues' *Becoming a Nation of Readers* (1985), Jeanne Chall's *Learning to Read* (1967), Marie M. Clay's *Becoming Literate* (1991), and George R. Klare's *The Measurement of Readability* (1963).

In short, there is a huge body of reading research available. The questions asked by the research are at varying levels of specificity from the legibility of typefaces to the role of reading in the reader's quest for identity. Here are some of the questions that have been asked and the findings that have emerged.

- **What factors of type, line spacing, and line width make reading easier?**

  Typefaces in common use are all equally legible. Readers dislike very short and very long lines as well as material set solid, that is, set with no leading, or extra space, between the lines.

  Tinker, Miles A. 1963. *Legibility of Print.* Ames: Iowa State University Press.

- **What are the characteristics of readable texts?**

  Most of the work on readability has been directed toward developing a formula for counting some easily identifiable characteristic of a sample text. Readability formulae typically calculate the average number of words per sentence or the ratio of polysyllabic words to one-syllable words. The Fog Index combines both these factors to produce a score that is intended to indicate readability. Such measures have been criticized because they fail to take into account complexity of sentence structure or the fact that some familiar polysyllabic words such as "watermelon" can be easier to read than some short words such as "weald." More able to take into account the variety of complex factors that determine readability, the cloze procedure works by measuring the predictability or redundancy of a passage. Subjects are asked to complete a passage from which words have been deleted at fixed intervals such as every fifth word. The more successful readers are at filling in the missing words, the more readable the passage is judged to be.

  Monteith, M. 1976. "Readability Formulas." *Journal of Reading* 20, 2: 604–17.

  Klare, George R. 1984. "Readability." In *Handbook of Reading Research.* Edited by D. P. Pearson. New York: Longmans.

- **What do our eyes do as we scan a page?**

College students reading texts that are appropriate to their reading skill level fixate on about two-thirds of the words and are more apt to fixate on content words (83 percent) than function words (38 percent). Carpenter and Just claim that the reader tries to interpret each word as it is encountered rather than holding off assigning meaning until reaching the end of the meaning unit.

Carpenter, P. A., and Marcel A. Just. 1983. "What Your Eyes Do While Your Mind Is Reading." In *Eye Movements in Reading: Perceptual and Language Processes*, 275–93. Edited by Keith Rayner. New York: Academic Press.

- **What are readers actually doing when they read a sentence, paragraph, page, or whole text?**

Psycholinguistic theories emphasize the evidence for functional parallelism: fluent readers must carry on many operations simultaneously as they take in printed information with their eyes, draw on linguistic knowledge in their heads about how sentences work, use their knowledge of the world to fill in gaps in the text, and integrate what they have just read with what they can remember from earlier parts of the text.

Smith, Frank. 1978. *Understanding Reading: A Psycholinguistic Analysis of Reading and Learning to Read.* 2nd ed. New York: Holt, Rinehart and Winston.

- **What methods work best at teaching children initially how to read?**

Jeanne Chall's synthesis of fifty years of research suggests that teachers of beginning reading should present well-designed phonics instruction.

Chall, Jeanne S. 1983. *Learning to Read: The Great Debate.* 2nd ed. New York: McGraw-Hill.

See also Anderson, Richard C., E. H. Hiebert, J. A. Scott, and I. A. G. Wilkinson. 1985. *Becoming a Nation of Readers: The Report of the Commission on Reading.* Washington, DC: US Department of Education, National Institute of Education.

- **What are skillful readers like?**

The single most striking characteristic of skillful readers is that they speed through stretches of text with apparent effortlessness (Adams 1990, 19).

Adams, Marilyn J. 1990. *Beginning to Read: Thinking and Learning about Print. A Summary.* Center for the Study of Reading. University of Illinois at Urbana, Champagne.

- **What is the most important factor in the making of readers?**

In 1983, a national commission in the United States called the Commission on Reading was organized by the National Academy of Education and the National Institute of Education. The Commission spent two years winnowing some 10,000 research reports and concluded the following: "The single most important activity for building the knowledge required for eventual success in reading is reading aloud to children" (Anderson et al. 1985, 23).

See also Anderson, Richard C., E. H. Hiebert, J. A. Scott, and I. A. G. Wilkinson. 1985. *Becoming a Nation of Readers: The Report of the Commission on Reading.* Washington, DC: US Department of Education, National Institute of Education.

- **What factors help children to become proficient readers?**

Access to books and other interesting reading materials is a critical factor in becoming a good reader. Jeff McQuillan (1998, 86) concludes, "There is now considerable evidence that the amount and quality of students' access to reading materials is substantively related to the amount of reading they engage in, which in turn is the most important determinant of reading achievement." Libraries have an important role to play because low-income families especially are likely to have very few books in their home.

McQuillan, Jeff. 1998. *The Literacy Crisis: False Claims, Real Solutions.* Portsmouth, NH: Heinemann.

See also:

Wells, Gordon. 1987. *The Meaning Makers.* London: Hodder & Stoughton.

Tizzard, Barbara, and Martin Hughes. 1984. *Young Children Learning.* Cambridge, MA: Harvard University Press.

- **Is there a fall-off in reading skills of the present generation in comparison with previous generations?**

No. Comparative data of students' performance on standardized NAEP reading tests indicates that students are reading better now than they did thirty years ago. Average scores of nine, thirteen, and seventeen year olds were higher in 1996 than were those of their counterparts in 1971. In the 1998 NAEP assessment of students in Grades 4, 8, and 12, female students in all three grades had higher reading scores than their male peers, and a higher percentage of girls than boys reached each of the reading achievement levels of basic, proficient, and advanced. In all three grades in 1998, students who reported talking about their reading activities with family or friends once or twice a week or at least monthly had higher average reading scores than did those who reported doing so rarely or not at all (National Assessment of Educational Progress 1997, 1998). The percentage of fourth- and eighth-graders who performed at or above the Proficient level in reading was higher in 2002 than in 1992, whereas the twelfth-grade percentage at this level was lower (The Nation's Report Card, 2002).

National Assessment of Educational Progress. 1997. *Report in Brief: NAEP 1996 Trends in Academic Progress.* Washington, DC: National Center for Education Statistics.

National Assessment of Educational Progress. 1998. *Reading: An International Focus. The IFLA Reading Survey,* 84–115. Washington, DC: National Center for Education Statistics.

The Nation's Report Card. 2002 Reading Assessment Results. Available at http://nces.ed.gov/nationsreportcard/pubs/main2002/2003521.asp (Accessed January 5, 2005).

- **What are the gender differences in reading?**

Boys take longer to learn to read than girls do. Once they are able to read, boys spend less time reading than girls do and are less likely to value reading for pleasure. On the other hand, boys do better than girls at information retrieval and work-related literacy tasks and are far more likely than girls are to read for utilitarian purposes. Significantly more boys than girls describe themselves as "nonreaders" (Smith and Wilhelm 2002, 10). As adults, women on average read a greater variety of books and spend more time reading than men (Tepper 2000, 255).

Smith, Michael W., and Jeffrey D. Wilhelm. 2002. *"Reading Don't Fix No Chevys": Literacy in the Lives of Young Men.* Portsmouth, NH: Heinemann.

Tepper, Steven J. 2002. "Fiction Reading in America: Explaining the Gender Gap." *Poetics* 27: 255–75.

- **Why do children from professional families do better in school than children from working-class or welfare families?**

Hart, Betty, and Todd Risley (1996; see also Hart and Risley 2003) tape-recorded and coded samples of time in the homes of forty-two children from differing socioeconomic groups over a longitudinal period from age seven to nine months to thirty-six months. They discovered that that by age three, there was already a 30-million-word gap between the words that the children in families on welfare had heard and the words that children in professional families had heard. "By the time the children were three years old, trends in amount of talk, vocabulary growth, and style of interaction were well established and clearly suggested widening gaps to come. Even patterns of parenting were already observable among the children. When we listened to the children, we seemed to hear their parents speaking; when we watched the children play at parenting their dolls, we seemed to see the futures of their own children." During the period studied, welfare children had received half as much language experience (616 words heard on average per hour) as working-class children (1,251 words per hour) and one-third as much language experience as the children of professionals (2,153 words per hour). Another key difference was in the quality of language experience: on average welfare children heard five encouragements and eleven prohibitions per hour, whereas the professional child heard thirty-two encouragements and five prohibitions per hour. Extrapolated, this data suggests that in the first four years of life the child from the professional family would have heard 560,000 more instances of encouragements than discouragements, whereas the child from the welfare family would have heard 125,000 more prohibitions than encouragements.

Hart, Betty, and Todd R. Risley. 1996. *Meaningful Differences in the Everyday Experience of Young American Children*. Baltimore, MD: Brookes.

Hart, Betty, and Todd R. Risley. 2003. "The Early Catastrophe: The 30 Million Word Gap by Age 3." *American Educator* (spring 2003). Available at http://www.aft.org/pubs-reports/american_educator/spring2003/catastrophe. html (accessed January 5, 2005).

- **What is the connection between childhood reading and reading in adulthood?**

Nicholas Zill and Marianne Winglee (1990; see also Tepper 2002) found that people who were encouraged to read as children were four times more likely to be fiction readers as adults compared with people who were not encouraged to read as children.

Zill, Nicholas, and Marianne Winglee. 1990. *Who Reads Literature? The Future of the United States as a Nation of Readers*. Washington, DC: Seven Locks.

Tepper, Steven J. 2002. "Fiction Reading in America: Explaining the Gender Gap." *Poetics* 27: 255–75.

- **How do people feel about books as objects?**

When asked, "What are the things in your home which are special to you?" 22 percent mentioned books (36 percent mentioned furniture, 26 percent mentioned visual art, 23 percent photographs, 21 percent the television set, and 15 percent plants) (Csikszentmihalyi and Rochberg-Halton 1981, 58). The authors sum up the value of books that makes them special: "books, more than any other kind of objects, are special to people because they serve to embody ideals and to express religious and professional values" (71).

Csikszentmihalyi, Mihaly, and Eugene Rochberg-Halton. 1981. *The Meaning of Things: Domestic Symbols and the Self.* Cambridge, England: Cambridge University Press.

With so many studies on reading being published each year, reading is obviously a complex field. However, there are a number of core findings that should be emphasized as significant for library professionals, parents, and community members.

- Although we speak of readers and nonreaders, in modern societies the ability to read is not really a binary variable. That is, it is *not* the case that you either can read or you can't. In fact, almost everyone in modern societies *can* read at a very basic level. The problem is that many can't read well enough to cope with the increasing literacy demands of an information society. Reading is a skill with many gradations of proficiency.

- Reading is an acquired skill. People learn to read by doing lots and lots of reading.

- Pleasure is the spur that motivates beginning readers to spend the thousands and thousands of hours reading that it takes to become a proficient reader. Readers who become proficient are those who enjoy reading and who do it by choice as a voluntary activity in their leisure time. Children who dislike reading and avoid it whenever possible never get the hours of practice that it takes to become a good reader. With each year, the proficiency gap grows between children who enjoy reading and do it voluntarily and those who dislike and avoid reading.

- Beginners are more likely to choose to do an activity when they feel they are successful at it and when they get pleasure from participation in the activity right from the start. This is why reading aloud is such a winning strategy in the making of readers. The novice reader experiences the pleasure of stories in a risk-free environment where it is impossible to fail or appear incompetent.

- The experience of confident and successful readers is a beneficent circle: 1) an initial experience with texts and stories that is pleasurable; 2) an acquired knowledge about reading that comes from exposure to texts and stories; 3) a desire to repeat the pleasurable experience at first by hearing more stories and later by reading on one's own; 4) achievement of competency in reading acquired through lots of practice listening to and reading texts; 5) the reader's sense of himself or herself as a skilled and successful reader who is good at reading and therefore wants to engage in more of it.

Research Tells Us

Research shows that when beginning readers read lots of meaningful, connected text, they become much better readers. In an extensive study of independent reading, Anderson, Wilson, and Fielding (1988) investigated a broad array of activities and their relationship to reading achievement and growth in reading. They found that the amount of time students spent in independent reading was the best predictor of reading achievement and also the best predictor of the amount of gain in reading achievement made by students between second and fifth grade. Out-of-school reading turns out to be very important. "Research also shows that the amount of reading done out of school is consistently related to gains in reading achievement" (Anderson et al. 1985, 7). Because students do more independent reading when they have easy access to books in the home, libraries have a crucial role to perform, especially for children whose families cannot afford to buy books.

To Read More on Making Sense of Reading Research

Kaestle, Carl F. 1991. "Readers and Reading in America: Historical and Critical Perspectives." In *Literacy in the United States: Readers and Reading since 1880,* 33–72. Edited by Kaestle, Carl F., Helen Damon-Moore, et al. New Haven, CT: Yale University Press.

Purves, Alan C., and Richard Beach. 1972. *Literature and the Reader. Research in Response to Literature, Reading Interests, and the Teaching of Literature.* Urbana: University of Illinois.

> This bibliographic survey provides extensive coverage of empirical studies of actual readers' responses to literature. An especially helpful appendix provides summaries of thirty-three studies conducted between 1929 and 1970 that are considered "touchstones" for reader response in relation to the teaching of literature.

Radway, Janice. 1994. "Beyond Mary Bailey and Old Maid Librarians: Reimagining Readers and Rethinking Reading." *Journal of Education for Library and Information Science* 35, no. 4 (fall): 275–96.

> Written originally as a talk for librarians, this article summarizes research on reading as a context for arguing for a new way of thinking about pleasure reading.

References

Adams, Marilyn J. 1990. *Beginning to Read: Thinking and Learning about Print. A Summary.* Urbana/Champagne: Center for the Study of Reading, University of Illinois.

Anderson, Richard C., E. H. Hiebert, J. A. Scott, and I. A. G. Wilkinson. 1985. *Becoming a Nation of Readers: The Report of the Commission on Reading.* Washington, DC: US Department of Education, National Institute of Education.

Anderson, Richard C., P. T. Wilson, and L. G. Fielding. 1988. "Growth in Reading and How Children Spend Their Time Outside of School." *Reading Research Quarterly* 23: 285–303.

Bissex, Glenda L. 1980. *GNYS AT WRK: A Child Learns to Write and Read.* Cambridge, MA: Harvard University Press.

Butler, Dorothy. 1975. *Cushla and Her Books.* Boston: Horn Book.

Carpenter, P. A., and Marcel A. Just. 1983. "What Your Eyes Do While Your Mind Is Reading." In *Eye Movements in Reading: Perceptual and Language Processes,* 275–93. Edited by Keith Rayner. New York: Academic Press.

Chall, Jeanne S. 1983. *Learning to Read: The Great Debate.* 2nd ed. New York: McGraw-Hill.

Clark, Margaret M. 1976. *Young Fluent Readers.* London: Heinemann Educational Books.

Clay, Marie M. 1991. *Becoming Literate: The Construction of Inner Control.* Portsmouth, NH: Heinemann.

Cochran-Smith, Marilyn. 1984. *The Making of a Reader.* Norwood, NJ: Ablex.

Crago, Maureen, and Hugh Crago. 1983. *Prelude to Literacy: A Preschool Child's Encounter with Picture and Story.* Carbondale and Edwardsville: Southern Illinois University Press.

Darnton, Robert. 1982. "What Is the History of Books?" *Daedalus* (summer): 65–83.

Darnton, Robert. 1984. *The Great Cat Massacre and Other Episodes in French Cultural History.* New York: Basic Books.

Davidson, Cathy N. 1986. *Revolution and the Word: The Rise of the Novel in America.* New York and Oxford: Oxford University Press.

Durkin, Delores. 1966. *Children Who Read Early: Two Longitudinal Studies.* New York: Teachers College Press.

Fry, Donald. 1985. *Children Talk about Books: Seeing Themselves as Readers.* London: Open University Press.

Gallup Organization. 1978. *Book Reading and Library Usage: A Study of Habits and Perceptions.* Conducted for the ALA. Princeton, NJ: Gallup Organization.

Gilmore, William. 1989. *Reading Becomes a Necessity of Life: Material and Cultural Life in Rural New England, 1790–1835.* Knoxville: University of Tennessee Press.

Gold, Joseph. 1990. *Read for Your Life: Literature as a Life Support System.* Markham, ON: Fitzhenry and Whiteside.

Heath, Shirley Brice. 1983. *Ways with Words: Language, Life and Work in Communities and Classrooms.* New York: Cambridge University Press.

Huey, Edmund Burke. 1908. *The Psychology and Pedagogy of Reading.* Reprint, Cambridge, MA: MIT Press, 1962.

Klare, George R. 1963. *The Measurement of Readability.* Ames: Iowa State University Press.

Long, Elizabeth. 2003. *Book Clubs: Women and the Uses of Reading in Everyday Life.* Chicago and London: University of Chicago Press.

Radway, Janice. 1984. *Reading the Romance: Women, Patriarchy and Popular Literature.* Chapel Hill: University of North Carolina Press.

Ryan, Barbara, and Amy M. Thomas, eds. 2002. *Reading Acts: Readers' Interactions with Literature, 1800-1950.* Knoxville: The University of Tennessee Press.

Shanahan, Timothy. 2000. "Research Synthesis: Making Sense of the Accumulation of Knowledge in Reading." In *Handbook of Reading Research,* 209–26. Vol. III. Edited by Michael L. Kamil et al. Mahwah, NJ: Lawrence Erlbaum Associates.

Street, Brian. 1995. *Social Literacies: Critical Approaches to Literacy in Development, Ethnography and Education.* London: Longman.

Train, Briony. 2003. In *Reading and Reader Development: The Pleasure of Reading.* Edited by Judith Elkin, Briony Train, and Debbie Denham. London: Facet.

1.6. Reading as a Transaction

People used to think they knew what reading is. First you learned to read, and then you read to learn. This seemed quite straightforward—simple really. In the reading-to-learn phase, the emphasis was on the text and on what the text contained. You'll notice that this approach to reading elevates the object of reading—the text or the book—but has little interest in the processes of reading or in the historical contexts for reading or in the individual differences of actual readers. More recently, however, the activity of reading and the agency of the reader has attracted a great deal of attention. Although these controversies may seem remote from the day-to-day concerns of librarians or readers, in fact they have influenced how the library profession has gone about its business in areas such as collection development and readers' advisory. For this reason, it is worth taking a look at some different models of reading.

Although there are a great many such models of reading, Brian Cambourne (1979) has argued that they all boil down to two major types, depending on whether the flow of information is thought to be "outside-in" or "inside-out." In the outside-in model, meaning is thought to reside within the text, and the readers' job is to decode what's right there on the page and then take it in. This is the Little-Jack-Horner approach, where the reader puts in his thumb and pulls out a plum, which he then swallows. When this theory is applied to teaching young children to read, much emphasis is placed on readers as accurate "pattern-matchers" and "word-identifiers" who have mastered decoding skills and can successfully transform the written word into its corresponding spoken form. Outside-in theorists put a lot of stock in developing the child's ability to discriminate the shapes of words and letters and emphasize repetition, drills on discrete skills, and flashcards. A good reader is one who can correctly identify words on a prescribed list.

The inside-out model, in contrast, emphasizes the knowledge that is in the head of the reader—knowledge about the way the world works, the way language functions, and the way that stories work. The emphasis is on meaning making, and the reader is seen as an active agent in making sense of the text. According to inside-out theorists, a good reader is one who has acquired a lot of experience with print in meaningful situations and who understands that print and books are sources of enjoyment and information.

Although this contest between "outside-in" and "inside-out" theorists has taken place on the terrain of teaching children to read, we can identify a similar set of contesting theories that has affected the teaching of reading at the other end of the spectrum—university classrooms. Here again there is a division between theorists who emphasize meaning as something that resides in the text and those who emphasize what's in the heads of the readers. The New Criticism is usually taken as the case, par excellence, of a model of reading that emphasizes the text. The New Criticism was a theory of reading and of teaching literature that dominated English Departments in the English-speaking world from the 1930s to the 1960s. Several generations of literary students were taught to perform "close readings" of texts, following the lead of influential models such as Cleanth Brooks and Robert Penn Warren's *Understanding Poetry* (1932).

For the New Critics, the production of meaning was thought to be the result of the impersonal operation of a system of signs organizing the form of the text. The text was viewed as an autonomous object with an objective existence that was out there in the world, apart from any reader. The proper way to read was to pay close attention to the formal elements of the text—its images, themes, patterns of sound, and use of literary conventions—with a view to uncovering the text's unity. Especially admired by the New Critics were complex and difficult texts, such as the poetry of John Donne or T. S. Eliot, which repaid this intense and reflective style of reading.

A key doctrine in New Critical theory was that a text's meaning does *not* depend on its effects on its readers. The notion that it does was dismissed by Wimsatt and Beardsley (1954, 21) as the "Affective Fallacy" of confusing the poem or text with its results—that is, of confusing "what it *is* and what it *does*." The job of the literary student was to try to avoid idiosyncratic responses and view the text as objectively as possible. It goes without saying that readers were definitely not encouraged to talk about their own individual responses to the text, how it made them feel, whether they were interested or bored, or how it was related to their own lives (for a contrasting approach to reading, see section 4.3). More generally the New Criticism denied that either the author's intentions concerning the text or the reader's activity in interpreting it has any importance for establishing the text's meaning.

By the early 1970s, the New Criticism had run its course and literary theorists had begun to be interested in the activities of the reader who interprets the text. Influential critics such as Wolfgang Iser, Hans Robert Jauss, Norman Holland, David Bleich, Stanley Fish, and others wrote about the role of the reader in studies that came to be called reader-response criticism or reception theory. By 1980, three influential books focusing on reader-response signaled that a marked shift of attention had occurred from the autonomous text to the active reader (Fish 1980; Suleiman and Crosman 1980; Tompkins 1980). "The words *reader* and *audience,*" writes Susan Suleiman, "once relegated to the status of the unproblematic and obvious, have acceded to a starring role" (Suleiman and Crosman 1980, 3).

Summarizing some of this work on the reader, Jonathan Culler (1982, 69) draws attention to what he calls different "stories of reading":

> There are, of course, many different stories of reading. Wolfgang Iser tells of the reader actively filling in gaps, actualizing what the text leaves indeterminate, attempting to construct a unity, and modifying the construction as the text yields further information. . . . Norman Holland . . . tells of readers merrily using the work to "replicate themselves."

Culler goes on to say that when we consider the stories of reading that are told by these different literary critics, two key questions emerge. One is the issue of control. Who is in charge here—the reader or the text? Do active readers dominate the text by their constructive and creative activities of reading? Or does the text provoke certain responses in the reader through manipulative strategies put there by the scheming author? And the second, closely related question arises from these stories of reading is: What is "in" the text? Culler (1982, 71–73) asks, "Is it so rich a plenitude that no reader can ever grasp it at all? a determinate structure with some gaps the reader must fill in? a set of indeterminate marks on which the reader confers structure and meaning?"

Reader-response critics were not of course typically interested in actual empirical readers. With the exception of a few researchers such as Norman Holland, they focused on the role of some idealized reader as constructed by the text. They found implied readers, intended readers, mock readers, narratees, competent readers, superreaders, and readers who are members of implied audiences or interpretive communities. Depending on their interests, theorists have tried to account for the variation in readers' responses to texts as well as for the similarities in readers' interpretations. Wolfgang Iser (1978) thought of the text as a set of instructions for meaning production, which readers will follow according to their competencies. Even with competent readers, however, variations in interpretations occur because there are always "gaps" in the text that readers have to fill in by drawing on their own experience and imagination. According to Iser (1978, 169), "Whenever the reader bridges the gaps, communication begins. . . . Hence the structured blanks of the text stimulate the process of ideation to be performed by the reader on terms set by the text."

Others, especially feminists and cultural theorists, are interested instead in those refusals by readers to read the text on its own terms. Judith Fetterley's *The Resisting Reader* (1978) makes the case that canonical American fiction requires readers to identify with a perspective that is male, which gives female readers the choice of suppressing their own female perspective or of reading against the grain of the text. Also interested in readers' compliance with or resistance to hegemonic texts, Stuart Hall (1980) has identified "dominant," "negotiated," and "oppositional" styles of reading.

The importance of this work is that it asks questions about the agency of the reader: What is the reader doing when she reads? What is the relation between the reader and the text? Where is meaning—in the text or in the reader? Are readers cultural dupes who meekly absorb messages whole and intact, or are they actively trying on roles and experimenting with identities in what Janice Radway has called "the safe space of the imaginary" (2002, 187). Theorists now question the notion of the compliant reader as a receptacle for meanings produced by others. In an influential essay titled "Reading as Poaching," Michel de Certeau (1984, 169–70) argues that the reader "invents in texts something different from what [their authors] 'intended'. . . . He combines their fragments and creates something un-known. . . . Whether it is a question of newspapers or Proust, the text has a meaning only through its readers; it changes along with them; it is ordered in accord with codes of perception that it does not control." Radway (2002) talks about "narrative gleaning" but is referring to the same process of the reader's picking and choosing, fashioning the self from a selection of all the diverse materials that come to hand. She says that readers "sift and select" (2002, 186).

A wrestling match seemed to be going on between the determinant text and the active, constitutive reader. As one way out of this impasse, many people, especially in educational circles, have turned to the work of Louise Rosenblatt and her model of reading as a transaction. In 1938, Louise Rosenblatt published *Literature as Exploration,* which developed the model of reading as a transaction between a text and an active reader. The black marks on the page are important, of course, but the meaning is constructed by the reader on the basis of his or her past experience with reading texts and with living in the world. If you ask different readers to read the same text, you have to take into account the fact that each reader is creating from the words on the page a somewhat different meaning.

What difference does it make in practice to adopt a transactive model rather than a model that gives most of the power to the text? Perhaps the most important difference is the importance given to the experience of actual, not idealized, readers. If you take the view that meaning is fixed in an objective and autonomous text, then the reader's individual experience is not really very interesting. Either readers achieve the normative interpretation or they don't. Failures to achieve correct interpretations can of course be examined, as I. A. Richards did in *Practical Criticism* (1929) in which he got undergraduate English students at Cambridge to produce response statements, or what he called "reading protocols," to poems such as John Donne's sonnet, "At the round earth's imagined corners blow" or D. H. Lawrence's "Piano." Richards examined the students' deviations from the normative reading and classified them according to the reasons for the incorrect reading—"stock responses," "sentimentality," "doctrinal adhesions," "technical preconceptions," and so on.

Louise Rosenblatt was impressed by the work of I. A. Richards in *Practical Criticism* but came to a completely different conclusion from the one reached by the New Critics. She accepted Richards's finding that readers came to the text with a set of preconceptions. But instead of viewing what was in the reader's head as a source of error, Rosenblatt saw it as a necessary part of reading. The reading of a text is an active event that necessarily entails the reader's bringing prior knowledge to bear on what is read. Alan Purves (1988) says that subsequent research has demonstrated that Louise Rosenblatt was right about the transactive model of reading: "Beginning with I. A. Richards, and continuing with the work of James Squire, Arthur Applebee, Norman Holland, Charles Cooper, and myself (see Purves and Beach 1972), there is a steady stream of findings that readers bring something with them when they read texts. What they bring is a sense of the appropriate content of literary texts, as well as a sense of the structure, form, and style of literary works."

Rosenblatt had the misfortune to publish her work on the transactive model of reading just when the New Criticism was establishing itself as the dominant approach to the teaching of literature. Outside of faculties of education, her work was ignored for forty years. In his Foreword to the 5th edition of *Literature as Exploration* (Rosenblatt 1995, vii), Wayne Booth says, "I doubt that any other literary critic of this century has enjoyed and suffered as sharp a contrast of powerful influence and absurd neglect as Louise Rosenblatt. . . . She has probably influenced more teachers in the ways of dealing with literature than any other critic. But the world of literary criticism and theory has only recently begin to acknowledge the relevance of her arguments." The edited collections on reader-response criticism by both Tompkins and Suleiman and Crosman acknowledged Rosenblatt in a footnote as an afterthought in their introductions, each saying that they had encountered Rosenblatt's pioneering work too late for inclusion.

So why should librarians or readers care about any of this? Because models of reading influence practice, especially when those models are taken for granted and not examined. If you believe that meaning lies in the texts themselves, you can build collections and recommend books without taking into account the reader. You can draw up lists called "Good Books You Should Read" because you believe that texts have an objective value in themselves. You don't need to ask, Good books for what? or Good books for whom? The most direct connection between the transactive model of reading and library practice is in the area of readers' advisory work.

Within the library field, the growing body of work on readers' advisory service has viewed reading as a transaction and has emphasized the importance of the interview to find out what the reader considers to be a good book. For example, Saricks and Brown's *Readers' Advisory Service in the Public Library* (1997, 35–55) puts emphasis on "appeal factors," which they identify as pacing, characterization, storyline, and frame. They stress that fast pacing or slow leisurely unfolding should not be regarded as a virtue in itself on some absolute scale of value. The important point is to find out, during the readers' advisory interview, what appeal factors are important to that individual reader and then match the reader to an appropriate book (for more on Readers' Advisory, see section 4.8).

The transactive model of reading underlies the approach taken in this book to the topic of reading, the reader's experience, and what libraries and communities can do to foster reading.

Case 5: Meaning Constructed in the Encounter

What goes around comes around. Here's what Edith Wharton (1903) said at the beginning of the last century about the transactional relationship between reader and book:

> What is reading, in the last analysis, but an interchange of thought between writer and reader? If the book enters the reader's mind just as it left the writer's—without any of the additions and modifications inevitably produced by contact with a new body of thought—it has been read to no purpose. In such cases, of course, the reader is not always to blame. There are books that are always the same—incapable of modifying or of being modified—but these do not count as factors in literature. The value of books is proportionate to what may be called their plasticity—their quality of being all things to all men, of being diversely moulded by the impact of fresh forms of thought. Where, from one cause or the other, this reciprocal adaptability is lacking, there can be no real intercourse between book and reader. In this sense it may be said that there is no abstract standard of values in literature: the greatest books ever written are worth to each reader only what he can get out of them. The best books are those from which the best readers have been able to extract the greatest amount of thought of the highest quality; but it is generally from these books that the poor reader gets least.

Comments

Wharton's essay emphasizes the dialogic nature of reading—reading as a conversation between author and reader. She says, "Works—even the greatest works, especially the greatest works—have no stable, universal, fixed meaning. They are invested with plural and mobile significations that are constructed in the encounter between a proposal and a reception."

What Libraries Can Do

1. Examine library practices in the light of a theory that views reading as a transaction. One obvious implication is the need to put more emphasis on the reader in the readers' advisory interview by always including a question such as, "Can you tell me about a book you have read and enjoyed?" or "What kind of reading experience are you in the mood for now?"

2. If the reader's prior knowledge is an important element in making sense of a text, readers' advisors need to have a lively sense of what those elements of prior knowledge may be, for any given type of book. Children's librarians are aware that some books demand a level of vocabulary beyond the reach of beginning readers and recommend the rule of five. Read a page at random and every time you come to a word you don't understand, hold up a finger. If you get to five fingers, it's a sign that unless the topic is absolutely riveting, you will probably not enjoy the book.

3. Be skeptical of any claim that you can determine the value or the meaning of a reading experience from the text alone.

To Read More on Models of Reading

Fish, Stanley. 1980. *Is There a Text in This Class? The Authority of Interpretive Communities.* Cambridge, MA: Harvard University Press.

> For Fish, the meaning taken from a text is the product of an interpretive strategy sanctioned by the reader's particular interpretive community.

Marshall, James. 2000. "Research on Response to Literature." In *Handbook of Reading Research,* 381–402. Vol 3. Edited by Michael L. Kamil, Peter B. Mosenthal et al. Mahwah, NJ, and London: Lawrence Erlbaum Associates.

> A useful overview that brings together "into one conversation" three traditions of thought about readers' responses to literature: the political tradition that looks at the moral dimensions of reading for individuals or communities; the critical tradition conducted mostly by literary theorists; and the empirical tradition that examines the reading responses of actual readers, usually mediated by think-aloud protocols or accounts provided by readers of their reading.

Radway, Janice. 1984. *Reading the Romance: Women, Patriarchy, and Popular Literature.* Chapel Hill: University of North Carolina Press.

> Radway contrasts her own study of real readers of romance to the work of previous writers who ignore what romance readers themselves say and privilege their own readings and explanations for why romance is read (usually that female readers are passive consumers of some harmful message that is contained within the text itself). Like de Certeau who talks of readers as poachers, Radway discovers that readers "appropriate the texts for their own purposes" (16).

Rosenblatt, Louise. 1938. *Literature as Exploration*. New York: Appleton-Century; 5th edition 1995. New York: Modern Language Association.

> Rosenblatt is interested in describing the readers' processes of engagement as they use an array of strategies to construct meaning from the black marks on the page. "The special meaning, and more particularly, the submerged associations that these words and images have for the individual reader will largely determine what the work communicates to him. The reader brings to the work personality traits, memories of past events, present needs and preoccupations, a particular mood of the moment, and a particular physical condition. These and many other elements in a never-to-be-duplicated combination determine his response to the peculiar contribution of the text" (30–31).

References

Brooks, Cleanth, and Robert Penn Warren. 1932. *Understanding Poetry*. New York: Harcourt Brace.

Cambourne, Brian. 1979. "How Important Is Theory to the Reading Teacher?" *Australian Journal of Reading* 2, no. 2: 78–90.

Culler, Jonathan. 1982. *On Deconstruction: Theory and Criticism after Structuralism*. Ithaca, NY: Cornell University Press.

de Certeau, Michel. 1984. "Reading as Poaching." In *The Practice of Everyday Life*. Translated by Steven F. Rendall. Berkeley and London: University of California Press, 165–76.

Fetterley, Judith. 1978. *The Resisting Reader: A Feminist Approach to American Fiction*. Bloomington: Indiana University Press.

Fish, Stanley. 1980. *Is There a Text in This Class? The Authority of Interpretive Communities*. Cambridge, MA: Harvard University Press.

Hall, Stuart. 1980. "Encoding/decoding." In *Culture, Media, Language: Working Papers in Cultural Studies, 1972–79*. Edited by Stuart Hall et al. London: Hutchison University Library.

Holland, Norman N. 1975. *5 Readers Reading*. New Haven, CT, and London: Yale University Press.

Iser, Wolfgang. 1978. *The Act of Reading: A Theory of Aesthetic Response*. Baltimore and London: John Hopkins University Press.

Pawley, Christine. 2002. "Seeking 'Significance': Actual Readers, Specific Reading Communities." *Book History* 5, 143–60.

Purves, Alan C. 1988. "The Aesthetic Mind of Louise Rosenblatt." *Reader* 20: 68–77. Available at http://www.hu.mtu.edu/reader/online/20/purves20.html (Accessed January 5, 2005).

Purves, Alan C., and Richard Beach. 1972. *Literature and the Reader: Research in Response to Literature, Reading Interests, and the Teaching of Literature*. Urbana, IL: National Council of Teachers of English.

Radway, Janice. 2002. "Girls, Reading and Narrative Gleaning: Crafting Repertoires for Self-Fashioning Within Everyday Life." In *Narrative Impact: Social and Cognitive Foundations,* 183–204. Edited by Melanie C. Green et al. Mahwah, NJ: Lawrence Erlbaum.

Richards, I. A. 1929. *Practical Criticism: A Study of Literary Judgment.* New York: Harcourt, Brace.

Rosenblatt, Louise. 1938. *Literature as Exploration.* New York: Appleton-Century. Reprint, 5th edition, New York: Modern Language Association, 1995.

Rosenblatt, Louise. 1978. *The Reader, the Text, the Poem: The Transactional Theory of the Literary Work.* Carbondale, IL: Southern Illinois Press. 2nd ed., Carbondale, IL: Southern Illinois Press, 1994.

Saricks, Joyce, and Nancy Brown. 1997. *Readers' Advisory Service in the Public Library.* 2nd ed. Chicago and London: American Library Association.

Suleiman, Susan R., and Inge Crosman, eds. 1980. *The Reader in the Text: Essays on Audience and Interpretation.* Princeton, NJ: Princeton University Press.

Tompkins, Jane P., ed. 1980. *Reader-Response Criticism: From Formalism to Post-Structuralism.* Baltimore and London: Johns Hopkins University Press.

Wharton, Edith. "The Vice of Reading." *North American Review* 177 (October 1903): 513–21.

Wimsatt, William K., and Munroe Beardsley. 1954. "The Affective Fallacy." In William K. Wimsatt. *The Verbal Icon: Studies in the Meaning of Poetry.* Lexington: University Press of Kentucky.

1.7. Reflecting on Reading

One good way to think about the role of the reader is to begin with your own experiences and reflect on your own reading history. Were you read to as a child? Who read to you? What can you remember about the first stages of reading on your own? Did you have a favorite book that you read and reread and maybe still have to this day safely somewhere in a cupboard or bookcase? Did you come from a reading family or did you discover reading on your own later, perhaps with the help of a teacher who read aloud a lot of stories? Aidan Chambers in *The Reading Environment* says that he was born into a house where there was little reading of any kind but a lot of oral storytelling, and a primary school teacher read to him every day (1991, 87). When you recall the experience of being read to, does your memory include a physical experience—being held in a mother's lap or bounced to the rhythm of a nursery rhyme or seated side-by-side with a sibling? Growing up, did you think of reading as something you excelled at? Or did you dread being called on to read aloud in class, expecting that you would make a mistake in the first sentence and have to sit down? Can you remember being spellbound by a story read aloud by a teacher or librarian? What was your first experience of going to the library?

To develop a reading autobiography, a good place to start is with the question that initiates almost all the interviews in Ross's study of reading for pleasure: "What's the first thing that you can remember about reading?" In these interviews conducted by Ross and her students in a graduate course on genres of fiction and reading, interviewers tried to achieve an open-ended and exploratory conversation that captured the individual reader's unique history and experience of pleasure reading. Avid readers were asked, among other questions, the following:

- What is the first book that you can remember either having read to you as a child or reading yourself? What can you remember about it?

- Can you think of a book/story that really stands out in your memory? What was special about it?

- What do you remember reading next? Next? After that?

- Was there anything in your childhood experience that you would say fostered reading? Discouraged reading?

- When you were a child, did you think of yourself as a reader? (probe: If not, then when did you start to think of yourself as reader? What made the difference?)

- How, if at all, did your reading interests change as you reached adolescence?

- How do you choose a book to read?

- Where do you get the books that you read?

- Are there types of books that you do *not* enjoy and would not choose?

- Has there ever been a book that has made a big difference to your life in one way or another? (probe: What kind of a difference? How did it help you?)

- What would it be like for you if for one reason or other you *couldn't* read?

- If you could get an author to write for the "Perfect Book," what would it be like? What elements would it include?

- What would you say is the role of reading in your life?

Whether your early childhood was rich in books or whether you read reluctantly as a child and came to book reading later in life, you will probably be able to remember the feelings, positive or negative, associated with childhood reading. As Margaret Meek says in *How Texts Teach What Readers Learn* about a similar exercise in constructing an autobiography of reading, "Summon up your best recollections and you will probably remember two things above all others— the difficulties and successes you had on your way, and the important turning points in your understanding of what reading was all about" (Meek 1988, 4).

Reflecting on reading can happen most felicitously in the context of rereading, as Wendy Lesser discovers in her book *Nothing Remains the Same* (2002). The title comes from a quotation from an 1887 letter from Mark Twain to William Dean Howells quoted as an epigraph (Lesser 2002, vii). Twain is reflecting on the felt sense of both loss and compensation in revisiting a monument of childhood, whether a book or a house: "When a man goes back to look at the house of his childhood, it has always shrunk. . . . Well, that's a loss. . . . But there are compensations. You tilt the tube skyward and bring planets and comets and corona flames a hundred and fifty thousand miles high into the field. Which I see you have done, and found Tolstoi."

In her forties, Lesser rereads books that had meant a lot to her when she first read them twenty or thirty years earlier. Revisiting *Don Quixote,* Wordsworth's "Immortality Ode," *Education of Henry Adams, Middlemarch, Anna Karenina,* George Orwell's *The Road to Wigan Pier, The Winter's Tale,* Ian McEwen's *The Child in Time,* and *Huckleberry Finn,* among others, she juxtaposes two readings performed by the older and younger reading selves. She says, "You know there are two of you because you can feel them responding differently to the book. Differently, but not entirely differently: there is a core of experience shared by your two selves" (Lesser 2002, 4). Rereading two of her favorite books from adolescence *Lucky Jim* and *I Capture the Castle,* Lesser finds that she can no longer respond to the core emotions—resentment, withheld fury, embarrassment, and righteous vindication—that she now sees at the heart of *Lucky Jim.* The opposite happens when Lesser rereads Dodie Smith's novel about two English sisters, Rose and Cassandra Mortmain, who fall in love with two American brothers and whose experiences are captured in Cassandra's journal entries. Lesser is startled by how similar her own views of life and her own beliefs and preferences have become to Cassandra's and wonders, "Did I, at thirteen, absorb the book so fully that it shaped my habits and superstitions as I grew older? Or was I drawn to Cassandra's personality precisely because it mirrored my own gradually emerging character?" (Lesser 2002, 35).

Many avid readers keep lists of books they have read, often with annotations that record the date of reading, summarize impressions of the book, and sometimes include quotations considered especially apt. Going one step further, Sara Nelson and Alberto Manguel have each written reading diaries for one year of reading. For each month, Manguel uses the rereading of favorite books as the starting point for exploring the connection between his reading and events—both current and remembered—in the everyday world. The resulting book, *A Reading Diary* (2004), is a series of diary entries that record reflections on friends, travel, and public and private events—all as elicited by his reading. In the entry written one year after September 11, 2001, Manguel reads

Chateaubriand's *From Beyond the Grave* and reflects on memory, efforts to recapture the past, climates of hatred, and the loss of empire. December's reading is Kenneth Grahame's *The Wind in the Willows,* in which Mole's losing of his familiar home triggers Manguel's elegiac reflection on the recent death of a friend and unwanted nature of change: "I want my friends to be there always. . . . I want the places I like to stay the same. . . . I don't want to keep missing voices, faces, names." In a life that has included travel from a childhood in Buenos Aires, Argentina, to residences in Italy, England, Tahiti, Canada, and France, the books in Manguel's library are the home that can be transported everywhere.

With the goal of reading a book a week and recording the experience, Sara Nelson similarly ends up reflecting on the intersection of the reading and the personal life. Senior contributing editor of *Glamour,* mother of three, wife, daughter of a Jewish mother, younger sister of a writer of literary fiction, best friend of another avid reader, Nelson says, "What I am doing, I think, is trying to get down on paper what I've been doing for years in my mind: matching up the reading experience with the personal one and watching where they intersect—or don't" (7). In *So Many Books, So Little Time: A Year of Passionate Reading* (2004), Sara Nelson starts the year with a list of books that she wants to read (*The Autobiography of Malcolm X, Cakes and Ale, The House of Mirth, A Tale of Two Cities, In Cold Blood, Empire Falls,* etc.), but the plan falls apart within the first week when she can't get into Ted Heller's *Funnymen.* She concludes, "I don't always choose the books. . . . Sometimes the books choose me" (14).

Keeping a reading diary is an ideal medium for reflection on reading and life. In *Reading Lolita in Tehran,* Azar Nafisi describes the reading diaries kept by the chosen seven of her former students who met in her Tehran home each Thursday to discuss forbidden fiction in the repressive regime of revolutionary Iran: "Each would have a private diary, in which she should record her responses to the novels, as well as ways in which these works and their discussions related to her personal and social experiences" (Nafisi 2003, 18).

Case 6: Some Books Change

This discussion of rereading happened at the end of an interview on memory and childhood reading conducted with Alice Munro in 1988 at her home in Clinton, Ontario (Ross 1989). Growing up in a community in Huron County, Ontario, where reading was considered a suspect if not shameful activity, Munro was a secret addict, reading and rereading certain favorite books in a desire for absolute possession.

Ross: Let me end the interview on the topic of rereading. Some people say, "There are so many books out there that I don't have time for rereading."

Munro: That's like saying, "There are so many flavours of ice cream, I'll never have chocolate again." Or "There's so many nice men to make love to, I'll never stay with this one." I don't take that approach to life. You either see things that way or you don't. I don't see reading in that sense. The books that are important to me, I figure on rereading some time. Most of the books I own I probably have reread, or reread in part.

Also some books change according to your own age and your situation in life. I've read *Anna Karenina* several times and the first time I read it I really identified with the young girl, Kitty, and her illness and her dreadful humiliating love for Vronsky. And when I read it again, I identified with Anna. And then I reread it and I identified with Dolly. [laughter] This was at the height of my mother period—poor Dolly's always worried about getting the washing done and she can never rise to the occasion because of her constant preoccupations. The book had just shifted this much. And then I read it again and I didn't identify with any of the women. I read it in a much calmer, overall way. And so there are books like that that change for you.

Ross: Probably any really good book will do that, if it's rich enough. As you change, you respond to levels in the book that you hadn't noticed before.

Munro: Yes. And there are ways that certain writers have of looking at the world that I sometimes want to reexperience. You read a few pages of Proust and you no longer think that ordinary things, like stuff on this coffee table, are boring. There is that feeling of everything being so deeply absorbing. Every true writer's voice seems to come out of a special conviction, a way of looking at experience, which you sometimes just feel like getting in touch with.

Comments

Many readers have reported their sense that *Anna Karenina* is a shape-shifter. Like Alice Munro, Wendy Lesser (2002, 76) also finds the book transformed through rereading: "I was amazed to see the once-disdained Levin parts—the parts I had skimmed through rapidly. . . so as to get back to the engrossing love story—taking over the book; the chapters devoted to Levin and his love for Kitty, Levin and his land, Levin and his peasants, Levin and his religious feelings are fully half the book, it turns out, and to me, now, they are the far more interesting half."

Inspirational Reading on Reading

Readers sometime talk about "reading their way into reading." Having read one good book, they want to start on another one right away, so as to repeat the pleasurable experience. At the same time, other people's enthusiasms for books or for reading can be contagious. Here are some books and essays that in one way or another celebrate reading so persuasively that, after reading them, you may want to drop everything and immerse yourself in a good book.

Butler, Dorothy. 1975. *Cushla and Her Books.* Reprint, Boston: The Horn Book, 1979.
This classic work is an account of Cushla, a child with a genetic disorder that severely retarded her physical development, whose first contact with the outside world was through books. When she was about eight months old, her family started to use picture books with Cushla as a way of occupying her waking hours. "Cushla's books have surrounded her with friends; with people and warmth and colour during the days when her life was lived in almost constant pain and frustration" (102). Reflecting on the interconnections among story, language, pleasure, and learning, Butler says, "Cushla was not 'taught' to read, unless the provision of language and story, in books and out of books, can be called a method. I believe it can, and that it is the best method of all. It produces children who experience reading as a joyous process, natural to the human state; children who absorb ideas as sponges absorb water" (105). Butler's account is one of a growing number of case studies of individual children's experience with books, a genre that notably includes Dorothy Neal White's *Books before Five* (1954) and Maureen and Hugh Crago's *Prelude to Literacy* (1983).

Calvino, Italo. 1986. *If on a Winter's Night a Traveller.* Translated by William Weaver. Toronto: Lester & Orpen Dennys.
Calvino has written a novel about reading that is a must-read for anyone interested in the phenomenology of reading and readers. This metafiction about reading alternates chapters about the protagonists' quest for an ideal reading experience with first chapters of novels that correspond to the readers' varying descriptions of their preferred genres: "I rather enjoy that sense of bewilderment a novel gives you when you first start reading it" (p. 30); "The novel I would most like to read at this moment . . . should have as its driving force only the desire to narrate, to pile stories upon stories, without trying to impose a philosophy of life on you, simply allowing you to observe its own growth, like a tree, an entangling, as if of branches and leaves" (p. 92); "The novels that attract me most . . . are those that create an illusion of transparency around a knot of human relationships as obscure, cruel, and perverse as possible" (p. 192).

Fadiman, Anne. 1998. *Ex Libris: Confessions of a Common Reader.* New York: Farrar, Straus & Giroux.
Daughter of Clifton Fadiman, the author grew up in a strenuously literary family and came naturally by her passion for language. In her preface, Fadiman introduces this collection of twelve personal essays on reading with a quote from Virginia Woolf's *The Common Reader*: "[The common reader] reads for his own pleasure rather than to impart knowledge or correct the opinions of others. Above

all, he is guided by an instinct to create for himself, out of whatever odds and ends he can come by, some kind of whole."

Kingsolver, Barbara. 1996. "How Mr. Dewey Decimal Saved My Life." In *High Tide in Tucson,* 45–53. New York: HarperCollins.

    The opening sentence of this personal essay on how Kingsolver changed her career goal in high school from motorcycle moll to writer who "ended up roaring hell-for-leather down the backroads of transcendent, reeling sentences": "A librarian named Miss Truman Richey snatched me from the jaws of ruin, and it's too late now to thank her."

Manguel, Alberto. 1996. *A History of Reading.* New York: Viking.

    This erudite and eminently readable book is doubly satisfying, being both a scholarly history of reading and an engaging personal memoir of reading. The chapter titles themselves beckon to book enthusiasts—for example, "Reading Shadows," "The Silent Readers," "The Book of Memory," "Being Read To," "The Shape of the Book," "Private Reading," "Reading the Future," "Stealing Books," "The Book Fool." For readers who expect a histories to be developed chronologically, Manguel has provided as a last page a pullout, "The Reader's Timeline," listing some reading milestones from c. 4000 B.C. when the first clay inscription occurred to 1996 when the Library of Congress's collection numbers more than a million items. My favorite is c. 1000: "To avoid parting with his collection of 117,000 books while travelling, the avid reader and Grand Vizier of Persia, Abdul Kassem Ismael, has them carried by a caravan of four hundred camels trained to walk in alphabetical order."

References

Chambers, Aidan. 1991. *The Reading Environment: How Adults Help Children Enjoy Books.* Stroud, England: The Thimble Press.

Crago, Maureen, and Hugh Crago. 1983. *Prelude to Literacy.* Carbondale and Edwardsville: Southern Illinois University Press.

Lesser, Wendy. 2002. *Nothing Remains the Same: Rereading and Remembering.* Boston: Houghton Mifflin.

Manguel, Alberto. 2004. *A Reading Diary.* New York: Farrar, Straus & Giroux.

Meek, Margaret. 1988. *How Texts Teach What Readers Learn.* South Woodchester, England: Thimble Press.

Nafisi, Azar. 2003. *Reading Lolita in Tehran: A Memoir in Books.* New York: Random House.

Nelson, Sara. 2003. *So Many Books, So Little Time: A Year of Passionate Reading.* New York: Berkley Books.

Ross, Catherine Sheldrick. 1989. "An Interview with Alice Munro." *CCL: Canadian Children's Literature,* 53: 15–24.

White, Dorothy Neal. 1954. *Books before Five.* New York: Oxford University Press.

Chapter 2

Becoming a Reader: Childhood Years

Lynne (E.F.) McKechnie

In *Voices of Readers: How We Come to Love Books*, Carlsen and Sherrill (1988) share excerpts from more than one thousand reading autobiographies completed by their students of education and librarianship. These reading accounts give us a vivid sense, from the perspective of readers themselves, of the complex task of learning to read, as in this example:

> My first recollection of reading was the wonderful experience of having stories read to me by my parents and older sister. My sister read to me from a primer so much that I memorized the book and by looking at the pictures I could recite it verbatim. Oh, the sheer joy of reading a book! Although I couldn't actually read, I think that this was the motivation I needed. I wanted to read more than anything else in the world. (Carlsen and Sherrill 1988, 30)

This chapter looks specifically at children and reading. It begins with a brief overview of what is known about children and reading—what surveys and other large studies tell us. It continues with a description of how children become readers. Two topics of current interest follow: the contentious issue of series book reading and the "problem" of boys and reading. The chapter concludes by looking at the relationship among children, public libraries, and reading.

2.1. What We Know about Children and Reading

Surveying Childhood Reading

Although most of the large-scale national surveys of reading have targeted adults, many have included questions about the state of children's reading. The following findings, which tend to agree across constituencies, are typical.

- *United States:* A survey of media use by 2,032 youth 8 to 18 years old (Rideout, Roberts, and Foehr 2005) found that young people spend an average of 6.5 hours per day using media. Although the amount of time spent with media, particularly new media such as computers, the Internet, and video games, had increased significantly since a previous survey in 1999, the amount of time spent reading remained steady at about forty-three minutes per day. Additionally, three-quarters of the children and teens reported daily reading for pleasure.

- *Australia:* A national telephone survey (Nielsen 2001) of 1,503 adults conducted in June 2001 found that 74 percent of parents with children under age thirteen had read to the children in the previous week for an average of five of the seven days. Parents were more apt to purchase books for their children than for themselves. Those more likely to read to and purchase books for their children were those who had higher levels of education and were themselves avid readers.

- *Canada:* In a 1991 survey (Ekos Research 1992) of more than seven thousand respondents, parents reported reading to their children (aged thirteen years and younger) an average of 1.6 hours per week. "Most parents strongly agreed that reading is a healthy alternative to television viewing and that it is important for children to read for pleasure in order to succeed in school" (Ekos Research 1992, 34).

- *England:* A research study from Oxford Brookes University of more than five thousand pupils between 1998 and 2001 revealed "that despite the rise in 11-year-olds' national test scores, reading and reasoning tests set by the National Foundation for Educational Research suggest that standards have remained unchanged" (United Kingdom National Literacy Trust 2003, 1).

- *International:* The Progress in International Reading Literacy Study (PIRLS), a large comparative study conducted in 2001 (National Center for Education Statistics n.d.), compared the reading literacy of Grade 4 students across thirty-five countries. Sweden, the Netherlands and England had the highest scores, with Canada and the United States also scoring in the top quarter. In all thirty-five countries, girls outperformed boys.

Still More . . . and More . . . and More . . . Studies of Children's Reading

An enormous body of empirical studies, primarily in the field of education, has explored a wide variety of variables related to reading and children. Among other things, educators are interested in the mechanics of learning to read, classroom strategies for teaching reading, and effective interventions for children experiencing difficulty in reading. For those wanting to look more closely at individual studies of reading, Stephen Krashen's (2004) *The Power of Reading: Insights from the Research* provides succinct summaries of many studies and an overview of their findings. Although a review of this literature is beyond the scope of this book, a discussion of a few studies of particular interest to parents, librarians, and other adults concerned about children's reading serves to give a sense of the range and type of studies that have been conducted.

Using a stratified sample of 18,185 American children in Grades 1 through 6, McKenna, Kear, and Ellsworth (1995) found that attitudes toward reading became more negative as children grew older. Negative attitudes toward reading were correlated with weaker ability, with the least able readers being the least interested in reading. Girls had more favorable attitudes toward reading than did boys and this gap widened with increasing age.

Statistics Canada's (2004) "National Longitudinal Survey of Children and Youth" (NLSCY) tested four- and five-year-old children, using the Peabody Picture Vocabulary Test, designed to test a child's level of oral vocabulary. Children of immigrants whose parents' first language was neither English nor French (Canada's two official languages) started school with less developed reading and writing skills than did children of Canadian-born parents. In the early grades, reading skills were found to be about 20 percent lower and writing skills 30 percent lower compared to classmates of Canadian-born parents. The Statistics Canada study found this gap did not disappear until the immigrant children were ten or eleven years old. Reporting on data collected in 1996–7 by Statistics Canada for its National Longitudinal Survey of Children and Youth, Lipps and Yiptong-Avila (1999) note that children who participated in formal early childhood care and education programs such as structured daycare, nursery schools, playgroups and mom-and-tot programs, performed better in both reading and writing in kindergarten and grade one. These results held across varying family income and parental education levels. Children who had been read to daily and had early exposure to books did substantially better in kindergarten than those who had not.

Reading Preferences

Any parent, librarian, or teacher knows that finding a book that interests a child is one of the best ways to motivate a child to read. A logical way to support children's reading would seem to be to conduct studies to determine what children prefer to read. Over the last fifty years, many researchers have done just that. Adele Fasick (1985) provides a review of childhood reading preference studies. Not surprisingly most agree that children report liking mysteries, adventure stories, and ghost stories. Reading interests vary with age, with older children in Grades 5 to 7 liking fantasy, science fiction, and sports stories. Typically studies have found that reading interests vary by gender, with one study noting that across all ages boys say they dislike love stories and girls say they dislike war stories. Although interesting, these findings are not particularly useful. Reading preference is highly personal. Understanding group trends is unlikely to be helpful when an individual child asks you for "a good book to read."

More recent studies of childhood reading preference and motivation focus on general principles rather than on specific titles or genres. Ivey and Broaddus (2001, 356) surveyed "1,765 sixth-grade students in 23 schools" in both an urban and a rural/small city area to learn what made them want to read. They did follow-up interviews with thirty-one of the children. Classroom reading activities most enjoyed were free reading time (63 percent of respondents) and the teacher reading out loud (62 percent). Classroom book discussion groups were liked by only 16 percent of the children and reading stories from the reading text by only 8 percent. To the question "What makes you want to read in this class?" many of the students (42 percent) responded that they were motivated by finding good materials to read and having choice in the selection of these reading materials (361). "Bad" reading was reported as being directly related to assigned reading, which was experienced as boring and difficult. One of the respondents gave a good example: "I had to read *O Pioneers!* It was the longest most boring book ever" (363). Ivey and Broaddus (367) conclude, "having a rich supply of texts and many opportunities to experience text through independent reading and through teacher read-alouds may be universal needs for diverse students across a range of contexts."

When adults preselect books for a child without knowing that child very well, things tend to go wrong. Carter and Harris (1981) compared the child-chosen titles on selected "Children's Choice" lists published by state library associations with lists of best books for children published by reviewing journals such as *School Library Journal* and *Booklist*. Only one-quarter of the children's choices were found on the journal lists.

Although it is important that children have access to high-quality, literary works, it is clear that they also want to read more popular materials. A more recent study by Worthy, Moorman, and Turner (1999) confirms the discrepancy between the materials provided in school and public libraries and what children themselves choose to read. Sixth-grade students completed questionnaires about what they liked to read. Preferred reading included scary stories, comics and cartoons, magazines, drawing books, series books, funny books, and other materials from the realm of popular rather than of literary culture. To access what they wanted to read and did read, these sixth graders said their main sources were bookstores and subscriptions rather than libraries (school, public, or classroom).

What the Experts Say

Much of what we know about children and their reading comes through the expert observation and reflection of skilled parents and practicing teachers and librarians as well as scholars who have been working in this area for long periods of time. Here are two experts who are wise observers of children reading. Margaret Meek is a parent, teacher and internationally recognized reading expert. She states firmly that helping a child learn to read is fundamentally an uncomplicated task:

> To learn to read, children need the attention of one patient adult, or an older child, for long enough to read something that pleases them both. A book, a person, and shared enjoyment: these are the conditions of success. The process should begin at an early age and continue as a genuine collaborative activity until the child leaves school. Understanding the reading process may help, but there is nothing so special about it that any interested adult cannot easily grasp it by thinking about why he or she enjoys reading. (Meek 1982, 9)

For Donald Fry, a scholar of reading, the central issue in becoming a reader is to see oneself as a reader:

> Even before we can read, we behave like readers. Very young children borrow books from libraries, go to bookshops, and number books amongst their possessions. They pick up their comics at the newsagents, choose from catalogues, and begin to make out the differences between timetables and maps and recipes and other things that they see their parents using. They handle and arrange books, turning over the pages which they cannot yet read, but which they recognise. They play at reading, accompanying their turning of pages with their own version of the story: perhaps they read aloud to toys, to an imaginary playgroup or an invisible friend. They play at writing, too, making 'books', or seeing their own words made into writing by adults and being read. They already know about books, naming titles, recognising books and series

of books. And, of course, they attend to stories that are read to them, at home and elsewhere, feeling themselves to be part of a community that reads, and coming into the sure possession of what story is and what a story does. They see themselves as readers, and we could say that unless they do so, and are encouraged to do so, they will not learn to read. (Fry, 1985, 94)

To Read More

Carlsen, G. Robert, and Anne Sherrill. 1988. *Voices of Readers: How We Come to Love Books*. Urbana, IL: National Council of Teachers of English.

Using excerpts from more than one thousand reading autobiographies, the authors provide insight into a number of questions asked of their participants including the following: "What did they remember about learning how to read? What books did they remember reading? Who, if anyone, had been important in developing their attitudes toward reading? When and where did they read?" (1988, x) A fascinating book in which the voices of readers are central to understanding childhood reading.

Meek, Margaret. 1982. *Learning to Read*. London: Bodley Head.

Intended for parents, this book examines what happens as children learn to read and shows how parents can best help them at each stage. Meek (1982, 25) describes her book as follows: "An alternative viewpoint, that reading is too important to be left to experts, is presented in this book. Reading is whole-task learning, right from the start. From first to last the child should be invited to behave like a reader, and those who want to help him should assume that he can learn, and will learn, just as happened when he began to talk. Once a child knows that print has meaning and that he can make it mean something, he will learn to read. The adult's job is to read with him what both can enjoy, to let him see how the story goes, to help him observe what is there to be read, and to tell him what he needs to know when he finds it difficult. Learning to read in the early stages, like everything else a child has come to know, is an approximation of adult behaviour with a genuine, meaningful function."

References

Carlsen, G. Robert, and Anne Sherrill. 1988. *Voices of Readers: How We Come to Love Books*. Urbana, IL: National Council of Teachers of English.

Carter, Betty, and Karen Harris. 1981. "The Children and the Critics: How Do Their Book Selections Compare?" *School Library Media Quarterly* 10, no. 1: 55–58.

Ekos Research. 1992. *Reading in Canada 1991*. Ottawa, ON: Ekos Research Associates.

Fasick, Adele. 1985. "How Much Do We Know about What Children Are Reading?" *Emergency Librarian* 12, no. 3: 17–24.

Fry, Donald. 1985. *Children Talk about Books: Seeing Themselves as Readers*. Milton Keynes, England: Open University Press.

Ivey, Gay, and Karen Broaddus. 2001. " 'Just Plain Reading': A Survey of What Makes Students Want to Read in Middle School Classrooms." *Reading Research Quarterly* 36, no. 4: 350–77.

Krashen, Stephen D. 2004. *The Power of Reading: Insights from the Research.* 2nd ed. Westport, CT: Libraries Unlimited.

Lipps, Garth, and Jackie Yiptong-Avila. 1999. *From Home to School: How Canadian Children Cope.* Statistics Canada Catalogue No. 89F0117XIE. Ottawa, ON: Culture Tourism and the Centre for Education Statistics.

McKenna, Michael C., Dennis J. Kear, and Randolph A. Ellsworth. 1995. "Children's Attitudes towards Reading: A National Survey." *Reading Research Quarterly* 30, no. 4: 934–56.

Meek, Margaret. 1982. *Learning to Read.* London: Bodley Head.

National Center for Educational Statistics (United States). n.d. *Preprimary and Primary Education: International Comparisons of Reading Literacy in Grade 4.* Available at http://nces.ed.gov/surveys/international (accessed June 15, 2005).

Nielsen, A. C. 2001. *A National Survey of Reading, Buying and Borrowing Books.* Melbourne, Australia: Books Alive; Department of Communications, Information Technology and the Arts; Federal Government of Australia. Available at http://www.ozco.gov.au/arts_resources/publications/a_national_survey_of_reading,_buying_and_borrowing_books/ (accessed June 15, 2005).

Rideout, Victoria, Donald F. Roberts, and Ulla G. Foehr. 2005. *Generation M: Media in the Lives of 8–18 Year-olds.* Menlo Park, CA: Henry J. Kaiser Family Foundation. Available at http:// www.kff.org/entmedia030905pkg.cfm (accessed June 15, 2005).

Statistics Canada. 2004. *Children of Immigrants: How Well Do They Do in School?* Available at http://www.statcan.ca/english/freepub/81-004-XIE/200410/immi.htm (accessed June 15, 2005).

United Kingdom National Literacy Trust. 2003. "Oxford Brookes Research Suggests Reading Standards Haven't Improved." In *Research and Reading and Libraries*, 1–2. Available at http://www.literacytrust.org.uk/Research/libresearch2.htm (accessed June 15, 2005).

Worthy, Jo, Megan Moorman, and Margo Turner. 1999. "What Johnny Likes to Read Is Hard to Find in School." *Reading Research Quarterly* 34, no. 1: 12–27.

2.2. Becoming a Reader

With reading described as an essential skill for success throughout life and evidence that literacy is not universal, the question of *how* one becomes a reader is clearly important. The roots of literacy are grounded in childhood. A number of early landmark studies have investigated how children become readers.

Dolores Durkin (1966) surveyed almost 10,000 children just as they began to attend school and found that only 229 (2.4 percent) could read eighteen or more common words. She then interviewed a sample of parents from both the early reading and nonreading groups to find out how they differed. What distinguished the parents of the early readers was their involvement in activities with their children such as reading aloud to them; answering their questions; helping them with printing, spelling, and the sounds of letters; identifying words; and encouraging them to write. Durkin followed the early readers in a longitudinal study through to the end of Grade 6, discovering that they continued to do well academically.

Margaret Clark (1976) studied thirty-two children, all of whom could read before starting school, to explore the factors that contribute to children's progress in learning to read. Although these precocious readers had varying backgrounds in terms of family income and education levels, all came from families where books were read and stories were told. Glenda Bissex (1980) in *GNYS AT WRK* presents a case study of her own young son, showing how he considered himself to be a writer (a "genius at work") and underscoring the intricate and dynamic interplay between writing and reading. What is common to these studies and others like them is a sense that becoming a reader is a process that is complex and that is situated in early life experiences before the onset of formal education. The memories of childhood reading by the participants in Catherine Ross's study of avid adult readers confirm this.

Case 7: Cultivating Readers

Here's what the readers in Catherine Ross's study of avid adult readers said about the reading environments of their childhood that fostered a love of reading. The following is a sample drawn from many, many similar statements from readers:

Stella: Oh [my mom] read to me every night before I went to bed. . . . She opened the door to books for me, I suppose, and it was always such a pleasant experience to have somebody sit with you and read to you. . . . It certainly made an impression on me and I tried to duplicate that with my own children and I read to them. So I think the contact with the books and a parent are as important as the content of the books. (Librarian, age forty-nine)

Robert: I have read ever since I could do the alphabet. . . . Our house had a lot of books spread around. I know I began indiscriminately reading. It was never guided reading. Mother just left books around. So I never had any sense of censorship. Having books around is the most important thing, so far as I'm concerned, in a house. You can take your child to all sorts of organized visits to the library, and that's very good.

But if the books aren't around in the house, I doubt very much that you will cultivate a reader. (Professor of English, fifty-seven)

Sandra: Yes, I think all of my family pretty well tended to do a lot of reading. . . . I remember when I was a child being amazed that [my best friend's mother] was paying her for every book she would read in an effort to get her to read, and I thought that was amazing. I went and told my mother, "Why won't you pay me for every book I read?" It really amazed me that someone had to be bribed to read. (Graduate student, age twenty-six)

Arthur: We were very poor even by the standards of that day and living in a very backwoods area. Rural, so there weren't any—there were very few books in our home. However, both my father and mother read magazines and read the newspaper. They were avid readers, and I suppose there was something in me that brought me to read, because, as I went to school, I found most of the reading interesting. And a lot of the reading, of course, came from the schoolbooks themselves. (Director of a men's mission, age sixty-two)

Doreen: [Our family] had tons and tons of books. Any special event was always topped with a book. We had every kind of book you can imagine. Plus we lived at the library. Both of my brothers and me. My parents were avid readers. We had a cottage where we kept what we called our summertime books and they were reread every summer. . . . I had an Aunt Jean and she was the one who started me and every year she gave me a Lucy Maud Montgomery book. And then my grandmother had kept all my mother's books, and as she saw that I was at the age where I should have them, I got them. (Business consultant, age thirty-eight)

Craig: If you want to know how I started to read—our next-door neighbors had a pretty fair library for that time. Their aunt was a teacher. I started out with the Burgess books and then went on to the Alger books and then to Westerns, Edgar Rice Burroughs, and on into the more advanced books as I got older. . . . I was born in the country, and we didn't have a can to kick down the street. (Retired skilled tradesperson, age sixty-seven)

Tariq: There [were] about fifty books on the hall table every week or every two weeks from the library. (CBC office worker, age twenty-five)

Mark: The first memory I have of my mother, I think, is with a book in her hands. (Instructor in music education and composition, age forty-two)

Aaron: My dad read to me every single night. We used to lie on his bed and he'd read to me. . . . I looked forward to it, and he encouraged me to read too. He'd give me a chance to go ahead as well—he wouldn't just steal the show. (Master's student in English, age twenty-three)

Anita: Both my parents are great readers. I don't remember either of them saying, "You should read" or "Reading is a wonderful thing." I think we all just did it by following their example. . . . My mother was the sort who went to the library every week and got five books out and read them. And then, as soon as we were old enough, we had library cards and we would go with her. I just took [reading] for granted. I thought everybody did it. It didn't have to be sold to me. I just enjoyed it so much. And now, all of us are readers. (Master's of library and information science student, age twenty-five)

Carol: My parents both read a lot, and they always read to me at night. And they always really liked it when I read, so they made me feel good when I read. I would get lots of attention when I read. (Archaeologist, age twenty-five)

Comments

Aidan Chambers says, "Readers are made, not born. No one comes into the world already disposed for or against print" (Chambers 1973, 16). Nevertheless, the early years tend to set the pattern for what follows. An overwhelming majority of the committed adult readers in Ross's study came from families that strongly supported reading in childhood. Financial security mattered less than a family sense of valuing books and reading.

What We Know about Early Reading

Current research emphasizes a new approach to learning to read called emergent literacy. According to Teale and Sulzby (1986), the emergent literacy paradigm places the onset of literacy acquisition at birth rather than at the introduction of formal reading instruction in school. Listening, speaking, reading, and writing are seen as interrelated and develop concurrently. Literacy learning occurs in real-life settings in which literacy has real functions. From the perspective of emergent literacy, children's literacy is often learned through social interaction and the role modeling of others.

One thing we know about early reading is the importance of hearing stories read aloud. *Becoming a Nation of Readers: The Report of the Commission on Reading* (Anderson et al. 1985), a major U.S. Department of Education study, flatly states: "The single most important activity for building the knowledge required for eventual success in reading is reading aloud to children" (Anderson et al. 1985, 28). This assertion is strongly supported in the results of Gordon Wells's study, *The Meaning Makers* (1986). Wells placed tape recorders in the homes of 128 children, half of whom were fifteen months and the other half thirty-nine months old at the beginning of the study. On one day every three months for two and one-half years, 18 ninety-second audio recordings were made at random intervals to capture the naturally occurring conversations in the children's homes. The best indicator of later success at school was the child's knowledge of literacy and in particular the number of stories read aloud to the child. Wells estimated that Jonathon, a star reader in later years at school, had heard more than five thousand stories read aloud at home before he started school. In contrast, Rosie had heard almost no stories and in school experienced great difficulty with both her language and reading skills. Reading aloud to children has been described by many, including Aidan Chambers (1991), as being powerful for a number of reasons: it helps children learn how narratives work; it makes difficult materials accessible; it encourages children to read a text themselves; and it is a shared, social-bonding experience.

Margaret Meek provides a convincing argument for the importance of immersing children in stories and other texts. In *How Texts Teach What Readers Learn* (1988), Meek claims that the act of reading itself provides "private lessons in reading." Children who have been read to before school "can turn pages, tell a story from pictures, recognize advertisements on television, and know that print is common in their world (Meek 1988, 7). Reading aloud to children helps them see the relationship between print and speech. It gives them a sense of stories and how they work. Through being read to, children learn that book language differs from conversational language. "The most important single lesson that children learn from texts is the nature and variety of written discourse, the different ways that language lets a writer tell, and the many different ways a reader reads" (Meek 1988, 21). Joan Gibbons (1999, 209) agrees, stating, "Through hearing, reading and discussing stories, children begin to understand the nature of texts. Understanding different ways in which books are read and exploring the various ways in which meaning is expressed is a reading task that does not end with childhood; it continues for as long as the reader continues to tackle new kinds of reading experiences.

Although it is important to ensure that a parent or some other caring older person reads to children, there is some evidence to suggest that *how* parents read with their children may be just as important as *whether* they read to their children. Bergin, Lancy, and Draper (1994) videotaped thirty-two white, working-class parent-child pairs while the parent and child were sharing a picture book. They discovered that parents use widely variant approaches to this task and that specific behaviors were associated with positive and negative outcomes. Fluency and positive emotions associated with reading were found to be important in predicting success with reading. "[P]airs who view the child's reading as a source of fun, keep the story flowing without letting the child get bogged down in decoding (by using semantic-oriented rather than decoding-oriented correction tactics), encourage questions about the story, and express humor while reading have children who are more fluent and more positive about reading" (Bergin, Lancy, and Draper 1994, 72). They note that parents of successful readers tended to send the message that "Reading is fun!" whereas parents using negative behaviors broadcast a sense that "Reading is work."

Reading aloud to children varies across social class, with lower frequency of storybook sharing in low-income homes (Teale 1986) and lower availability and use of reading and writing materials in lower income families (Anderson, Teale, and Estrada 1980). Interventions have been tried, and there is some evidence to indicate that they work. In a study for which the purpose "was to test whether it was possible to enhance parent involvement in children's language and literacy development" (Svensson 1994, 84), twenty-five Swedish children received twice-yearly visits from 2.5 through 6.5 years of age. In each visit, the parents were given information about language and literacy development as well as books and other educational materials. These children were compared with a control group that received no intervention. Svensson found that the families in the experimental group read books, played with nursery rhymes, did fingerplays, and sang songs more than they had before the interventions and more than the parents in the control group.

In an overview of group intervention programs designed to increase the awareness and participation of parents in early literacy activities such as Running Start (funded by Chrysler in eight U.S. school districts) or Partnership for Family Reading (funded by Metropolitan Life in Newark, New Jersey), Lancy and Talley (1994) note that such efforts have been successful in at least creating a stronger and broader cultural awareness of the importance of early literacy activities. Carr (1994) found that encouraging parents to work with their children by assigning storybook reading and other daily literacy tasks to be completed at home, enriching the literacy environment of the classroom, and providing cross-age and peer tutors for children experiencing difficulty resulted in notice-able improvements in the literacy skills of an urban, low-income kindergarten class.

Factors That Foster Early Reading

The research has clearly established that particular contexts and activities are needed for children to become readers. As identified by many researchers including Chambers (1991), Clark (1976), Clay (1966), Hall (1987), Heath (1982), Meek (1982), and Sulzby and Teale (1991), the following factors foster early reading:

- Hearing stories read aloud by a parent or another caring adult
- Having opportunities to do emergent story readings ("reading" on one's own)
- Having ready access to reading materials at home, at school, or through a public library
- Having free choice of reading materials so that stories are enjoyed and the experience is pleasurable
- Having both the space and time for shared and individual reading
- Being part of a "readerly" family in which parents, siblings, and extended family act as role models
- Having opportunities to talk about reading both while being read to and in other contexts such as at the family dinner table
- Having a sense that reading is a valuable activity
- Having access to an enabling adult

Children and Adults Reading within the Zone of Proximal Development

The enabling adult turns up time and time again in studies of early reading acquisition. The work of Lev Vygotsky—in particular, his concept of the zone of proximal development—is helpful in explaining why the presence of a more experienced reader is so important. Vygotsky (1978, 86) described the zone of proximal development as

> the distance between the actual developmental level as determined by independent problem solving and the level of potential development as determined through problem solving under adult guidance or in collaboration with more capable peers.

Vygotsky held that children learn new cognitive skills by practicing them in social interaction with a more experienced person until the skill is mastered, internalized, and can be carried out independently. A number of studies have used the conceptual framework of Vygotsky's zone of proximal development as a way of understanding the joint adult-child collaboration in learning situations, including those involving stories and literacy. Tizard and Hughes (1984) compared the language experience of middle- and working-class four-year-old children at home and at nursery school by making audio recordings of their naturally occurring talk in both settings. They found that the home setting provided a very powerful environment for learning. The home setting had the advantage of its low adult-to-child ratio, the close emotional relationship between mother and child, the long-shared context, the wide range of activities engaged in, and the home setting's potential to embed learning in contexts meaningful to the individual child. Of particular interest here, "the longest conversations tended to occur in the context of story-reading and joint adult-child play, and . . . the context which provoked the most questions from children was story-telling" (Tizard et al. 1980, 74).

Two other research studies that look specifically at how literacy learning happens within the zone of proximal development are worth noting. Shirley Brice Heath (1982) speaks directly of the role of adult scaffolding in children's literacy development. She notes how adults help the children make text-to-life connections, encourage children to talk around a story, converse with children as they read stories together, and employ tactics such as pausing during reading to allow children to practice prediction. Lynne McKechnie (1996, 2000) conducted an observation study of 30 four-year-old girls and their mothers on an ordinary visit to their local public libraries. She discovered that one of the most important roles of the library was to support young children in their literacy development. The most frequently observed activity after the selection and checkout of library materials was shared reading of stories, with 21 or 70 percent of the girls being read to by their mothers or another adult while in the library. These story read-alouds were captured by the tape recorders the girls wore during their visits. The mothers proved themselves to be adept reading teachers as they shared stories with their daughters.

As David Lancy (1994, 3) points out, "those who are expert in the uses of literacy—parents and older siblings as opposed to reading teachers—model and introduce these uses to children. They create situations—dinner table conversations, interactive bedtime story rituals—where children can flap their stubby little literacy wings without fear of crashing to the ground." They read with their children within the zone of proximal development.

Case 8: The Important Role of Adults in Bringing Children to Reading

Elissa (age four) was a participant in McKechnie's (1996, 191) study of preschoolers using public libraries. In the following excerpt from an audio recording of their visit to the library, Elissa and her mother were reading *The Very Hungry Caterpillar*, a classic picture book written and illustrated by Eric Carle.

Elissa: You know what?

Mother: What?

Elissa: This is it. This is the caterpillar one.

Mother: What happens to him?

Elissa: Gets big.

Mother: And then what?

Elissa: Then . . . he gets bigger.

Mother: Uh huh?

Elissa: And then he gets fat.

Mother: Right! And when he finishes eating and getting big and fat, what happens at the end?

Elissa: Butterfly!

Observation Note: Mother laughs joyfully.

Comments

Elissa's recognition of the book reveals her growing knowledge of children's literature. Through the content of the story, she seems to have learned something about the life cycle of butterflies. Her ability to retell the story in the proper sequence shows that she understands something about the structure and conventions of stories. Elissa's mother supports her daughter's reading by asking open questions ("And then what?") and affirming Elissa's retelling of the story by repeating it using Elissa's own words ("big" and "fat"). Elissa's mother provided room and time for her to "read" this story, providing clues and cues as needed, and reinforcing the competence Elissa brought to the task. Elissa and her mother were working together in Vygotsky's (1978) zone of proximal development.

What Libraries Can Do

1. Provide large, rich collections.

2. Run story-time programs for babies, toddlers, and preschool children both in the library and through outreach to other community locations. These programs should include complementary activities such as crafts, songs, and finger plays that extend and reinforce the stories.

3. Facilitate access to reading materials through booklists and pathfinders, displays, and reader's advisory services.

4. Provide areas for reading, especially areas for young children and adults to read together.

5. Loan materials, either individual titles or specially prepared kits, and work cooperatively with other organizations such as nursery schools, day-care centers, "family literacy programs or other community-wide programs that serve children in their homes or in community locations" (Teale 1995, 116).

6. "[E]ducate parents, preschool teachers, or child-care professionals in what and how to read to preschoolers" (Teale 1995, 118).

What Parents Can Do

1. Read to your child.

2. Share a wide variety of books (fiction, nonfiction, poetry, picture books) in a wide variety of narrative genres with your child.

3. "Involve your child in the selection of books" (Bouchard 2001, 26).

4. Buy books for your child. "We like to possess copies of the books that mean most to us. Owning them allows us to reread them whenever we want, helps us to remember what is in them. Seeing them on our shelves and handling them now and then gives us pleasure" (Chambers 1991, 61).

5. Go to the library with your child—attend story time programs and borrow books.

6. Make books with your child.

7. Serve as a role model by reading yourself.

8. Provide time for reading. "Adults who care for children as readers must make sure that children have time for reading" (Chambers 1991, 36). It's equally important to provide quiet, comfortable spaces for reading.

9. Encourage early writing activities such as dictating stories for an adult to write down, making shopping lists, playing with magnetic fridge letters, scrapbook making, and play-dough letter modeling (Binkley 1988, 9–10).

To Read More about Becoming a Reader

Chambers, Aidan. 1991. *The Reading Environment: How Adults Help Children Enjoy Books*. Stroud, England: Thimble Press.

Chambers writes about the factors that contribute to a reading-friendly environment, including access to book stocks, displays, reading areas, reading time, storytelling, reading aloud, book owning, friends and peers, and the enabling adult. This book is full of practical suggestions for teachers, librarians, parents, and others who work with children and reading.

Immroth, Barbara Froling, and Viki Ash-Geisler, eds. 1995. *Achieving School Readiness: Public Libraries and National Education Goal No. 1*. Chicago: American Library Association.

With chapters on storytelling, play, social development, learning styles, oral and written language, and emergent literacy by leading scholars and practitioners, this book places the reading lives of young children within the larger context of their overall development. Drawing on the research literature, it includes suggestions for ensuring and enhancing healthy early literacy development.

Teale, William H., and Elizabeth Sulzby, eds. 1986. *Emergent Literacy: Reading and Writing*. Norwood, NJ: Ablex.

Teale and Sulzby explore young children and their reading and writing, covering the period from birth through five or six years. With chapters contributed from leading researchers in the field, they provide an excellent overview of early literacy development as a continuing and changing process. A landmark work.

Three Great Books for Parents

Full of inspiring stories and practical tips and written in highly accessible language, any of these three titles would help parents interested in fostering the development of their children as readers. The author of *Cushla and Her Books* (1980—see section 1.7) and *Babies Need Books* (1998), Dorothy Butler is widely acknowledged as the person most responsible for popularizing the importance of reading to babies. Marie Clay was the first to use the term *emergent literacy* in her doctoral research of 1966. Bernice Cullinan is a professor of early childhood and education at New York University. Mem Fox is an award-winning, Australian children's author and a passionate advocate of reading to children.

Butler, Dorothy, and Marie Clay. 1987. *Reading Begins at Home: Preparing Children for Reading Before They Go to School*. Portsmouth, NH: Heinemann.

Cullinan, Bernice E. 2000. *Read to Me: Raising Kids Who Love to Read*. New York: Scholastic.

Fox, Mem. 2001. *Reading Magic: Why Reading Aloud to Our Children Will Change Their Lives Forever*. San Diego, CA: Harvest Original/Harcourt.

References

Anderson, Alonzo B., William H. Teale, and Elette Estrada. 1980. "Low-income Children's Preschool Literacy Experiences: Some Naturalistic Observations." *The Quarterly Newsletter of the Laboratory of Human Cognition* 2: 59–65.

Anderson, Richard C., Elfrieda H. Hiebert, J. A. Scott, and I. A. G. Wilkinson. 1985. *Becoming a Nation of Readers: The Report of the Commission on Reading*. Pittsburgh, PA: U.S. National Academy of Education.

Bergin, Chris, David F. Lancy, and Kelly D. Draper. 1994. "Parents' Interactions with Beginning Readers." In *Children's Emergent Literacy: From Research to Practice*, 53–77. Edited by David F. Lancy. Westport, CT: Praeger

Binkley, Marilyn R. 1988. *Becoming a Nation of Readers: What Parents Can Do*. Indianapolis, IN: D.C. Heath with the U.S. Department of Education.

Bissex, Glenda. 1980. *GNYS AT WRK: A Child Learns to Read and Write*. Cambridge, MA: Harvard University Press.

Bouchard, David. 2001. *The Gift of Reading*. Victoria, BC: Orca Books.

Butler, Dorothy. 1980. *Cushla and Her Books*. Boston: Horn Book.

Butler, Dorothy. 1998. *Babies Need Books: Sharing the Joy of Books with Your Child from Birth to Six*. Portsmouth, NH: Heinemann.

Carr, Eileen M. 1994. "It Takes a Whole Village to Raise a Child: Supplementing Instruction for 'At-Risk' Kindergarten Students." In *Children's Emergent Literacy: From Research to Practice*. Edited by David F. Lancy, 238–49. Westport, CT: Praeger.

Chambers, Aidan. 1973. *Introducing Books to Children*. London: Heinemann Educational Books.

Chambers, Aidan. 1991. *The Reading Environment: How Adults Help Children Enjoy Books*. Stroud, England: Thimble Press.

Clark, Margaret M. 1976. *Young Fluent Readers: What Can They Teach Us?* London: Heinemann.

Clay, Mary M. 1966. *Emergent Reading Behaviour*. Ph.D. diss., University of Auckland, New Zealand.

Durkin, Dolores. 1966. *Children Who Read Early*. New York: Teachers College Press.

Gibbons, Joan. 1999. "Literature for Children." In *Learning to Read: Beyond Phonics and Whole Language*, 195–214. Edited by G. Brian Thompson and Tom Nicholson. New York: Teachers College Press.

Hall, Nigel. 1987. *The Emergence of Literacy*. Portsmouth, NH: Heinemann.

Heath, Shirley B. 1982. "What No Bedtime Story Means: Narrative Skills at Home and School." *Language in Society* 11, no. 1: 49–76.

Lancy, David F. 1994. "The Conditions That Support Emergent Literacy." In *Children's Emergent Literacy: From Research to Practice*, 1–20. Edited by David F. Lancy. Westport, CT: Praeger.

Lancy, David F., and Talley, Susan D. 1994. "Stimulating/Simulating Environments That Support Emergent Literacy." In *Children's Emergent Literacy: From Research to Practice,* 127–55. Westport, CT: Praeger.

McKechnie, Lynne (E. F.). 1996. *Opening the "Preschoolers' Door to Learning": An Ethnographic Study of the Use of Public Libraries by Preschool Girls.* Ph.D. diss. University of Western Ontario, London, Ontario, Canada.

McKechnie, Lynne (E. F.). 2000. "The Ethnographic Observation of Preschool Children." *LISR* 22, no. 1: 61–76.

Meek, Margaret.1982. *Learning to Read.* London: Bodley Head.

Meek, Margaret. 1988. *How Texts Teach What Readers Learn.* Stroud, England: Thimble Press.

Sulzby, Elizabeth, and William H. Teale. 1991. "Emergent Literacy." In *Handbook of Reading Research.* Vol. 2. Edited by Rebecca Barr, Michael L. Kamil, Peter Mosenthal, and P. David Pearson, 727–758. White Plains, NY: Longman.

Svensson, Ann-Katrin. 1994. "Helping Parents Help Their Children: Early Language Stimulation in the Child's Home." In *Children's Emergent Literacy: From Research to Practice*, 79–92. Edited by David F. Lancy. Westport, CT: Praeger.

Teale, William H. 1986. "Home Background and Young Children's Literacy Development." In *Emergent Literacy: Writing and Reading*, 173–206. Edited by William H. Teale and Elizabeth Sulzby. Norwood, NJ: Ablex.

Teale, William H. 1995. "Public Libraries and Emergent Literacy: Helping Set the Foundation for School Success." In *Achieving School Readiness: Public Libraries and National Education Goal No. 1*, 113–33. Edited by Barbara Froling Immroth and Viki Ash-Geisler. Chicago: American Library Association.

Teale, William H., and Elizabeth Sulzby, eds. 1986. *Emergent Literacy: Writing and Reading.* Norwood, NJ: Ablex.

Tizard, Barbara, Helen Carmichael, Martin Hughes, and Gill Pinkerton. 1980. "Four Year Olds Talking to Mothers and Teachers." In *Language and Language Disorders in Childhood.* Edited by Lionel A. Hersov and M. Berger (a book supplement to the *Journal of Child Psychology and Psychiatry*, vol. 2). Oxford, England: Pergamon Press.

Tizard, Barbara, and Martin Hughes. 1984. *Young Children Learning.* Cambridge, MA: Harvard University Press.

Vygotsky, Lev. 1978. *Mind in Society: The Development of Higher Psychological Processes.* Edited by Michael Cole, Vera John-Steiner, Sylvia Scribner, and Ellen Souberman. Cambridge, MA: Harvard University Press.

Wells, Gordon. 1986. *The Meaning Makers: Children Learning Language and Using Language to Learn.* Portsmouth, NH: Heinemann.

2.3. Series Books

In January 1929, *Wilson Bulletin* published an article titled, "Not to Be Circulated—A list, prepared by Mrs. Mary E. S. Root, of books in series not circulated by standardized libraries." This list included works by almost sixty authors such as Horatio Alger, Laura Lee Hope, and Edward Stratemeyer. Disdain for series books continues today. Margaret Beckman (1964, 39; 53) in "Why Not the Bobbsey Twins?" asserts that libraries do not have enough money even to buy the truly "good" books, that it would be a crime to "waste [the] few precious years children have to experience children's literature," and that "mind-stultifying series books" dull children's interest in reading. Marilyn Kaye (1990, 50) calls series "Twinkie books, books that are neither memorable or enduring . . . [and] . . . are the literary equivalent of fast food."

The actions and thoughts of readers stand in stark contrast to these assertions. In an interview and book inventory study of the personal collections of fifty-two children between the ages of four and twelve years, McKechnie (2004) found that forty-two (80.8 percent) owned series books. Some of the children in this study had voracious appetites for series books. Michael (pseudonym, twelve years) reported that he had read fifty-three of the fifty-four titles available in the Animorphs series. Many read series in numbered order. Mary (eight years), referring to her Boxcar Children books, told the researcher, "I am going to start reading this one [pointing to #27]. I just finished reading this one [pointing to #26]." Series books were described as easing the transition from picture books to novels. Tiffany (ten years) showed the interviewer her copy of the *New Adventures of Mary-Kate and Ashley;* she identified it as the first chapter book that she had ever read and finished.

Catherine Ross (1995), reporting on 142 open-ended interviews with adults who read for pleasure, found that about 60 percent of these avid readers had read series books as children, that a series book was often identified as the first real book read, and the reading of series books was universally described as pleasurable. Ross (1995, 201) concluded that series books provide lessons in reading and that "far from being harmful, might be for some readers an essential stage in their development as powerful literates."

> **Case 9: Series Readers Speak Out**
> Researchers report that it's not just adults recalling their childhood reading who routinely speak of the great pleasure associated with reading series. Children do as well.
> First two adults:
>
> I was introduced to the Bobbsey Twins under the Christmas tree at the age of eight. It is my impression that I went straight to my favorite chair with a sack of hard candies and didn't get up for three years, after reading all forty of the series at least a dozen times each. (A childhood

memory as reported by Bobbie Ann Mason [1975, 29] in *The Girl Sleuth: A Feminist Guide*.)

Our tiny drugstore got in a supply of Horatio Alger at fifteen cents each; my ambition was to own the complete series. During a siege of measles, I bullied my family into buying me six. (Excerpt from a reader autobiography cited in *Voices of Readers: How We Come to Love Books* by G. Robert Carlsen and Anne Sherrill [1988, 89].)

Here are two children:

Researcher: Why do you want to read the latest books in the series as soon as they're published?

Rachel: I want to know what R. L. Stine has come up with this time, and if the story will be more fun or scarier. I even like to collect them and they're not too expensive to buy from my allowance. (From "How about Asking a Child for a Change? An Interview with a Ten-Year-Old Goosebumps fan." 1995–96. *Bookbird* 33, no. 3/4: 23.)

When you begin a new novel . . . it is like going into a room full of strangers, but reading the latest book in a series which you already know is like going into a room full of friends. (Watson [2000, 6], interview with an 11 year old boy).

Comments

In these statements the readers identify several of the appealing features of series: they allow for almost never-ending engagement, they are inexpensive, you can collect them, they are easy to read, and their familiarity is comforting.

Why Children Love Series Books

A growing body of literature has helped us understand why children love series books. The following factors, identified by Barstow (1999), Blubaugh and Ball (1998), Deane (1991), Mackey (1990), Ross (1995), and Watson (2000), have been shown to contribute to the appeal of series. Series books

- are attractively packaged, with appealing covers, clever titles and intriguing blurbs.

- are inexpensive and can be purchased by children.

- have chapters and the same dimensions and shape as books for adults, a grown-up format that helps a child to see herself or himself as a more mature reader who has graduated from picture books to chapter books.

- provide a sense of continuity as they integrate elements of earlier titles (summary beginnings) and forecast coming titles (preview endings).

- involve characters and situations with which children can readily identify.

- feel familiar, comfortable, and safe.

- provide needed escape.

- act as a shared cultural currency and allow children to participate in a community of readers as they buy, trade, give, read, and discuss the same titles.

- give the reader the sense of being in control.

- leave the reader with a sense of accomplishment and success as a reader.

This research also points to the nature and structure of series books, which make them accessible and easy for developing readers. Textual factors accounting for the success of series books with their intended audience typically include

- Informative titles and descriptive chapter headings that provide clues to the content

- Shorter length, large clear type, wide margins, shorter paragraphs, shorter sentences, and fewer lines per page

- Conventional, first-person narrative style

- Inclusion of lots of dialogue and few long, descriptive passages

- Repetition and redundancy

- Predictable, uncomplicated plots

- Exclusion of ambiguity

Series books provide practice in some key skills associated with reading such as making patterns, putting stories together, and extrapolating meaning. They help the reader develop confidence and speed. In short, they can be seen as acting like "training wheels" for reading development, all within the larger context of an experience described by readers to be very pleasurable.

As Makowski (1998) suggests, it's time for libraries and parents to get "Serious about series." Here are some suggestions for action.

What Libraries Can Do

1. Actively acquire and manage collections of current and popular series.

     Purchase complete sets.

     Use standing and pre-publication orders to ensure that new titles are available immediately after publication.

     Flag series for priority cataloguing and processing to get new titles on the shelf quickly.

     Allow, encourage, and teach children how to place holds on titles.

     Purchase enough copies of each title to satisfy demand in a timely manner.

     Replace titles that wear out or go missing.

2. Purchase collection development and reader advisory tools such as Thomas and Barr's *Popular Series Fiction for K–6 Readers* or Volz et al.'s (2000) *Junior Genreflecting*.

3. Enhance reader access to series.

     Include entries in the catalogue for and allow searching by both series title and the number of individual titles within a series.

     Prepare and distribute pathfinders that list titles in a series by number and suggest other series that the reader might enjoy.

     Shelve series separately from other fiction and in numbered order within each series.

     Create displays to showcase series.

     Provide reader's advisory services.

4. Encourage professional journals to review series using criteria appropriate to the genre.

What Parents Can Do

1. Purchase series books for their child and provide shelving for them in the child's bedroom.

2. Share stories about their own childhood reading of series.

3. Read the first book of a series that is new to your child aloud with him or her.

To Read More on Children and Series Books

Mackey, Margaret. 1990. "Filling the Gaps: *The Baby-Sitters Club*, the Series Book, and the Learning Reader." *Language Arts* 67, no. 5: 484–9.

Here's how Mackey describes the flurry and intrigue surrounding the appearance of a new title in the Baby-Sitters Club series:

> Anyone involved in encouraging children to read would have found our neighbourhood a cheering sight over the past few months. Both in school and at home, there has been a ferment over the gradual acquisition of a particular collection of children's books. Neighbouring children have rushed breathless to our door, waving a new purchase under the envious noses of our daughters. There have been excited phone calls: "It's in—I saw it at Greenwood's! Are you going to get it? You can borrow mine, but you'll have to wait till I've finished—and my sister." (484)

After this wonderful description, Mackey provides a brief research-derived overview of the characteristics of the texts of series books that appeal to children and help them develop as readers.

Makowski, Silk. 1994. "Serious about Series: Selection Criteria for a Neglected Genre." *VOYA* 16: 349–51.

Regarding series as a genre unto themselves, Makowski provides a rationale for collecting series and describes appropriate selection criteria, including those related to setting, characters and continuity, that can be used by libraries to build collections.

Ross, Catherine Sheldrick. 1995. " 'If they read Nancy Drew, so what?': Series Book Readers Talk Back." *LISR* 17, no. 3: 201–36.

A well-written and fascinating account of series books and their readers. Ross begins with a history of series book publishing from their nineteenth-century forerunners to today. She goes on to describe how real readers, as evidenced through 142 open-ended interviews with adults who read for pleasure, talk about their own childhood reading of series. She closes with a discussion of how the texts work to provide reading lessons for "apprentice" child readers. Ross persuasively argues that "Series books can be seen as allies in the making of readers" (233) and encourages libraries, teachers, and parents to make them accessible for children. If you can only read one item about series, choose this article.

References

Barstow, Barbara. 1999. Foreword to *Reading in Series: A Selection Guide for Children*, vii–xi. Edited by Catherine Barr. New Providence, NJ: R. R. Bowker.

Beckman, Margaret. 1964. "Why Not the Bobbsey Twins?" *Library Journal* 89, no. 20: 38–39, 53.

Blubaugh, Penny, and Sharon S. Ball. 1998. "The Series Controversy and How It Grew." *Public Libraries* 37, no. 1: 48–50.

Bud, Rita. 1995–96. "How about Asking a Child for a Change? An Interview with a Ten-Year-Old Goosebumps Fan." *Bookbird* 33, no. 3/4: 22–24.

Carlsen, G. Robert, and Anne Sherrill. 1988. *Voices of Readers: How We Come to Love Books*. Urbana, IL: National Council of Teachers of English.

Deane, Paul. 1991. *Mirrors of American Culture: Children's Fiction Series in the Twentieth Century*. Metuchen, NJ: Scarecrow Press.

Kaye, Marilyn. 1990. "The Twinkie Collection: Books That Have No Apparent Redeeming Value but Belong in the Library Anyway." In *Lands of Pleasure: Essays on Lillian H. Smith and the Development of Children's Libraries*, 49–61. Edited by Adele M. Fasick, Margaret Johnson, and Ruth Osler. Metuchen, NJ: Scarecrow.

Mackey, Margaret. 1990. "Filling the Gaps: The Baby-sitters Club, the Series Book, and the Learning Reader." *Language Arts* 67, no. 5, 484–9.

Makowski, Silk. 1998. "Serious about Series: Selection Criteria for a Neglected Genre." *VOYA* 16: 349–51.

Mason, Bobbie Ann. 1975. *The Girl Sleuth: A Feminist Guide*. New York: Feminist Press.

McKechnie, Lynne (E. F.). 2004. " 'I'll Keep Them for *My* Children" (Kevin, nine years): Children's Personal Collections of Books and Other Media." *Canadian Journal of Information and Library Science* 28, no. 4: 75–90.

Moran, Barbara B., and Susan Steinfirst. 1985. "Why Johnny (and Jane) read Whodunits in Series." *School Library Journal* 31, no. 3: 113–17.

Root, Mary E. "Not to be circulated: A list, prepared by Mrs. Mary E. S. Root, of books in series not circulated by standardized libraries." 1929. *Wilson Bulletin* 3, no. 17: 446.

Ross, Catherine Sheldrick. 1995. " 'If they read Nancy Drew, so what?': Series Book Readers Talk Back." *LISR* 17, no. 3: 201–36.

Thomas, Rebecca L., and Catherine Barr. 2004. *Popular Series Fiction for K–6 Readers: A Reading and Selection Guide*. Westport, CT: Libraries Unlimited.

Volz, Bridget Dealy, Cheryl Perkins Scheer, and Lynda Blackburn Welborn. 2000. *Junior Genreflecting: A Guide to Good Reads and Series Fiction for Children*. Englewood, CO: Libraries Unlimited.

Watson, Victor. 2000. *Reading Series Fiction: From Arthur Ransome to Gene Kemp*. London: Routledge.

2.4. The Boy Problem

In both the popular press and the research literature on gender differences in reading and school achievement, it used to be the *girls* who were thought to be the problem. Until recently both research and practice were most interested in uncovering and addressing the unfair, unequal treatment of girls. But times have changed. Everyone agrees that girls have improved on almost all performance indicators, while boys have not. Boys are now identified as lagging behind girls, especially in reading and writing, skills seen as crucial for later success.

Surveying Boys' Reading: The Numbers

In a literature review of gender differences in education, Rowe (2000) found that on the average, boys' literacy skills, general academic achievements, attitudes, behaviors, and experiences of schooling are significantly poorer than those of girls. A number of national and international surveys support this finding.

- The U.S. Department of Education's National Assessment of Educational Progress (NEAP) surveys of 1998 and 2000 found that fourth-grade girls scored higher in reading than boys, with the boys lagging behind the girls by about 1.5 years (as reported in Sommers 2000).

- The Department for Education and Employment (1999) in the United Kingdom conducted national testing of seven, eleven, and fourteen year olds. Whereas 86 percent of girls reached level two (acceptable) or higher in reading, only 77 percent of boys did. Scores were similar for writing with 87 percent of girls but only 78 percent of boys achieving level two or higher. The gaps widened with increasing age.

- In its national literacy testing completed in 1996, Australia's Department of Employment, Education, Training and Youth Affairs (1998) found a similar gender gap: 66 percent of boys as opposed to 77 percent of girls met the national benchmark for reading in year three at school with similar differences (65 percent of boys, 85 percent of girls) for meeting the national benchmark in writing.

- The International Association for the Evaluation of Educational Achievement in a cross-national study of thirty-two countries, including Canada, the United States, and Great Britain, found that girls consistently do better than boys in standard tests of reading at age nine (Wagemaker 1996).

A significant amount of other research paints a similarly unsettling picture of boys and reading. For example, Sullivan (2003, 1) reports that "Boys are two to three times more likely than girls to be diagnosed with a reading disability." The American Psychiatric Association (1994) notes that five out of six children and adolescents diagnosed with attention-deficit disorder and attention-deficit/hyperactivity disorder are boys. Phillips (1994) asserts that 85 percent of special education students in the United States are boys, a statement that is confirmed by the National Center for Education Statistics (2000), which claims that boys are three to five times more likely to receive special education than girls. Finally,

Kleinfield (1999) tells us that boys are 59 percent more likely to fail a grade than girls.

Surveying Boys' Reading: What Counts as Reading?

Studies of reading preferences suggest that boys frequently have different interests than girls. Collins-Standley et al. (1996) report that at ages as young as two years, boys and girls display different preferences in fairy tales, with boys liking scary, violent stories and girls liking romantic ones. School librarian Glenda Childress monitored the book selection choices of kindergarten and Grade 1 students. In a sample of more than one thousand choices, she found that whereas girls chose fiction 80 percent of the time, boys chose nonfiction as frequently as they chose fiction. Childress (1985, 71) concluded "that boys and girls show rather divergent patterns in materials selection even before they begin to read independently."

Case 10: What Counts as Reading?

Mary Alice Wheeler conducted in-depth interviews with the mothers of three nine-year-old boys. Although the boys had been read to since an early age, had parents who read, and lived in print-rich environments (all indicators of success in reading), their mothers were concerned about a recent and sudden decline in their reading. Wheeler (1984, 610) reports on the interviews as follows.

The boys' daily activities are revealing. All, of course, are exposed to print in each school day. At home, their mothers stated, all three read at least the sports and comics in the newspaper. One mother stated that she prepares her son's breakfast which he allows to "sit there and get cold while he reads the newspaper. He goes over almost all of it. Not the want ads and the personal columns . . . but the rest of the newspaper." Two of the boys collect baseball cards and have books which tell them how much cards are worth. These two boys read the figures and records on the backs of the cards. All three have personal subscriptions to children's magazines. One boy is attending typing classes and often uses his family's word processor. All three are Cub Scouts and must read manuals to complete achievements for badges. One boy attends Sunday school where he reads worksheets, memorizes Bible verses, and learns songs. This boy also began music lessons during the past summer and is learning how to read music. As the mothers spoke, they articulated these numerous encounters with print that their sons were constantly experiencing, yet the mothers did not think the boys were reading.

Comments

Wheeler concludes that the boys indeed were reading. But they were reading texts different from the ones they had shared earlier with their mothers and different from the ones that were presented at school. The findings of this study suggest that we need to rethink what counts as reading. It seems that boys are reading but are choosing texts that are different from those privileged in school and those commonly considered to be "real" reading.

Boys' traditional favorites have been identified in a variety of studies (Childress 1985; Kelly 1986; Langerman 1990; Odean 1998) and include information books, humor, science fiction, and action stories. The forty-nine adolescents who participated in Smith and Wilhelm's (2002) study of literacy practices all reported reading texts in diverse media and forms such as magazines, newspapers, driver education manuals, video game manuals, rock videos, animated cartoons, and Web sites. The problem, as identified by Newkirk (2002, 70), is that the genres and media forms that boys prefer "are often treated as subliterature, something that a reader should move beyond." He contends that teachers, librarians, parents, and other adults who work with children create a hierarchy of texts (see section 4.5 for more on the notion of hierarchies of taste). "Some forms of literary activity have status; other forms are barely recognized as literacy at all. But, as we used to say on the playground, 'Says who?' " (Newkirk 2002, 91).

So What's Really Going on with Boys and Reading?

A number of explanations have been provided concerning the boy problem. Here are three that have received the most attention. Of course, whatever the underlying cause of the boy problem, teachers, librarians and parents need to work hard to address it.

The Essentialist Approach

Boys are just different. Citing Freud's claim that boys have an inborn drive to master their world while girls seek to understand it, Langerman (1990) contends that boys learn differently from girls and therefore read differently as well, favoring reading for information rather than for communication and cooperation. This essentialist approach points to nature and genetics as the factors underlying reading differences. It is supported by recent research identifying gendered differences in brain structures, developmental rates and patterns, and our own everyday observations of boys and girls from birth through childhood. Identifying and providing boy-friendly reading materials and encouraging boys to interact with texts in male-appropriate ways is consistent with the essentialist approach to gender differences in reading.

The Construction of Literacy as Feminized

Boys are taught to think reading is for sissies. According to Young (2000) and Newkirk (2002), the cause of the boy problem is the construction of literacy as feminized. Basow (1992) and Delamont (1990) found that almost all early childhood educators are female. Newkirk (2002) claims this same gender imbalance is also true for elementary school reading and writing teachers. Piper and Collamer (2001) report that in 1998, 83.4 percent of children's librarians were women. Pottorff, Phelps-Zientarski, and Skovera (1996) note that mothers read more often to their children then do fathers; furthermore, mothers themselves are ten times more likely to read books than are fathers, who are ten times more likely to read newspapers than are mothers. According to Jon Scieszka, children's author and founder of Guys Read (a literacy program focusing on the needs of boys), "[t]he problem is that we don't have enough men teaching elementary school, and being role models for boys. We tell boys reading is important. But what we show them is that reading is important if you are a girl and want to grow up to be a woman teacher or librarian" (Bafile 2001).

The feminization of reading is exacerbated by the lack of boy-friendly books. Kelly (1986) and Newkirk (2002) contend that school-sanctioned narratives are those typically read by girls. "Preference is given to books that are morally functional, that assist personal development and socialization. Books trump magazines; print trumps the visual; the serious trumps the humorous; fiction trumps nonfiction" (Newkirk 2002, 171). In a survey of reading preferences and access to materials by sixth-grade students, Worthy, Moorman, and Turner (1999) found that only one-third of school libraries carried the genres that boys prefer. Nicolle (1989) notes that this is also true for public libraries. Kelly (1986) and Worthy (1996) suggest that lack of texts of interest may lead some boys not to read at all. Parental attitudes may also contribute to the feminization of reading. In an ethnographic study of reading in a small town in North America, Cherland (1994) found that most parents did not view reading as an appropriate activity for boys. Some fathers vehemently denied that their boys ever read fiction. Most parents felt, however, that reading was a valuable pastime for girls.

Rejection of Schoolish Forms of Literacy

Reading don't fix no Chevys. This third approach to the boy problem is offered by Smith and Wilhelm (2002, 83–84). The results of their study of forty-nine adolescent boys convinced them "that the reason boys reject schoolish forms of literacy is not that they see literacy as feminized, but because of its very schoolishness—that is, its future orientation, its separation from immediate uses and functions, its emphasis on knowledge that is not valued outside of school."

In contrast to school reading, the home reading of the boys in Smith and Wilhelm's study usually had a clear and immediate purpose (for example, to find out about dirt bikes or new movie releases), was often related to problem-oriented work, and allowed for choice and response to interests. It might be best described as pragmatic reading. Smith and Wilhelm (2002, 94) conclude by emphasizing "the sharp difference between the literate practices inside and outside of school. . . . [T]he literate lives of all the boys outside of school were surprisingly varied and rich, but this home/outside/real-world literacy was practiced in ways that looked quite different from the literacy they were asked to practice in school."

Case 11: Connecting Reading with Life outside of School

The boys interviewed and observed by Smith and Wilhelm (2002, 150) provide expert evidence about their reading. Here's what three of them had to say.

Rudy   *(Grade 7, European American, private school, high achiever) talking about music:*

Sometimes when I get bored doing my homework, like a lot of research on the Internet, I will get an MPS file or listen to a CD. Or I will look at the back of a CD and kind of read some of the lyrics to see if I know the song, and then I will program the songs that I want to hear. (2002, 150)

Johnny   *(Grade 11, suburban, African American, average achiever) talking about nonbook reading:*

I like the music part—the songs, and whenever you have Rap CDs, they use metaphors. I like when rappers use metaphors. (2002, 150)

Robert   *(Grade 11, urban, African American, low achiever) talking about reading at school:*

Researcher: Of all the reading that you do in school, what's your least favorite, would you say?

Robert: English.

Researcher: And why is that?

Robert: Because after we finish reading, we just go on to something else. We go on to something else to do. Like, she'll give us some different work. After we read, we just close the book and do different work.

Researcher: And you would rather do what?

Robert: Do work, like, responding to the story, like that. (2002, 107)

Comments

Rudy and Johnny make it clear that boys often choose nonbook texts, texts they are unlikely to encounter at school. All three, but especially Robert, express the idea that reading is not over when the text is put aside; readers need to explore the text further through discussion, programming, handling the package, dramatic reading, reenactment, and other activities. Such activities are not encouraged enough in either schools or libraries.

What Libraries Can Do

1. Find out what boys like to read by looking at lists developed by others, surveying the boys in your community, or using automated circulation systems to track boys' borrowing patterns.

2. Build collections with titles of interest to boys, including information books and nonbook media such as magazines, graphic novels, music, and video recordings.

3. Remember that libraries are particularly well positioned to address boys' interest in nonfiction. Information books are less frequently published in paperback editions and less frequently stocked by bookstores and so typically cost more and are less available outside of libraries than are fiction titles.

4. Include male images on publicity and promotion materials to help boys see the library as a place for them.

5. Plan programs that will attract boys as well as girls. Among the many possibilities are visits by authors of nonfiction and the inclusion of nonfiction in the thematic reading lists for summer reading programs.

6. Encourage fathers to help their sons choose library materials to borrow. Hire male children's librarians. This will help boys identify reading as a masculine as well as a feminine activity.

7. Provide space and opportunities for boys to interact with and respond physically to books.

8. Help parents understand boys' reading by building collections and preparing booklists and pathfinders about boys' reading and using opportunities provided through library programming and readers' advisory interactions to share information and advice.

What Parents Can Do

1. Read to your son.

2. Provide strong male role models for your son so that he will begin to identify reading as both a male and a female endeavor. It is important for boys to be read to by their fathers, older brothers, and other male relatives. It is equally important for boys to see their fathers, brothers, and other male relatives reading.

3. Purchase and borrow well-chosen, male-friendly materials, both book and nonbook, for your son to read.

4. Whenever possible, allow your son to freely choose *his* own reading materials and celebrate *his* choices.

5. To address the unfortunate, commonly held perception that reading is not for boys or is not cool, provide quiet spaces and opportunities for reading undercover, in private.

6. Work with the idea of reading as a social activity by encouraging your son and his friends to recommend titles to each other.

7. Attend story time at your local public library with your son. As Sullivan (2004, 38) notes:

> Now picture the ideal reading environment for boys—the public library's story hour. Here, boys join their peers as well as some of the adults they love and respect—one of whom reads them an illustrated story. Boys are encouraged to get up and sing, and maybe even dance. Then it's time for the craft project that reinforces the story—an activity that leans heavily on boys' natural desires to build, create, and use tools to solve problems. For a guy, reading doesn't get any better than that.

To Learn More about Boys and Reading

Booth, David. 2002. *Even Hockey Players Read: Boys, Literacy and Learning.* Markham, Ontario: Pembroke Publishers.
    Based on research but written for practitioners, *Even Hockey Players Read* provides an overview of the reading lives of boys, offers suggestions for how to help boys become strong readers and writers, and includes an extensive list of recommended books for boys. Excerpts from the reading diary Booth maintained while his son Jay grew up as well as quotations from other male readers enliven the text. The author is a faculty member at the Ontario Institute for

Studies in Education at the University of Toronto where he teaches in the areas of reading and writing.

Smith, Michael W., and Jeffrey D. Wilhelm. 2002. *"Reading Don't Fix No Chevys": Literacy in the Lives of Young Men*. Portsmouth, NH: Heinemann.

This interesting study of forty-nine teenage boys in Grades 7 through 12, drawn from a variety of racial backgrounds and urban, rural, and suburban American communities, looked at literacy activity inside and outside of school. The study included equal numbers of high, average, and low achievers. The boys were asked to rank literacy activities, to respond to profiles of males engaged in literacy activities, to maintain logs of their reading and writing for three months, and to respond to stories through think-aloud protocols; they were also interviewed about all the data collection measures throughout their participation in the study. In "Meet the Crew" sections distributed throughout the book, the authors provide profiles of individual participants. What emerges is a deep and rich picture of the literacy practices of male adolescents. Smith and Wilhelm discovered that boys value reading. Rather than identifying it as "feminine," they describe it as being "schoolish." Although the boys had rich literary lives, these reading transactions did not look like the literacy valued in schools. Boys chose different texts and approached them in terms of the social relations central to their lives. Through the voices of the boys who participated in their study, Smith and Wilhelm provide a compelling argument for boy-centered approaches to literacy.

Odean, Kathleen. 1998. *Great Books for Boys: More than 600 Books for Boys 2 to 14*. New York: Ballantine.

An excellent source for libraries wishing to build boy-friendly collections and for parents seeking advice on recommended titles. Odean, using her own experience as a children's librarian as well as research about boys' reading preferences, chose titles from genres and topics known to appeal to boys. She strove to include "outstanding books populated by fully rounded (male) characters whose stories reflect feelings and issues that affect boys" (1998, 7).

Two Recommended Web Sites

Scieszka, Jon. Guys Read. Available at http://www.guysread.com (accessed June 12, 2005).

Award-winning children's author Jon Scieszka describes Guys Read as "a web-based literacy program I've made to help boys find stuff they like to read." The site includes titles recommended by boy readers as well as by Scieszka.

Sullivan, Michael. Tales Told Tall. Available at http://www.geocities.com/talestoldtall (accessed June 12, 2005).

Includes an overview of boys and reading, a list of recommended books for boys, and tips for parents interested in supporting their sons' reading.

References

American Psychiatric Association. 1994. *Diagnostic and Statistical Manual of Mental Disorders*. 4th ed. Washington, DC: American Psychological Association.

Bafile, Cara. 2001. "Guys Read: Helping Boys Become Better Readers, Better Students, Better Guys." *Education World.* Available at http://www.education-world. com/a_issues/issues204.shtml (accessed June 2005).

Basow, Susan A. 1992. *Gender Roles and Stereotypes.* Pacific Grove, CA: Brooks/Cole.

Booth, David. 2002. *Even Hockey Players Read: Boys, Literacy and Learning.* Markham, ON: Pembroke Publishers Ltd.

Cherland, Meredith R. 1994. *Private Practices: Girls Reading Fiction and Constructing Identity.* London: Taylor.

Childress, Glenda T. 1985. "Gender Gap in the Library: Different Choices for Girls and Boys." *Top of the News* 42, no. 1: 69–73.

Collins-Standley, Tracy, Su-Lin Gan, Hsin-Ju J. Yu, and Dolf Zillmann. 1996. "Choices of Romantic, Violent, and Scary Fairy-tale Books by Preschool Girls and Boys." *Child Study Journal* 26: 279–302.

Delamont, Sara. 1990. *Sex Roles and the School.* London: Routledge.

Department of Employment, Education, Training and Youth Affairs. 1998. *Literacy for All: The Challenge for Australian Schools.* Canberra: Australian Government Publishing Service.

Department for Education and Employment, United Kingdom. 1999. *National Curriculum Assessments of 7, 11 and 14 Year Olds by Local Education Authority 1999.* London: Department for Education and Employment.

Kelly, Patricia R. 1986. "The Influence of Reading Content on Students' Perceptions of the Masculinity or Femininity of Reading." *Journal of Reading Behavior* 18: 243–56.

Kleinfield, Judith. 1999. "Student Performance: Males versus Females." *Public Interest* 134: 3–20.

Langerman, Deborah. 1990. "Books and Boys: Gender Preferences and Book Selection." *School Library Journal* 36, no. 3: 132–6.

National Center for Education Statistics. 1998. *The Condition of Education, 1998.* Washington, DC: U.S. Department of Education.

National Center for Education Statistics. 2000. *Trends in Educational Equality of Girls and Women.* Washington, DC: U.S. Department of Education.

Newkirk, Thomas. 2002. *Misreading Masculinity: Boys, Literacy, and Popular Culture.* Portsmouth, NH: Heinemann.

Nicolle, Ray. 1989. "Boys and the Five-year Void." *School Library Journal* 35, no. 7: 130.

Odean, Kathleen. 1998. *Great Books for Boys: More than 600 Books for Boys 2 to 14.* New York: Ballantine.

Phillips, Angela. 1994. *The Trouble with Boys.* New York: Simon & Schuster.

Piper, Paul S., and Barbara E. Collamer. 2001. "Male Librarians: Men in a Feminized Profession." *Journal of Academic Librarianship* 27: 406–11.

Pottorff, Donald D., Deborah Phelps-Zientarski, and Michelle E. Skovera. 1996. "Gender Perceptions of Elementary and Middle School Students about Literacy at School and at Home." *Journal of Research & Development in Education* 29: 203–11.

Rowe, Kenneth J. 2000. " 'Problems' in the Education of Boys and Exploring 'Real' Effects from Evidence-based Research: Useful Findings in Teaching and Learning for Boys and Girls." Australia ERIC Document 450873.

Smith, Michael W., and Jeffrey D. Wilhelm. 2002. *"Reading Don't Fix No Chevys": Literacy in the Lives of Young Men.* Portsmouth, NH: Heinemann.

Sommers, Christina Hoff. 2000. *The War against Boys: How Misguided Feminism Is Harming Our Young Men.* New York: Simon & Schuster.

Sullivan, Michael. 2003. *Connecting Boys with Books: What Libraries Can Do.* Chicago: American Library Association.

Sullivan, Michael. 2004. "Why Johnny Won't Read." *School Library Journal* 50, no. 8: 36–39.

Wagemaker, Hans, ed. 1996. *Are Girls Better Readers?* Amsterdam: International Association for the Evaluation of Educational Achievement.

Wheeler, Mary Alice. 1984. "Fourth Grade Boys' Literacy from a Mother's Point of View." *Language Arts* 61, no. 6: 607–14.

Worthy, Jo. 1996. "Removing Barriers to Voluntary Reading: The Role of School and Classroom Libraries." *Language Arts* 73: 483–92.

Worthy, Jo, Megan Moorman, and Margo Turner. 1999. "What Johnny Likes to Read Is Hard to Find at School." *Reading Research Quarterly* 34, no. 1: 12–27.

Young, Josephine Peyton. 2000. "Boy Talk: Critical Literacy and Masculinities." *Reading Research Quarterly* 35, no. 3: 312–37.

2.5. Children, Libraries, and Reading

The public library is the only local government-funded, educational, and social service freely available to children from birth through adolescence. For that reason, according to Armstrong et al. (1997), it plays a very important role in supporting children in their development as readers. One of the most important services of the public library is provision of large and rich collections for children of all ages. Many studies (see, for example, McQuillan 1997; Gottfried, Fleming, and Gottfried, 1998; Pack 2000; Allington 2002; Krashen 2002) indicate that access to books and magazines is correlated with higher reading achievement.

Case 12: The Public Library as a Haven for Book Addicts

In McKechnie's (1996) study of the use of public libraries by four-year-old girls and their mothers, she encountered many examples of children's insatiable appetites for books. In one such episode, Genevieve had been left by her mother in the children's area with the instruction to select five books for borrowing. When her mother returned, Genevieve was sitting cross-legged on the floor, looking through one book from a large pile of picture books that she had collected in front of her.

Mother: Genevieve! How many books do you have?

Genevieve: One more.

Mother: Just one more! Remember how many books I said?

Genevieve: Yup.

Mother: How many?

Genevieve: Four.

Mother: I said five. And I think you've got more than five.

Genevieve: I do. I do have more.

Mother: Ya. We're going to have to put some back.

Genevieve: [Picking up and looking at the books one at a time] I want this one. Where's that one? That one. That one.

Mother: OK. I leave you for three minutes and look, you've cleaned out the library.

Genevieve: That one. I need a book like that one and that one.

Comment

Genevieve eventually talked her mother into six books. The two of them examined the pile together to figure out which six would be the best to take home. This extract from a library visit transcript is interesting because it shows how important the library's collections—especially the picture books—were to the children who participated in this study ("I need a book"). The public library was uniquely able to satisfy Genevieve's addiction to books.

Usherwood and Toyne (2002) interviewed public library users to identify what readers value in public library services. "The principle of equity of access was seen as crucial, in that it provided everyone (especially children) with the opportunity to encounter reading material." One participant in the study, a thirty-year old mother, said, "it's really exciting [for children] to go and have the experience of a place where there's lots of books. They see other readers as well. I think it engenders reading into their culture" (Usherwood and Toyne 2002, n.p.). Another (female, age fifty-five) spoke of getting the library habit as a child: "I joined the library when I was eight years old. I used to spend all of Saturday mornings there choosing my three books. I loved it. It's a habit that has stayed with me" (Usherwood and Toyne 2002, n.p.).

The opportunity to try out a book with no risks and the importance of no-cost use, the assistance of knowledgeable staff, wide choice, and the ability to browse and freely choosing reading material independently support readers of all ages. With school libraries in crisis (Haycock 2003), their stocks being tied to curriculum, and their lack of accessibility to preschoolers, public libraries are often the best place for children to find materials for the free voluntary reading that Krashen (2004) has identified as crucial to reading success.

References

Allington, Richard L. 2002. "What I've Learned about Effective Reading Instruction: From a Decade of Exemplary Elementary Classroom Teachers." *Phi Beta Kappan* 83, no. 10: 740–7.

Armstrong, Chris, Debbie Denham, Judith Elkin, Margaret K. Evans, Roger Fenton, Peggy Heeks, and Ray Lonsdale. 1997. "A Place for Children: The Qualitative Impact of Public Libraries on Children's Reading. Interim Report." *The New Review of Children's Literature and Librarianship* 3: 93–103.

Gottfried, Adele E., Jane Fleming, and Allan W. Gottfried. 1998. "Role of Cognitively Stimulating Home Environments in Children's Academic Intrinsic Motivation: A Longitudinal Study." *Child Development* 69, no. 5: 1448–60.

Haycock, Ken. 2003. *The Crisis in Canada's School Libraries: The Case for Reform and Re-investment.* Toronto: Association of Canadian Publishers; Canada Heritage, Government of Canada.

Krashen, Stephen D. 2002. "What Do We Know about Libraries and Reading Achievement?" *Book Report* 20, no. 4: 38.

Krashen, Stephen D. 2004. *The Power of Reading: Insights from the Research.* Westport, CT: Libraries Unlimited.

McKechnie, Lynne (E. F.). 1996. *Opening the "Preschoolers' Door to Learning": An Ethnographic Study of the Use of Public Libraries by Preschool Girls.* Ph.D. diss. University of Western Ontario, London, Ontario, Canada.

McQuillan, Jeff L. 1997. *Access to Print and Formal Instruction in Reading Acquisition.* Ph.D. diss., University of Southern California, Los Angeles.

Pack, S. 2000. "Public Library Use, School Performance and the Parental X-Factor: A Biodocumentary Approach to Children's Snapshots." *Reading Improvement* 37: 161–72.

Usherwood, Bob, and Jackie Toyne. 2002. "The Public Library and the Reading Experience." Proceedings of *Libraries for Life: Democracy, Diversity and Delivery*, 68th IFLA General Conference and Council, August 18–24, 2004, Glasgow, Scotland. Available at http://www.ifla.org/IV/ifla68/ (accessed June 15, 2005).

Chapter 3

Young Adults and Reading

Paulette Rothbauer

3.1. What We Know about Young Adults and Reading

We still hear a lot about young adults and the "reading problem." Newspaper headlines routinely alert us about declining reading scores. Here's a sample of recent headlines:

- "Students' scores rise in math, not reading" (Schemo 2003).

- "Tests find reading scores flat, but math improved" (Toppo 2003).

- "Is reading becoming more of a lost art?" (Noland 2004).

- "[S]tudents make the grade in math, writing; reading skills a concern" (*Canadian Press Newswire* 2002).

- "[T]eens have a lot competing for their attention. Who has time to read?" (Linwood 2004).

Young people are surveyed again and again by various governmental and nongovernmental bodies only to find that reading levels are on the decline. Many surveys are based on standardized testing and other methods of benchmarking, and the concern is almost always about making better readers. But a somewhat different picture emerges from research that takes seriously the reading preferences and genres chosen by young people themselves. The myth of the "reading problem" encompasses a number of common assumptions that run something like this:

> *Young adults don't read.* Young adults do not read because they haven't got the time to read, at least not enough to read the kinds of books adults would like them to be reading. They have too much homework and poor adult role models who also don't read. Some young adults don't read because they do not possess the requisite level of reading fluency that enables them to read for pleasure.

> *Young Adults don't like to read.* Related to the first assumption is the notion that young adults do not *like* to read. Reading for pleasure is simply not enjoyable; it is dull, difficult, and too much like school work.

> *Young Adults prefer to watch television, play with computers, and listen to music rather than read.* Young people would much rather engage with a variety of multimedia such as television, film, computer games, the Internet, and music. They prefer to do this in the company of friends. These media compete with traditional books and win because they are trendy, easy, and confer an esteemed status among peers.

> *Real reading means the reading of certain kinds of books.* When we hear about "the reading problem," often what is meant is a lack of interest in the type of literature read in English class (although in fact reading scores are often derived from tests of functional literacy such as instructions, maps, and menus). Sustained engagement with magazines, comics, graphic novels, newspapers, and a variety of online texts typically counts for little or nothing when it comes to assessments of the reading behavior of young adults. Yet many young people who reject books do read comics and magazines.

Pauline Heather (1981, 81) found in an early British study of the leisure reading of young people between thirteen to fifteen years of age that nearly 80 percent of the sixty participants read magazines. The popularity of magazines as reading material for young adults has been confirmed in study after study (SmartGirl.org; Mellon 1990; Statistics Canada 1998; Book Marketing Limited 2000). Studies conducted around the world confirm that this preference for reading magazines is not limited to North America.

In a study of manga reading in Japan by Allen and Ingulsrud (2003), young adults gave four reasons for engaging in this kind of recreational reading: 1) to pass the time, 2) for pleasure, 3) to learn something new, and 4) because it is easy. The authors insightfully challenge this last point, citing the sophisticated conventions of the genre, which include the following: four kinds of script, variance in presentation and layout, symbolic image systems, and diversity of point of view. Allen and Ingulsrud speculate that readers downplay the complexity of the genre because they understand that manga is not considered serious reading.

Popular genres of reading such as series books, horror, and romance and popular formats such as magazines are often discounted as inappropriate and trivial, even by the readers who enjoy them. In a report of leisure reading among rural teens, Constance Mellon (1990, 224) elaborates on this phenomenon of discounting:

> Somehow teens have assimilated the idea that magazines are not legitimate reading. And that's too bad. For this is reading that teens enjoy, that they do without any adult prodding—regularly, extensively, and with great attention to detail. Teens spend their own money on magazines, they keep them as reference material (often in large, ragged piles that are the despair of house-proud mothers), and they share them with friends.

In short, commonly held assumptions about the young adult "reading problem" construct the reader as reluctant and unwilling—forced to read for school but likely, if given the chance, to choose anything but reading as a leisure activity. There are variations on the so-called reading problem, but they all amount to the same thing: young adults have the problem that they cannot or do not like to read. This despite claims of such prominent reading advocates as Stephen Krashen (2004) who says that, contrary to popular belief, teenagers and children *are* reading and they actively choose to read for pleasure.

Unfortunately some librarians, teachers, parents, and other concerned adults promote reading in outmoded frameworks that take little account of the actual reading interests and motivations of young people. Reading—even the reading of novels and comics—is often promoted in an instrumental way that privileges reading for "information" rather than reading for pleasure. However, Patrick Jones (2002), another prominent youth advocate, challenges this approach in a collaborative book on the provision of library services to young adults that calls for more respect for the reading choices of teens:

> We learn about teen reading and contribute to improving adolescent literacy when we show respect for the reading choices of young people. We compliment; we don't condemn. If a young adult is reading comic

books, we provide access to comic books and graphic novels. To say or to convey the attitude of "at least they are reading something" is to show disrespect for what the teen, for whatever reason, has chosen to read.

If we examine each of the assumptions listed earlier in light of various studies of the recreational reading practices of adolescents, we can tell a different story about young adult readers. Far from being disaffected and reluctant readers, young people actively choose to read because they find it relaxing, pleasurable, entertaining, informative, and fun.

Young Adults *Do* Read

Study after study of reading habits gives strong evidence that young people *are* reading. What's more, they are *choosing* to read. The term "young people" is variously defined, usually signifying those under the age of twenty-four years. Recent large-scale national surveys of book buying and borrowing from Britain, the United States, Canada, and Australia all lend support to the statement that the majority of young adults do read.

The Book Study Industry Group reported in their *2001 Consumer Research Study on Book Purchasing* that the demand for books for teens reached its highest level since 1997. Roughly 36 million books were purchased for the fourteen- to seventeen-year-old age group. Some of those books must be getting into the hands of adolescent readers! More than two-thirds of books bought for teenagers were intended as gifts (IPSOS Book Trends 2002, 78–81). A National Education Association (NEA) poll on the reading habits of adolescents surveyed some five hundred young Americans between the ages of twelve and eighteen. More than half of the respondents (56 percent) read more than ten books a year, and 41 percent read more than fifteen books a year. Forty-two percent said that they read for "fun and pleasure" (Peter D. Hart Research Associates 2001). Since 1999, the Young Adult Library Services Association of the American Library Association and SmartGirl.org Teen Read Week surveys have consistently shown that young people, both male and female, do read and claim they would read more if they had more time (SmartGirl.org). Tellingly, in the 2002 survey, 30 percent of the 6,458 respondents indicated that they read to stave off boredom.

In Britain, 26 percent of young adult respondents between the ages of twelve and sixteen years read books for three to five hours a week (Book Marketing Limited 2000). In Canada, Nancy Duxbury found that the duration of reading is identical for young people between the ages of fifteen and twenty-four years: 26 percent read for three to five hours a week; 51 percent of those surveyed read for five hours a week or more (Duxbury 1995). A Statistics Canada survey revealed that more than 71 percent of Canadians between the ages of fifteen and nineteen read books regularly, a higher percentage than any other age category; almost 27 percent of young people read at least one book a week (Statistics Canada 1998). These numbers, although encouraging, should be taken with a grain of salt. There is no way to know, for instance, how young people tallied their reading time per week. Did they count the reading they did while watching television, while sitting on the bus, or while hanging out with friends? Did they count only the books they read for class? Did they count graphic novels and comic books as "books"?

An Australian study reveals that teenagers were the most active group of borrowers of all groups surveyed (Guldberg 1990). Sixty-one percent of respondents under the age of twenty were reading a book at the time of the study. Readers under twenty also indicated that the main purpose for buying a book was "relaxation or general enjoyment" (Guldberg 1990, 78), and most young people (58 percent) still borrow books from libraries rather than purchase them (26 percent).

Young Adults Like to Read and Choose to Read for Pleasure

Why do young adults read? A large percentage of young people surveyed say that they choose to read for pleasure, relaxation, or entertainment. Their answers vary depending on who is asking the question: surveys conducted by educational researchers tend to frame the question to take some account of "schooled reading" or the reading that young people have to do to succeed in school. Many studies discuss authorized or recommended readings but make no mention of popular reading materials such as comics or magazines.

In a Canadian study, "The Reading and Purchasing Public" (Duxbury 1995), readers in the fifteen- to twenty-four-year age range cited "reading for relaxation" as the chief reason for reading, ranking pleasure higher than reading for career development information. In Australia, 68 percent of people younger than twenty years bought a book in 1990 for the main purpose of "relaxation or general enjoyment" (Guldberg 1990, 78). The 2001 NEA survey shows that 40 percent of the five hundred teens polled read primarily for pleasure (Peter D. Hart Research Associates 2001). In their survey of leisure reading among young people, Moffitt and Wartella (1992) found that 85 percent of girls reported reading for pleasure, compared to 65 percent of boys.

The notion of reading for pleasure is rarely explored in any depth in the large-scale surveys. However, several qualitative studies on the reading practices of adolescent women ask questions about what it means to read for pleasure. What is the pleasure of reading—of engaging with certain kinds of texts? In a study of the magazine reading of girls between the ages of thirteen and seventeen, Dawn Currie found that girls' engagement with magazines had less to do with their desire to escape reality than with their yearning for content that addressed the realities of teenage life (Currie 1999, 158). In an earlier study, Linda Christian-Smith (1990, 106–7) surveyed seventy-five young women who were avid readers of the romance genre who experienced pleasure through vicarious identification with the heroines and their romantic journeys.

Reading *Relates* to Other Leisure Activities of Young People

The literature on young people and reading often sets up an antagonistic relationship of competition among popular leisure-time activities. We hear about reading versus television viewing, reading versus computer gaming, reading versus playing sports, reading versus Internet surfing, and reading versus social engagement. In these accounts, reading is isolated from other leisure activities and also from other information-seeking practices. Often little systematic attention is paid to the relationships among reading and other leisure activities.

However, longitudinal studies can give us a sense of how adolescents might alter their reading practices in relation to other leisure events. In her two-year study of young people's leisure reading, Pauline Heather (1981, 51) provides a case study of Graham, an adolescent reader who said he "read less over the Summer holidays," but at another later interview he reported "reading a bit more because there was less to watch on television." Other reasons given by participants for changes in the amount of reading included the "pressure of examinations," "Christmas activities," "family commitments," baby-sitting, housework, or "going out" (Heather 1981, 60, 77). Heather also found that just over a third of her participants read books that were related to their other leisure interests. For example, young people interested in air training, army cadets or war-gaming, read war books (Heather 1981, 78).

We need to consider reading practices in the context of other leisure activities. "Getting into a book" can be demanding and require its own best time. In the words of Joanne, a fifteen-year-old reader studied by Donald Fry, "you can't read enough to get into the book before it's time to put it down" (Fry 1985, 89). Joanne prefers films to books, but this preference does not make her a nonreader. She reads different cultural texts (e.g., books versus films) for different purposes at different times according to her own preferences. Donald Fry (1985, 90) explains further:

> As with many in her class, there is a close relationship between the films she watches and the books she reads. When the reading of the book follows the viewing of the film, then that enables the viewer/reader to extend the world of the film, to make it last longer: it brings to mind again the film itself, as the reader recognizes a scene or detects something new, matching the images of the film against the text of the book; where the book is not the same as the film, it still perpetuates the story world of the film, and the remembered pictures help the reader "get into" the new book. The images of the film help to create a visual reference point that the reader needs to construe the text. When the reading of the book precedes the viewing of the film, then the film brings the story to life: more experienced readers may feel critical of film versions of novels, but for Joanne it is the film that authenticates the book, confers realism upon it . . . as though the experience of reading needs the experience of viewing to be entire.

Much of the research on young adults' reading comes from those interested in literacy practices associated with education and school contexts. As a result, the acquisition of literacy skills and development of reading fluency are primary targets of concern. Although many young people are doubtless enjoying the texts that they must read for school, just as many do not find pleasure in curriculum based texts. When the research lens shines directly on the reading preferences and reading interests of young people, as stated by young people, a different picture of reading and the role of reading in their lives emerges. Research that asks questions about young people and leisure reading consistently shows that:

- Young adults read regularly.

- Young adults like to read for pleasure.

- Young adults like to read magazines, but they also like to read books.

- Reading relates to other leisure activities of young adults.

Research Tells Us: Young Adults and Newspaper Reading

In a large-scale study of 1,200 Belgian youth between the ages of sixteen to eighteen years, Karin Raeymaeckers (2004) found that teen readers were not keen on innovative layout changes designed by editors to reach a youth market—for example, increased use of color and other "flashy" design strategies or the inclusion of youth inserts. Instead these young readers expressed a desire to be treated as "mature partners" in the communication process. In terms of content, young people preferred local news and articles about film or crime and had little interest in economics and politics. However, as Raeymaeckers (2004, 228) explains, this lack of interest in what might be called "hard news" is not necessarily cause for hand wringing:

> These results are in line with the conclusions of the focus group discussions where young participants argued that their moderate interest in political news was not a sign of apathy. They explained that this kind of newspaper content has little in common with their personal lifestyles. By contrast, the interest in local news is rather high. This kind of news is more attractive for young readers, since it is about people and situations with which they are familiar: moreover this kind of news is judged to concern their everyday life.

Although 20 percent of the study participants never read newspapers, the remainder of young people in the sample read them occasionally (43 percent), regularly (17.5 percent), and daily (19.5 percent).

To Read More on Young Adults and Reading

Fry, Donald. 1985. *Children Talk about Books: Seeing Themselves as Readers*. Milton Keynes, England: Open University Press.

    In this accessible and readable book, Fry uses a case-study approach and conversations with six young readers between the ages of eight and fifteen years to examine what happens when these young readers see (or do not see) themselves as readers. In the chapters on Sharon and Joanne, each fifteen years old, Fry uses insights from his conversations with them to explore the social function of popular reading and the transition from children's fiction to adult books. He makes a very strong argument, still valid nearly twenty years later, that adults who promote reading among young people need to be alert to what young people say about reading and that the only way we can do that is to ask questions and listen.

Krashen, Stephen, and Debra Von Sprecken. 2002. "Is there a decline in the reading romance?" *Knowledge Quest* 30, no.3: 11–17.

    The authors provide continued support for Krashen's ongoing arguments that children at all stages and ages like to read. A critique is offered of inadequate methods of investigation of reading among young people, and an analysis of some recent studies counters the notion of a decline in reading interest among adolescent readers.

SmartGirl.org. 1999. *Smartgirl Survey Archives: Teen Read Week Survey: Summary of Major Findings.* Available at http://www.smartgirl.org/speakout/archives/trw1999/trwsummary.html (accessed January 31, 2005).

SmartGirl.org. 2001. *Smartgirl Survey Archives: Teen Read Week Survey 2001.* Available at http://www.smartgirl.org/speakout/archives/trw/trw2001.html (accessed January 31, 2005).

SmartGirl.org. 2002. *Latest Survey Results – Teen Read Week 2002 Summary.* Available at http://smartgirl.org/reports/1493716.html (accessed January 31, 2005).

SmartGirl.org. 2003. *Latest Survey Results – Report on Teen Read Week 2003.* Available at http://www.smartgirl.org/reports/2734196.html (accessed January 31, 2005).

    These surveys are products of Smartgirl.org and the Young Adult Library Services Association of the American Library Association. The surveys provide overwhelming and ongoing evidence that young people, both young women and young men, "read constantly for their own satisfaction." Extremely large numbers of adolescents respond to this survey (nearly 6,500 respondents in 2002).

References

Allen, Kate, and John E. Ingulsrud. 2003. "Manga Literacy: Popular Culture and the Reading Habits of Japanese College Students." *Journal of Adolescent and Adult Literacy* 46, no. 8: 674–83.

Book Marketing Limited. 2000. *Reading the Situation: Book Reading, Buying & Borrowing Habits in Britain.* Library and Information Commission Research Report 34. London: Library and Information Commission.

Canadian Press Newswire. 2002. "B.C. Students Make the Grade in Math, Writing; Reading Skills a Concern." 1 October.

Christian-Smith, Linda K. 1990. *Becoming a Woman through Romance.* New York: Routledge.

Currie, Dawn. 1999. *Girl Talk: Adolescent Magazines and Their Readers.* Toronto: University of Toronto Press.

Duxbury, Nancy. 1995. *The Reading and Purchasing Public: The Market for Trade Books in English Canada 1991.* Toronto: Ekos Research.

Fry, Donald. 1985. *Children Talk about Books: Seeing Themselves as Readers.* Milton Keynes, England: Open University Press.

Guldberg, Hans Hoegh. 1990. *Books—Who Reads Them? A Study of Borrowing and Buying in Australia.* Sydney: Australia Council for the Arts.

Heather, Pauline. 1981. *CRUS Occasional Paper 6: Young People's Reading: A Study of the Leisure Reading of 13–15 Year Olds.* Sheffield, England: University of Sheffield, Western Bank, British Library Board.

IPSOS Book Trends. 2002. *2001 Consumer Research Study on Book Purchasing.* Book Industry Study Group.

Jones, Patrick. 2002. *New Directions for Library Service to Young Adults.* Chicago: American Library Association.

Krashen, Stephen. 2004. *The Power of Reading: Insights from the Research.* 2nd ed. Westport, CT: Libraries Unlimited.

Linwood, Gayle. 2004. "To Read . . . or Not to Read? With Internet, Schoolwork, Television, DVDs and the Latest Hit Movies in the Theaters, Teens Have a Lot Competing for Their Attention. Who Has Time to Read?" *South Florida Sun-Sentinel,* 13 February, 5.

Mellon, Constance A. 1990. "Leisure Reading Choices of Rural Teens." *School Library Media Quarterly* 18, no. 4: 223–8.

Moffitt, Mary Anne S., and Ellen Wartella. 1992. "Youth and Reading: A Survey of Leisure Reading Pursuits of Female and Male Adolescents." *Reading Research and Instruction* 31, no. 2: 1–17.

Noland, Hope. 2004. "Bookin' It: Is Reading Becoming More of a Lost Art?" *Charleston Gazette,* 7 August, 7.

Peter D. Hart Research Associates. 2001. *NEA: National Education Association (NEA) Poll on the Reading Habits of adolescents.* Available at http://web.archive.org/web/20020805122811/http://www.nea.org/readingmatters/readpoll.html (accessed January 31, 2005).

Raeymaeckers, Karin. 2004. "Newspaper Editors in Search of Young Readers: Content and Layout Strategies to Win New Readers." *Journalism Studies* 5, no. 2: 221–32.

Schemo, Diana Jean. 2003. "Students' Scores Rise in Math, Not in Writing." *New York Times,* 14 November, A18.

Statistics Canada. 1998. *General Social Survey: Canadians' Reading Habits.* Available at http://www.statcan.ca/english/Pgdb/arts13a.htm (accessed January 27, 2005).

Toppo, Greg. 2003. "Tests Find Reading Scores Flat, but Math Improved." *USA Today,* 14 November, AO6.

3.2. Young Adults and Fiction Reading

When asked about the books they like to read and choose to read, young adults have been remarkably consistent in their responses. In a pioneering study of children's reading preferences, Lewis Terman and Margaret Lima (1931, 39) surveyed Canadian young people aged six to sixteen. They found that boys liked adventure stories, and girls showed a preference for domestic dramas. At fourteen years of age, both male and female readers enjoyed reading periodicals, and young women in particular were reading adult books (Terman and Lima 1931, 42–43). However, far from supporting the independent selection of popular reading materials by young people, these authors warned of the dangers of "worthless" reading:

> The next step in the encouragement of good reading habits is to keep away from the child objectionable or worthless books. It is of course difficult if not impossible to control a child's reading to such an extent that he will never read a book that is undesirable. One who attends the public schools and reads the books that are passed around among children is almost certain to read some things that would better be left unread. However, if enough good reading is constantly put before him, he will usually find so much of interest in it that undesirable books will make little appeal. There are, of course, exceptions to this rule. An occasional child may be continually exposed to good literature in the home and yet turn to cheap and sensational books. Such a child, however, is likely to need special attention not only to his reading but to his activities, his companions, and his environment in general. (Terman and Lima 1931, 5–6)

More than forty years later, George Norvell (1973) made a cautious—yet radical —call for the selection of reading materials based on popularity and pleasure. He conducted a study that collected massive amounts of data on ranked preferences of nearly five thousand titles chosen by secondary school students. He writes:

> [T]here has been increasing recognition of the role played in learning and habit formation by the factor of interest. Granting the dominance of this factor, it seems the high objective—a love of good reading—might be attained through providing young people with an ample supply of literary selections which stand where the lines of student popularity and critical approval converge. The major difficulty in testing this plan has been the lack of knowledge as to which selections pupils genuinely enjoy. (Norvell 1973, 4)

Happily, we no longer lack knowledge of the reading preferences of young people. We can paint a picture of these preferences using broad strokes. In some cases we can even make claims based on enduring interest in specific authors. Studies of readers' preferences are scattered across disciplines and levels of scholarship from tidy studies of a single library branch's young adult patron base to the large-scale national surveys of reading mentioned in section 3.1. We also know that narrative forms of reading material such as fiction and biography remain generally more popular than expository forms of nonfiction. Decades of reading research give strong evidence that young adults of all ages and genders prefer to read mysteries, thrillers, humorous stories, fantasies, adventures, and various popular series. Since the mid-1980s boom in young adult horror along with the rise of the immense popularity of Stephen King, horror has also been a consistent favorite. At the same time, there are marked gender differences in reading preferences—boys have historically avoided romances, a favorite genre of young women. If given a choice, young male readers consistently choose books with suspenseful, action-driven plots—books that seldom appear in school curricula or on recommended book lists (Sullivan 2003; Williams 2004).

Although fiction is popular with both males and females, recent studies have taken a second look at the role of pragmatically oriented texts in the reading histories of young men (see Smith and Wilhelm 2002; Love and Hamston 2003). Nonfiction and factual texts have emerged as an important and not-to-be-ignored reading preference among young people, especially among boys (Sullivan 2004), but more studies are needed to take serious account of this phenomenon.

Research Tells Us: How Young Adults View Libraries

A 1962 study of library usage among young adults aged fourteen to twenty years listed the following deterrents to their obtaining preferred reading materials from libraries (Bearman 1962, cited in Heather 1981, 12):

- Public libraries did not have the right sort of books for young people.

- Librarians were viewed as definitely unapproachable and as being like schoolteachers.

- It was easier to borrow from friends than to negotiate the public library hurdles of borrowing.

- Libraries were too quiet.

- Lack of time kept them from traveling to the library.

- Respondents had enough books at home.

In 1998, The DeWitt Wallace-Reader's Digest Fund enabled a large-scale study into how libraries could improve services to youth during nonschool hours (Yohalem and Pittman 2003). Libraries in ten urban U.S. areas surveyed teens in their community about their views on the public library. Thirty-seven years after the Bearman study, teens apparently still find public libraries to be restrictive, alienating, and not particularly helpful. Here's what they said (Meyers 1999):

- Libraries are not cool; they are frequented by nerds, dorks, and dweebs.
- Library staff is not helpful or friendly.
- Libraries need to provide better books and materials.
- Teens need welcoming spaces—not morgues.
- Library hours of service are not convenient to teens.
- Libraries need to get rid of restrictive rules and fees.

These negative perceptions indicate that libraries still have a lot of work to do if they want to be seen by young adults as friendly places to get interesting materials to read.

Case 13: Reading to Escape

When Paulette Rothbauer asked the young women in her study to "Describe the role that reading plays in your life," here's what they said. The following excerpts are a sample of responses made by young women between the ages of eighteen and twenty-three years, all participants in Rothbauer's (2004) doctoral research into the intersection of information, identity, and voluntary reading:

- It represents a guilty pleasure. Because books are that much better to me when I don't have—like I really shouldn't be reading them. It's a little bit more delicious because I know that I have a textbook sitting next to me that I should be reading. . . . I guess it's a bit of fantastical escape, even if I'm reading something ordinary.

- I think it's just an escape for me . . . any time anything bothers me I'll read something. . . . I get consumed in it, so in a way it's bad because I don't deal with the problem. But it's good because it's like, I could do drugs to do that, but I'd just rather read. . . . So I think it's always really escape, 'cause I didn't ever really read for knowledge; I think [knowledge] was just a by-product.

- I think I read for knowledge . . . I'm really for equality so I like to read to understand the different areas of the world, and like different people's conflicts . . . It's also kind of an escape. And you get to be alone by yourself at the same time—it's like a little secret too, like you get to know this other world and it's like your own little secret. You can't explain it unless someone else reads it.

- It's a comfort to me . . . when I was younger, when things were bad or something, I could, you know, go in my room, close the door and read . . . It's almost even comfortable to see [the books]. Because I'll see my Anne of Green Gables books and I'll remember. . . . There's a comfort just to have them, like when I go away . . . I'm going to bring them with me.

Comments

These excerpts illuminate the power of voluntary reading to create new possibilities in young people's lives, while at the same time giving no small measure of comfort.

To Read More on the Reading Preferences of Young People

Christian-Smith, Linda K. 1990. *Becoming a Woman through Romance*. New York: Routledge.

Seventy-five adolescent girls were surveyed about their romance-reading habits. Their top reasons for reading romances include escape or a way to get away from the pressures of home and school; better reading than school materials; simply for enjoyment and pleasure; and to learn what romance and dating are about (1990, 105). Christian-Smith theorizes her participants' resistant reading strategies in light of class and gender politics.

Sarland, Charles. 1991. *Young People and Reading: Culture and Response*. Milton Keynes, England: Open University Press.

This remains one of the best studies of popular literature preferences of young adults. Sarland talks to young people about their voluntary reading, and he privileges popular literature claiming that pulp horror, romance, adventure thrillers, and so on provide as valuable reading experiences as so-called quality literature. The voices of real readers are emphasized throughout the book.

Smith, Michael W., and Jeffrey Wilhelm. 2002. *"Reading Don't Fix No Chevys": Literacy in the Lives of Young Men*. Portsmouth, NH: Heinemann.

This is a groundbreaking and long overdue book-length exploration of the writing and reading practices of young men. These authors interrogate what they call the "mantra that boys are in trouble" in relation to literacy and schooling. They directly ask young men what they like to do, why they like to do it, what they like to read, and why they enjoy it.

References

Heather, Pauline. 1981. *CRUS Occasional Paper 6: Young People's Reading: A Study of the Leisure Reading of 13–15 Year Olds.* Sheffield, England: University of Sheffield, Western Bank, British Library Board.

Love, Kristina, and Julie Hamston. 2003. "Teenage Boys' Leisure Reading Dispositions: Juggling Male Youth Culture and Family Cultural Capital." *Educational Review* 55, no. 2: 161–77.

Meyers, Elaine. 1999. "The Coolness Factor: Ten Libraries Listen to Youth." *American Libraries* 30, 10: 42–45.

Norvell, George Whitfield. 1973. *The Reading Interests of Young People.* East Lansing: Michigan State University Press.

Rothbauer, Paulette M. 2004. *Finding and Creating Possibility: Reading in the Lives of Lesbian, Bisexual and Queer Young Women.* Ph.D. diss., faculty of Information and Media Studies, University of Western Ontario, London, Canada.

Smith, Michael W., and Jeffrey Wilhelm. 2002. *"Reading Don't Fix No Chevys": Literacy in the Lives of Young Men.* Portsmouth, NH: Heinemann.

Sullivan, Michael. 2004. "Why Johnny Won't Read." *School Library Journal* 50, no. 8: 36–39.

Terman, Lewis M., and Margaret Lima. 1931. *Children's Reading: A Guide for Parents and Teachers.* 2nd ed. Toronto: Ryerson.

Williams, Bronwyn T. 2004. "Boys May Be Boys, but Do They Have to Read and Write That Way?" *Journal of Adolescent and Adult Literacy* 47, no. 6: 570–16.

Yohalem, Nicole, and Karen Pittman. 2003. *Public Libraries as Partners in Youth Development: Lessons and Voices from the field.* Washington, DC: The Forum for Youth Investment. Available at http://www.forumforyouthinvestment.org/papers/publiclibraries.pdf (accessed January 31, 2005).

3.3. Reading and Identity

Most researchers, librarians, teachers, social workers, and parents interested in adolescents' reading agree that reading is an ally in the construction of both personal and social identities at a crucial time in a young person's life. To be sure, "identity" is a contested term across a wide variety of disciplines. However, it is commonly held to be a process of defining the self in relation to others, based on self-categorization and group-identification. We generally consider the development of an individual identity to be one of the major tasks of adolescence, as young people negotiate the attachments and alienation of various friendships, peer groups, and families (Cotterell 1996, 5). Louise Rosenblatt (1994) suggests that the practice of reading can play a crucial helping role in this identity work:

> The sense of personal identity, as George Herbert Mead and his successors have made clear, comes largely from self-definition as against the "other," the external world of people and things. Literary texts provide us with a widely broadened "other" through which to define our world and ourselves. Reflection on our meshing with the text can foster the process of self-definition in a variety of ways (145).

Reading then helps us understand who we are and what our place in the world is and might become. Furthermore, self-identity is based on a shifting understanding of the self in relation to various social structures and social constraints. In the context of reading, the relationships that readers create with fictional characters and fictional worlds allow readers to test and explore interpretations of various and competing identities (see Sumara 1998). The activity of reading about other people and other experiences helps young adult readers understand themselves and their changing place in the world.

Reading can also take account of various identity markers such as race, ethnicity, class, sexual orientation, gender, and age. In an examination of the place of reading in the lives of immigrant youth in Dade County, Florida, Sandra Champion (1993) found that the reading of archetypal hero stories of struggle, initiation, transformation, and return helped young people cope with their own experiences of alienation and assimilation, while at the same time it allowed them to celebrate their difference and diversity. Kivel and Kleiber (2000) studied the role of leisure reading in the identity construction of gay and lesbian teens and determined that reading both helped them understand that there are others who feel as they do and gave them hope for their futures. Reading allows young people to negotiate identity without foreclosing on the possibilities for their lives. In his study of the voluntary reading of secondary school students, Charles Sarland (1991) contends that adolescent readers use a variety of fictional texts to invent or construct potential futures. Rothbauer's (2004a) research into the voluntary reading practices of young women who claim alternative sexual identities supports these findings.

Underlying these claims for reading is the assumption of a certain kind of reading. Most of the young people in these studies are speaking of the power of narrative to change their lives, the kind of narrative accounts of experience found in *stories*. Novels, biographies, autobiographies, and short stories "read" in a variety of formats (traditional hard covers and paperbacks, Web sites, film and video, music, poetry, comics and magazines) enable young people both to imagine new possibilities and to establish recognized boundaries for identity. The nature of this kind of reading affords a certain pleasure in finding oneself in the text while also functioning as a way to gather and organize information about the larger world and one's place in it. Dennis Sumara describes this process as a "re-weaving of the reader's self that alters the reader's interactions with the world" (1996, 80).

Research Tells Us: How Reading Helps in the Negotiation of Identity

Studies of reading that ask young people why they like to read and what they choose to read give overwhelming evidence that reading plays in an important role in helping young adult readers understand the world and their places in it. The following statements, which are derived from a synthesis of reading studies by Radway (2002), Sarland (1991), Sumara (1996), and Rothbauer (2004a, 2004b), correspond to the findings of the other studies mentioned throughout this chapter that take as their starting point what young readers themselves have to say about reading.

1. Reading allows young people to envision and create potential futures.

2. Reading means gathering and organizing information about the wider world and how it works and how one fits into it.

4. Reading enables young people to mediate competing claims for truth in their lives (Appleyard 1990).

5. Reading is an escape from the pressures of everyday life.

6. Reading transforms lives.

Case 14: Reading for Validation of Identity

Paulette Rothbauer (2004a, 2004b) explores how voluntary reading mediates the pressures of understanding and negotiating non-mainstream identities among young adult women. The starting point of this research is that reading provides a safe, self-regulating, private way to explore identity. Most of her participants actively sought to find themselves reflected in their reading choices. The following two excerpts are particularly salient articulations of this theme.

Keri (age 20): I think [reading] helps to validate my own life. That's what I look for in a book and that's what I gain from reading certain kinds of books . . . acceptance and validation. Even though I have it all around me, I still look for it. I like to read other people's experiences and say, yeah I'm having a similar experience. Or, yeah I can associate with this character; therefore what I'm feeling is normal. And so I think that is my number one goal when I'm looking for books and when I'm reading—I'm trying to associate with the book and kind of make myself feel better, make myself feel normal, I think.

Nicky (age 18): [Reading] is a way that I better understand myself . . . When I go out to get a book at the library because I want to read, that's generally what I'm looking for. Sometimes I just read because I'm bored or I read because there's nothing else to do, or sometimes I read because I want to know this information . . . but mostly the big purpose . . . is to be able to look at something from another perspective and kind of twist that around in my brain and see to better understand myself and better be able to interact.

To Read More on Reading and Identity

Hinchman, Kathleen A., Laura Payne-Bourcy, Heather Thomas, and Kelly Chandler-Olcott. 2002. "Representing Adolescents' Literacies: Case Studies of Three White Males." *Reading Research and Instruction* 41, no. 3: 229–46.

Using participant observation and interviews, the researchers found that the multiple literacy practices and perspectives of three adolescent boys resisted hegemonic notions of masculinity, class, and race. The detailed case studies show that each boy, in some way, resisted what the researchers call "the expected white male dominant story," while at the same time their engagement (both reading and writing) with a diverse range of cultural texts permitted the development of identities that ensured acceptance and survival among peers at school and within their communities.

Radway, Janice. 2002. "Girls, Reading, and Narrative Gleaning." In *Narrative Impact: Social and Cognitive Foundations*, 183–204. Edited by Melanie C. Green, Jeffrey J. Strange, and Timothy C. Brock. Mahwah, NJ: Lawrence Erlbaum.

Radway explores the intersection of the impact of reading for pleasure on the practices of what she calls "self-fashioning." She uses her own recollections of her girlhood reading history and looks at "riot grrrl" 'zine culture for contextual evidence of the insubordinate and creative power of reading.

References

Appleyard, J. A. 1990. *Becoming a Reader: The Experience of Fiction from Childhood to Adulthood*. Cambridge, England: University of Cambridge Press.

Champion, Sandra. 1993. "The Adolescent Quest for Meaning through Multicultural Readings: A Case Study." *Library Trends* 41, no. 3: 462–92.

Cotterell, John. 1996. *Social Networks and Social Influences in Adolescence*. London: Routledge.

Kivel, Beth D., and Douglas A. Kleiber. 2000. "Leisure in the Identity Formation of Lesbian/Gay Youth: Personal, but Not Social." *Leisure Sciences* 22, no. 4: 215–32.

Radway, Janice. 2002. "Girls, Reading, and Narrative Gleaning." In *Narrative Impact: Social and Cognitive Foundations*, 183–204. Edited by Melanie C. Green, Jeffrey J. Strange and Timothy C. Brock. Mahwah, NJ: Lawrence Erlbaum.

Rosenblatt, Louise M. 1994. *The Reader, the Text, the Poem: The Transactional Theory of Literary Work*. Reprint, Carbondale: Southern Illinois University Press, 1978.

Rothbauer, Paulette M. 2004a. "Finding and Creating Possibility: Reading in the Lives of Lesbian, Bisexual and Queer Young Women." Unpublished Ph.D. diss., Faculty of Information and Media Studies, University of Western Ontario, London, Canada.

Rothbauer, Paulette M. 2004b. " 'People aren't afraid anymore but it's hard to find books': Reading Practices that Inform the Personal and Social Identities of Self-identified Lesbian and Queer Young Women." *Canadian Journal of Information and Library Science* 27, 4.

Sarland, Charles. 1991. *Young People Reading: Culture and Response*. Milton Keynes, England: Open University Press.

Sumara, Dennis J. 1996. *Private Readings in Public: Schooling the Literary Imagination*. New York: Peter Lang.

Sumara, Dennis J. 1998. "Fictionalizing Acts: Reading and the Making of Identity." *Theory into Practice* 37, no. 3: 203–10.

3.4. Reading Diverse Media Forms

Once we accept that reading means more than just the reading of books, we must take some account of other modes of reading. Stephen Krashen (2004, 103–10) has made a strong case for the efficacy of comic books in recruiting pleasure-readers and argues for their inclusion in libraries and schools. Researchers have examined comic books, graphic novels, and magazines in the context of adolescent reading, but more research is needed on the newer formats for reading. How does reading change with the rise of electronic texts accessible via the Internet or read from DVDs and CDs? Should listening to music and watching television programs or films also be counted as reading?

There are several reasons we should pay attention to the multimedia texts that young people use and to the ways in which they use them. It does not matter if we call this engagement with alternative texts "reading" or if we call it something else. What does matter is that young people are engaging with text in ways that are meaningful, pleasurable, and voluntary. The power of story ties together all methods and forms of engagement with multimedia texts. For example, young people tell us they are drawn to anime fictions because they care about the characters, they want to know what happens to them, and when they can't know what happens (as is the case due to sporadic and haphazard access), they will fill in the blanks themselves, creating and distributing their own fanfictions. In the process they "have fun, exercise [their] imagination, and avoid boredom. . . . [they] develop and solidify relationships with various friends, online and otherwise" (Chandler-Olcott and Mahar 2003).

Alvermann and Hagood (2000) advocate building on the phenomenon of "fandom," or tastes and preferences of young people, to develop critical literacy skills. They suggest inviting adolescents to bring their music fan culture into the classroom. If public libraries similarly took steps to respect the various pop culture tastes and interests of adolescents, there would be two benefits. Young people would have evidence that libraries are more than repositories of what they see as mostly irrelevant books. Second, libraries themselves could become better informed about youth culture and therefore better able to respond to potential reading interests and tastes of young adults (see Rothbauer 2004).

Young people interacting with multiple narrative forms across different media still rely on traditional literacy skills, in some cases with considerable refinement, to make sense of new formats and media. Playing a favorite computer game well means "integrating information across multiple texts, relating textual meanings to personal experience, and composing complete messages in the form of stories and reports for actual audiences" (Guthrie and Metsala 1999, cited in Moje 2002). The "how" of reading matters less when the interests of young people motivate their reading choices. Margaret Mackey found that issues of personal salience were extremely important in the selection of texts by the young people in her study. The content of the text often outweighed considerations of format:

> In case after case, it is possible to observe them making a trade-off between issues of *personal salience* and issues of *fluency of access*. In other words, they checked out a story in any medium to see if it held any individual interest for them, and balanced this element against the question of how difficult or how easy it would be to gain access to that world. Too many long words, too obscure a video opening, too complex a set of controls for a computer game, and they were ready to switch off—unless such difficulties might be compensated for by a particular salient story. Similarly, many of them rejected texts that were too easy, unless they were extremely interesting to the individual making the choice. (Mackey 2002, 15)

Some researchers argue that popular and alternative forms of texts introduce students to stories that they might otherwise never encounter (see, for example, Schwartz 2002 on graphic novels). They tend to view the skills developed in reading multimedia texts as a kind of bridge to reading more traditional materials—Krashen (2004, 104) calls comics a "conduit to more challenging reading." The danger in this view of media is the tendency to privilege traditional print literacy and discount the value of popular cultural forms as valuable in themselves. What's more, according to David Buckingham (as cited in Williams 2003), young people quickly learn that conversations about media use take place in the "margins of school life" and that there is a certain amount of "institutional hostility" toward popular culture in general.

Other kinds of unsanctioned reading and writing may not attract hostile attention but tend to be invisible and go unnoticed by adults. These include the technology-mediated literacy practices associated with e-mail, various Web sites, chat rooms, and computer games. Young people do not seem to make the same distinction that librarians, teachers, and parents do among the varieties of textual experience. Or rather they are less likely, and perhaps less willing, to privilege book reading as the highest form of literacy. They consume and create meaning from a variety of popular media texts.

Research Tells Us: A Theory of Multimedia and Engaged Reading

David Reinking (2001) sees a unique and powerful potential for digital texts and contexts to promote enjoyable reading practices. He puts forward four key arguments as follows:

1. The reading experience is literally interactive or transactional. The reader manipulates the digital text in active ways according to his or her own motivation, thereby changing the text through the process of reading. This transaction between text and reader is virtually infinite.

2. Digital texts can mitigate the "Matthew effect" (in which early success in acquiring reading skills usually leads to later successes) in a reading context because more opportunities for help for struggling readers are embedded within the digital text itself. Digital texts can adapt to reading difficulties by responding with simplified vocabulary, syntax, content, or visual clues.

3. Electronic and digital texts can fulfill a broad range of psychological and social needs. In North America, the relative ease of access to such texts allows young people to explore topics of immediate interest in a timely way that cannot be matched by traditional print formats. Furthermore, even everyday activities such as e-mail messaging can extend to offline activities or can lead to collaborative writing and reading through the exchange of textual information, often with peers from the far-flung corners of the world. Reinking goes further, claiming that "Internet activities such as MUDs and MOOs allow students to adopt an imaginary persona in interacting with others in imaginative worlds or adventures. Likewise, students can grow plants remotely over the Internet, and they can interact with astronauts orbiting the earth. In short, electronic texts provide a wide array of need-fulfilling leisure activities not possible in printed materials, and they are thus more likely to increase engagement in reading" (2001, 207). (Note: MUDS are multiple-player online computer games; MOOs are text-based virtual reality programs.)

4. Electronic texts invite a playful and creative reading stance. In short, reading digital texts is fun.

Reinking tested his assertions in a study designed to assess whether middle school students read more books when introduced to the computer-based activity of creating multimedia book reviews. Overall, students' engagement with literacy activities increased while they participated in the online book review projects.

Reinking, David. 2001. "Multimedia and Engaged Reading in a Digital World." In *Literacy and Motivation: Reading Engagement in Individuals and Groups*, 195–221. Edited by Ludo Verhoeven and Catherine Snow. Mahwah, NJ: Lawrence Erlbaum.

Case 15: A Real Reader—Reading and Playing

Twelve-year-old Johnny begins an interview about his reading materials and habits by declaring, "Well, I don't read novels really, or anything like that." As the interview continued, however, it becomes apparent that his sustained engagement with computer games has clearly motivated him to read a diverse range of texts including magazines, comics, gaming manuals, and role-playing guides to get more from the game. With enthusiasm, Johnny described his reading as follows:

This is *Warhammer* and some other stuff, and I read short paragraphs and parts and stuff. . . . And I read little interesting stuff in those [points to computer game guides], but I don't read all the babble about history and whatever. I don't read all the history and all that boring stuff. I just read little paragraphs describing everything, characters, stories, whatever. They're describing—it's what these guys do [pointing to a shelf full of small plastic figurines: an army of lizards dressed in battle gear]. Those are Lizard men, but I have different ones. Some of them are dragons, but not all of them. But the books—there's all different ones like "Quest," and there's ones that are monthly releases. So they keep you updated on all kinds of *Warhammer*. (McKechnie 2004)

Comments

Even this small excerpt from the transcript illustrates Johnny's excitement and specialized knowledge. It also demonstrates his attraction to elements of the gaming narrative related to story: not the "history and boring stuff," but characterization, storytelling, and action adventures.

What Parents and Librarians Can Do

1. Become informed about the leisure interests of young people. Ask them, and observe them firsthand. Do not rely on outdated knowledge about the "cultural habits of teenagers." Find out what they are reading and how they get access to various texts.

2. Do not privilege traditional print literacy. Ask teens what they are watching on television and at the cinema, what they are playing and trading, what they are browsing and surfing.

3. Provide opportunities for young people to share their out-of-school interests with peers. Do this by providing space for young people to meet or by bringing together teens from across your region. Without a doubt these interests will involve some kind of reading across diverse media.

4. Provide access to electronic books through the collection, cataloguing services and programming. And if you can't provide access you can still know about them and talk about them with young people.

To Read More on Young People Reading Multimedia Texts

Alvermann, Donna E. 2001. "Reading Adolescents' Reading Identities: Looking Back to See Ahead." *Journal of Adolescent and Adult Literacy* 44, no. 8: 676–90.

    Alvermann explores the assumptions underlying the reading identity of the "struggling reader" and shows that if we give focused attention to the out-of-school literacies of young people our notions of "what counts as reading" might change. She presents the case of Grady, a ninth-grade African American and "struggling reader," who showed little interest in reading activities until his interest in becoming a Pokemon trainer was recognized and supported.

Mackey, Margaret. 2002. *Literacies across Media: Playing the Text*. London: Routledge Falmer.

    This is a must-read, book-length study of how sixteen young people, between the ages of ten and fourteen years, read a variety of texts from picture books and short stories to e-books, DVDs, and CD-ROM encyclopedias. Rich data were collected from interviews, observations, and diaries, and Mackey provides many fascinating excerpts that feature the voices of the young people themselves. A multifaceted picture emerges of young people as sophisticated and discerning users of multiple and varied texts.

References

Alvermann, Donna E., and Margaret C. Hagood. 2000. "Fandom and Critical Literacy." *Journal of Adolescent & Adult Literacy* 43, no. 5: 436–46.

Chandler-Olcott, Kelly, and Donna Mahar. 2003. "Adolescents' Anime-inspired 'Fanfictions': An Exploration of Multiliteracies." *Journal of Adolescent and Adult Literacy* 46, no. 7: 556–66.

Krashen, Stephen D. 2004. *The Power of Reading: Insights from the Research.* Westport, CT: Libraries Unlimited.

Mackey, Margaret. 2002. *Literacies across Media: Playing the Text.* London: Routledge Falmer.

McKechnie, Lynne (E.F.). 2004. " 'I'll Keep Them for My Children" (Kevin, Nine Years): Children's Personal Collections of Books and Other Media." *Canadian Journal of Information and Library Science* 28(4): 73–88.

Moje, Elizabeth Birr. 2002. "Re-framing Adolescent Literacy Research for New Times: Studying Youth as a Resource." *Reading Research and Instruction* 41, no. 3: 211–28.

Reinking, David. 2001. "Multimedia and Engaged Reading in a Digital World." In *Literacy and Motivation: Reading Engagement in Individuals and Groups*, 195–221. Edited by Ludo Verhoeven and Catherine Snow. Mahwah, NJ: Lawrence Erlbaum.

Rothbauer, Paulette. 2004. "The Internet in the Reading Accounts of Lesbian and Queer Young Women: Failed Searches and Unsanctioned Reading." *Canadian Journal of Information and Library Science* 27, 3.

Schwartz, Gretchen E. 2002. "Graphic Novels for Multiple Literacies." *Journal of Adolescent and Adult Literacy* 46, no. 3: 262–5.

Williams, Bronwyn T. 2003. "What They See Is What We Get: Television and Middle School Writers." *Journal of Adolescent and Adult Literacy* 46, no. 7: 546–54.

3.5. The Reading-Writing Relationship

The activity of writing for pleasure is the flip side of reading when we consider the literacy practices of young adults. We all understand the stereotype of the teenager, usually female, who writes in a journal about the intense longings and deeply personal feelings of dramatic and mundane experiences. We label teen poetry, teen lyrics, and other literature in this vein about teens as "angst literature." The phrase instantly conjures the tension between idealism and disillusionment, the *sturm und drang* of adolescence. However, the picture of the lone, angst-ridden adolescent writing in her journal for cathartic release and self-expression is incomplete because it denies the powerful social and communicative function of adolescents' writing activities. The writing that some young people do is an extension of their reading. Both are literacy practices and both are meaning-producing acts (Tierney and Shanahan 1991). Furthermore, both often fall well outside of the curriculum and the canon.

Margaret Finders has called the reading and writing that are enacted beyond the institutional vision of schools the "literate underlife" of young people. She contrasts these with systems of sanctioned literacies that are recognized and promoted by adults in authority (Finders 1997, 24–25). The literate underlife of many young adults includes the writing of poetry, songs and stories, and the reading of popular magazines, 'zines, comics and gaming manuals. Think of the reading and writing activities that typically occur in public libraries. There is the browsing, reading, and signing out of library materials, including a wide range of popular media texts such as magazines, games, music, and videos. There are also the browsing, reading, and writing activities conducted using computers and the Internet. These differ substantially from the activities of the classroom, where the curriculum holds sway. Perhaps more than any other institution, public libraries are able to support the literate underlife of young people as they engage in poetry-writing, role-playing games, and the creation of 'zines, personal Web sites, and weblogs (or "blogs") .

It perhaps seems obvious to say that a close connection exists between reading and writing. Too often, however, we concentrate on one activity or the other rather than considering the way that each feeds the other. Research indicates that, apart from reading, writing activities are the among the most popular literacy practices that young adults do. Following are three kinds of writing activities that are popular with young adults.

Writing for Oneself

Format, style, and content varies: poetry, prose, lyrics, scripts, weblogs, diaries, rants, graffiti, or comic strips. Whatever the format, writing for oneself is a way for young people to locate and create meaning about who they are, about what is going on in their lives, and about the possibilities for their lives. The difficulty for adults interested in promoting this kind of literacy is that young people are not likely to share this writing with them. Research indicates that there are very clear and distinct boundaries between the public writing required for school and the private writing for oneself. According to Finders (1997), for some young women, this private writing involving self-disclosure seemed so risky that they destroyed their poems and stories upon completion.

Writing for an Audience

Many young adults mount personal Web pages on the Internet to create a showcase for their writing. Others submit poetry and stories to traditional and online journals and magazines or send their work to be evaluated in writing competitions. The shift from private to public literacy can be subtle, such as might happen in the sharing of a poem with one's best friend or with a family member.

In other cases, as with a graffiti artist, the audience is more general. Elizabeth Birr Moje's recent research on graffiti writing and reading explores what counts as reading and writing and who count as readers. In her study of literacy among gang-connected youth, she discovered that graffiti writing "is central to who they are as people. It is a way of conveying, constructing, and maintaining identity, thought, and power" (Moje 2000, 651). In another article, she and Sarah McCarthey also write:

I have observed that mainstream readers discount graffiti as a textual form and label graffiti writers as violent, deviant, or at risk of school failure. Despite the fact that graffiti uses alphabetic letters and other symbol systems, many mainstream readers and writers do not count graffiti among real reading and writing practices. The failure of graffiti to be counted among legitimate literacy practices stems more from its identification with deviance than from its textual forms" (McCarthey and Moje 2002, 229).

Other studies on the literacy practices of gang youth and graffiti artists show that these young people, often written off by educational systems as low-literates or illiterates, are in fact highly experienced, and in some cases sophisticated, users of language (Weinstein 2002).

The findings of research studies such as these should inform the roles of librarians and libraries. Unless librarians and educators pay close attention to the cultural practices and markers central to the lives of many young people, young adults will continue find them irrelevant.

Writing by Teen Peers

Reading the work written by other young adults is an empowering experience for some. Weinstein (2002) tells the story of Yesenia, a student at a "second chance" alternative high school who was reading at a first- or second-grade level until she was inspired to contribute her own poetry to the school-distributed student writing books. Her inspiration came from reading the work of her peers. Weinstein explains that this story "shows the effect on students of seeing peers' writing as text, of reading not only 'official,' canonical writers but reading the writing of fellow students, and therefore seeing their peers as authors—someone like Yesenia can see herself in her peers in a way she can't in professional authors" (Weinstein 2002).

To Read More on the Relationship between Reading and Writing

Bitz, Michael. 2004. "The Comic Book Project: The Lives of Urban Youth." *Art Education* 57, no. 2: 33–39.

This short report of a truly inspiring project illustrates the powerful connection between creative literacies and the lived experiences of young people. The Comic Book Project engaged more than seven hundred inner-city youth, members of New York City after school programs, in the writing and illustration of fully designed and detailed comic books, developed with assistance by the comic publisher Dark Horse Comics. Young people emphasized the difficulties of their lives depicting gang violence, drug abuse, and dating.

Guzzetti, Barbara, Saundra Campbell, Corgan Duke, and Jeanne Irving. 2003. "Understanding Adolescent Literacies: A Conversation with Three Zinesters." *Reading Online* 7(1). Available at http://www.readingonline.org/newliteracies/lit_index.asp?HREF=/newliteracies/guzzetti3/ (accessed January 31, 2005).

> Guzzetti conducts a conversational interview with the three young women, cited as coauthors, who are creators of their own 'zines. It is a fascinating account of how these writers cultivate their work when faced with challenges both in and out of school.

What Librarians and Parents Can Do

1. Continue to provide access to materials that reflect up-to-the-minute cultural interests of young people: comics, graphic novels and other drawn books, including self-published 'zines and independent magazines. Especially important are publications that feature the works of young people as well as books on popular music, fashion, gaming, and film. Support and build collections of materials that aid creative writing and reading, such as anthologies of poetry, songs, photographs, along with books on how-to-get-published or produced, or how to make and mount Web sites and weblogs. Consider the "hidden literacies" of young people and take an expanded view of what writing is and what it means to read.

2. Create and distribute pathfinders that include Web resources and Web venues for youth writing. Create links on your Web sites and teen pages.

3. Using people from the community including youth experts, offer workshops on creative writing and support venues for publication, including making and distributing 'zines and newsletters. Young people want and need this practical information to gain experience on how to find exposure for their writing. Find experts who will read and offer critiques of participants' writing.

4. Provide access to "real live" writers who might inspire young people to write. Be sure to include successful young writers in this mix as well.

References

Finders, Margaret. 1997. *Just Girls: Hidden Literacies and Life in Junior High.* New York: Teachers College Press.

McCarthey, Sarah, and Elizabeth Moje. 2002. "Identity Matters." *Reading Research Quarterly* 35, no. 4: 548–552.

Moje, Elizabeth B. 2000. " 'To Be a Part of the Story': The Literacy Practices of Gangsta Adolescents." *Teachers College Record* 102, no. 3: 651–90.

Tierney, R. J., and T. Shanahan. 1991. "Research on the Reading-Writing Relationship: Interactions, Transactions and Outcomes." In *Handbook of Reading Research*, 246–80. Edited by Rebecca Barr, Michael L. Kamil, Peter B. Mosenthal, and P. David Pearson. New York: Longman.

Weinstein, Susan. 2002. "The Writing on the Wall: Attending to Self-motivated Student Literacies." *English Education* 35, no. 1: 21–45.

3.6. Young Adults Reading and Reaching Out

The activity of reading is commonly seen to be private, personal, and individual, conducted in solitude and privacy. Good readers are those who can read quietly, silently without moving fingers or lips. However, a growing body of research on the multiple literacies of young people throws into question this individualistic perception of reading. We can say with mounting certainty that even when young people—and all readers—read alone, the act of reading remains profoundly social (see section 4.9 for more on reading as a social activity). Books and other reading materials function as what sociologist James Paul Gee has called " 'artifacts' of thinking, feeling, believing, valuing, and acting that can be used to identify oneself as a member of a socially meaningful group or social network or to signal (that one is playing) a socially meaningful role" (Gee 1996, cited in Hinchman et al. 2002). Just think of the recent Harry Potter reading phenomenon where we witness myriad conversations held in various social arenas amongst a diverse readership about J. K. Rowling's immensely popular series. By reading these novels, readers are able to participate in these conversations, even if one never speaks a word of it to anyone—membership is granted as soon as one picks up the books (or buys the books, or views the movies, or writes a review, or recommends them to other readers).

In their book, *Reading Don't Fix No Chevys*, Smith and Wilhelm build a convincing case that "the social" is of the utmost importance to boys' literacy practices: "when the literate activity provided the occasion for social connections, the boys had intrinsic motivation for their engagement" (2002, 147). Friends, peers, and family members played key roles in the selection of texts and the development of relationships with favorite authors and characters. Smith and Wilhelm's work signals a renewed scholarly interest in boys and reading, but studies about girls and reading have reached similar conclusions. What all of these studies tell us in different ways is that certain kinds of reading materials confer social status of a particular kind. For example, Finders (1997) found a discrepancy between the books that junior high school girls carried with them for public display, which represented them in socially acceptable ways, and the books that they actually read.

Certain kinds of reading signify specific communities. Many of the examples of reading materials offered throughout this chapter suggest specific audiences of readers who share similar reading tastes, often related to genre boundaries: science fiction, romance, horror, comics, gaming, fan fiction, and poetry. Of course each possible genre suggests more specialized audiences, for example, readers who share a preference for reading materials based on television shows such as *Star Trek, The O.C., CSI,* or *Degrassi: The Next Generation.* Sometimes it works the other way around, too. Specific communities draw together certain kinds of readers: youth belonging to diverse ethnic backgrounds or those who claim alternative non-mainstream identities (e.g., lesbians and gays, Goths, punks); youth committed to various social and political causes such as environmental or labor movements, women's issues, racism and anti-oppression advocacy; or youth who share leisure and recreational interests such as sports, theater, arts, film, and music.

However diverse these communities of readers, the point is that social connections are frequently mediated through reading. Reading exists as another opportunity to establish or foster a membership in specific communities. There are three grounds on which to stake a claim to community: local, textual, and virtual.

Local Communities

Local communities are found in our neighborhoods, towns, cities, counties, provinces, and states and countries. They are sustained by personal and concrete social interactions with actual people met on a regular basis: neighbors, family members, friends, business owners and employees, teachers, classmates, teammates, librarians. Imagine two teenagers who share an interest in Stephen King novels. They live in the same neighborhood, maybe the same building. They can meet face to face to talk about King's latest offering. They might recommend and share books with one another. Perhaps they buy books at the same bookstore—perhaps a store that specializes in horror and fantasy or perhaps the only bookstore in town. They might meet one another at the public library and migrate to the paperbacks to note the sheer number of books that King has written and they have read. Or perhaps they attend a writing workshop structured on King's writing manual. They meet other people in their communities who also enjoy Stephen King. They are invited to join a reading group. They have movie nights where they watch film versions of King's novels.

Textual Communities

Textual communities, or fictional communities, are established when readers make connections with textual characters. Readers connect with characters with whom they share similar feelings or experiences. Writing about young female romance readers, Linda Christian-Smith observed that "the pleasure of the text involved reflecting on aspects of their social identities" (1990, 115). According to Smith and Wilhelm (2002), textual relationships also extend to the authors and the creators of various texts. Young people gain a sense of belonging and a sense of purpose that allows them to feel vitally connected to others. Even if these others are imaginary, fictional, or "made up," the process of identification fosters feelings of affinity and allows readers to stake a membership in the culture of reading.

Virtual Communities

Virtual communities encompass social connections among people who might never meet in a face-to-face interaction but whose communication with one another is mediated through electronic and digital technologies. There are many ways to foster virtual communities based on reading activities, the most common being Web-based gateways. These gateways feature young adult literature of various kinds, with links to authors, bookstores, chat rooms, mailing lists, gaming sites, reviews, and fan sites. The scope of an online community can be truly global in its reach, bringing together young adults from around the world. Or it may be much narrower in scope, linking teens from one neighborhood or one city. SmartGirl.org is just one example of a successful virtual community organized around literacy activities and youth.

Although we need more research on the rich connections between reading and community building among young people, studies cited throughout this chapter support the following statements:

1. Reading is a self-fulfilling, circular reward. Reading leads to social activities and social connections. Readers are motivated to do more reading.

2. Books are social artifacts that confer status and prestige, if put into the right hands at the right time. Time is critical here—trends change quickly, and what's hot one day is not hot the next. Books that are carried in public and read can signify social status.

3. Reading is more than a process of making sense or decoding or finding meaning, although it is that. Reading for pleasure constitutes an "event" or "experience" that, when shared with others, results in powerful and empowering social connections.

To Read More on Social Aspects of Reading

Kooy, Mary. 2003. "Riding the Coattails of Harry Potter: Readings, Relational Learning, and Revelations in Book Clubs." *Journal of Adolescent and Adult Literacy* 47, no. 2: 136–45.

This article chronicles the effects of shared reading experiences among preservice educators. Although not directly about young adult readers, it does provide a blueprint that, with modification, could be used to develop reading groups of interested adults and youth. The sheer joy and energy associated with reading builds connections with literature, with other adult readers, and, vitally, with audiences of young people.

Spires, Hiller, and Pru Cuper. 2002. "Literacy Junction: Cultivating Adolescents' Engagement in Literature through Web Optionality." *Reading Online* 6, no. 2. Available at http://www.readingonline.org/articles/art_index.asp?HREF=spires/index.html (accessed January 31, 2005).

The researchers designed a Web site called "Literacy Junction" that features Cyber Heights Middle School, a virtual learning center. Although this site is intended for teachers and students, it does provide a useful and interesting jumping off point for librarians because its main objective is to foster a socially oriented relationship between young adult readers and young adult literature. Actual, fictional, and virtual worlds converge in this model as students negotiate their identities and their role in their social worlds.

What Librarians and Parents Can Do

1. Foster connections among young adult readers by developing and supporting local and online book clubs and reading groups. Make reading social (and fun): sponsor letter-writing campaigns based on books and reading, art shows, theater, and reading events.

2. Foster connections with popular authors and textual characters by developing, promoting, and supporting venues for reviews written by youth, themed reading events, and author visits.

3. Don't be limited by physical space—move discussions online.

4. Recruit and train youth as peer tutors and reading buddies for younger children or elderly people to foster reading relationships in your local communities.

5. Share your successes (and failures) with others who are interested in young adults and reading at conferences, workshops, listservs, newsletters and newspapers, weblogs.

6. Start your own reading clubs based on young adult literature. Discuss its diverse genres and conventions with adult peers. Share yourself as a reader of these books, and talk about ways to introduce them to young people. Create your own culture of reading around the materials that young people like and want to read. A report of just such a book club can be found in *Canadian Children's Book News* (Doucet 2004).

References

Christian-Smith, Linda K. 1990. *Becoming a Woman through Romance*. New York and London: Routledge.

Doucet, Lisa. 2004. "A New Breed of Book Club." *Canadian Children's Book News* 27, no. 3: 16–17.

Finders, Margaret. 1997. *Just Girls: Hidden Literacies and Life in Junior High.* New York: Teachers College Press.

Hinchman, Kathleen A., Laura Payne-Bourcy, Heather Thomas, and Kelly Chandler-Olcott. 2002. "Representing Adolescents' Literacies: Case Studies of Three White Males." *Reading Research and Instruction* 41, no. 3: 229–46.

Smith, Michael W., and Jeffrey D. Wilhelm. 2002. *Reading Don't Fix No Chevys: Literacy in the Lives of Young Men.* Portsmouth, NH: Heinemann.

Chapter 4

Adult Readers

Catherine Ross

4.1. The Who, What, Why, Where, When of Reading

For more than half a century, large-scale studies of reading have asked "Who reads what and how much in what part of the country?" and have reached certain fairly stable conclusions. Women tend to read more than men; younger people tend to read more than those over age fifty; college-educated people and people with higher annual incomes tend to read more than those without a college education or with lower incomes; whites read more than nonwhites. As Table 4.1 indicates, studies have consistently found that the vast majority of the population reads *something*, about half the population reads books, and about 10 to 15 percent are avid readers for whom being a reader is a crucial part of their identity. Occupation group is more important than age when it comes to predicting whether a person is a book reader. The most robust single predictor of reading is level of education, which is of course related to income level and occupation group. Perhaps less to be expected, people who are "heavy readers" or "heavy book buyers" are somewhat more likely in the United States and Canada to live in the west rather than in the east of the country. In Europe, northerners read more books than those from the south (Eurobarometer 2002). Studies that examine literacy skills have found that younger adult readers have better literacy skills than older ones (despite the widespread belief that literacy rates are falling and that readers who are now aged sixty or seventy experienced a superior quality of elementary education compared with those readers of the present day).

Table 4.1

Percentage of the population that reads.

Study	All Readers (%)	Book Readers (%)	Heavy Readers (%)
Link and Hopf (1946)	50	20	
Leigh (1950)	85–90	50	25
Ennis (1965)	47	15	
Lorimer (1983)	92	58	34
BISG (1978)	94	55	25
Gallup (1978)	75	24	
Watson (1980)	63		
Lorimer (1981)	91	63	
Guldberg (1990)	54		
Graves/ Ekos (1991)	94	68	
BISG (1984)	94	50	17
Book Marketing Ltd. (2000)	96	70	12
Nielsen (2001)	96	72	
Eurobarometer (2002)	82	58	20
NEA (2004)	57	24	

The readership studies cited in Table 4.1 and others have been sponsored by organizations with different specific interests with respect to the who, what, why, when, and where of reading. Some studies look only at book reading, whereas others also include magazines and newspapers (but so far not much on-screen reading). Studies initiated by library associations or by book sellers and book publishers want to know *where* people get the books they read. Hence the 1978 Gallup study sponsored by the American Library Association asked questions about book reading and library use. A study sponsored by the Southam newspaper chain in Canada wanted to know about literacy levels and newspaper reading (Creative Research Group 1987).

For twenty-five years, the Book Industry Study Group (BISG) has sponsored a series of benchmark studies on the book reading and book buying practices of the American public, based on book-purchasing diaries filled out in 16,000 households. BISG reports have been published in 1978, 1983, 1991, and 2001 and are good sources on rates of book purchasing and types of books purchased. In 1991, for example, 60 percent of the households in the panel were "non–book buyers"—that is, in their diaries they did not report buying at least one book in the twelve-month period of the study.

Other studies specialize more narrowly in the particular type of book read. The National Endowment for the Arts limited its interest to "literary reading," which was defined as reading novels, short stories, plays, or poetry, but not nonfiction. In some studies, the nationality of the author or publisher also matters. In counties with smaller markets concerned to protect local authors and publishers from a flood of foreign materials, national studies want to know how many people are reading/ buying home-grown books and authors. For example, Nancy Duxbury (1995, 26) analyzed the 1991 data used in the Graves/Ekos study for a report prepared for the Association of Canadian Publishers and found that Canadian authors have a 20 percent market share in trade paperbacks and hard cover books in Canada. The Australian study *Books—Who Reads Them* (Guldberg 1990, 5) found that, of books bought in Australia in 1989, Australian books accounted for 9 percent of total fiction sales, 47 percent of nonfiction and 30 percent of children's books. In short, different studies have interested themselves in different questions and have defined reading in various different ways.

If we look just at North America, we find that adult leisure reading has been studied for decades in a variety of contexts. In a chapter on "Spending Leisure" in their celebrated book *Middletown in Transition,* Robert and Helen Lynd examined reading as a leisure activity during the depression in a middle American city and found that "Middletown reads more books in bad times and fewer in good times" (Lynd and Lynd 1937, 252). Because Middletown was not a book-buying city, book reading largely meant the reading of library books, the circulation of which doubled between 1929 and 1935 (253). And what were Middletown readers borrowing in such dramatically increased numbers? Fiction. While adult nonfiction circulation increased by 72 percent between 1929 and 1932, the circulation of fiction increased by 163 percent. The Lynds concluded that "Middletown was turning relatively more heavily to the anodyne of fiction in the depression than to nonfiction, conventionally regarded in this culture as 'serious' reading" (254).

This dichotomizing of reading into serious reading versus "the anodyne of fiction" was an approach taken by another pioneer of reading research, Douglas Waples, who is credited with introducing "stringent social science methods to the study of reading and librarianship" (Karetzky 1982, 95). During the 1930s, Waples and his coauthors published a steady stream of books and articles on reading, including *What People Want to Read About* (Waples and Tyler 1931), *People and Print: Social Aspects of Reading in the Depression* (Waples 1937), and *What Reading Does to People* (Waples, Berelson, and Bradshaw 1940). With serious social problems facing America in the 1930s—the Depression, the rise of fascism in Europe, the storm clouds of war on the horizon—Waples thought that people, if given the opportunity, would naturally want to read about these subjects of contemporary social concern. He was convinced that a vibrant democracy depended on an informed citizenry who read nonfiction books on such topics as economics, law, government, politics, and personal hygiene. His early work showed that people *said* on survey instruments that they wanted to read about these significant topics, but they *actually* read popular fiction and pulp magazines.

Perhaps Waples should not have been so surprised at the popularity of fiction, given his own finding in *What People Want to Read About* is "that *people like to read about themselves.* The more closely a subject relates to what is familiar to the given reader, the more interesting it is" (Waples and Tyler 1931, xxiii). Waples found that one out of every two Americans reads only newspapers, but not books. All this was troubling, but initially Waples blamed not the readers for failing to read serious nonfiction books but the publishers and distributors for not producing accessibly written nonfiction on socially important topics (Karetzky 1982, 109). As the 1930s wore on, Waples became discouraged and started to worry that citizens (now thought of as the "masses") were being seduced by propaganda and trash: "We have much to fear from the sordid escapist material aimed at frustrated youth, which primes them for the spiritual promises of a Hitler rather than the true solutions to their problems" (quoted in Karetzky 1982, 111).

While Waples was lashing out at librarians for increasing circulation by catering to a "public demand voiced most loudly by housewives and stenographers," research funded by publishers was just happy to see people reading and buying books of any kind. After World War II, U.S. publishers commissioned a study of reading habits to determine how to sustain book sales at the high volume they had enjoyed during the war. Link and Hopf (1946) interviewed four thousand people in 106 cities and towns in the United States and concluded that active book readers comprised 50 percent of the population. They also found, as have many later studies, that book-reading patterns follow a Bradford distribution: 70 percent of the books were read by 20 percent of the readers. Similarly the Public Library Inquiry, a major U.S. study on the public library and its users in the mid–twentieth century, found that 20 percent of borrowers accounted for 75 percent of the books borrowed (Leigh 1950, 32). These are the avid readers, identified in later studies variously as "heavy readers" or "frequent readers" or "strong readers."

Two other early studies of reading deserve special mention. In 1942, Ruth Strang published *Exploration in Reading Patterns*, based on case studies of 112 persons ranging in age from thirteen to over fifty and ranging in economic status from very poor to very wealthy. Her data included demographic data, test scores on the vocabulary test of the Terman-Merril intelligence test, reading test scores on three assigned articles, and interview data on the use of leisure time, magazines in the home, current reading, sources for books, and reading preferences and aversions.

Strang provides a generous summary of the responses of 21 individual readers drawn from the 112 cases studied. For example, Mrs. O. A. is a homemaker in her thirties with four children who left college in her freshman year to get married. Her vocabulary score put her in the Binet classification of "Superior Adult III." She has subscriptions to the *Reader's Digest, Time,* and *Ladies' Home Journal*. When interviewed, she was reading James Hilton's *Random Harvest* obtained from a rental library. She spends eight hours a week reading and enjoys articles on child care and child psychology as well as historical novels and good mystery stories. She "avoids western stories and depressing or sordid articles." She excelled in her responses to the three assigned articles and in short "of all our cases Mrs. O. A. perhaps most nearly approaches the ideal reader" (Strang 1942, 24–25).

From the analysis of these data based on case studies, Strang (1942, 2–5) derived seven generalizations including:

- Each person's reading pattern is complex and unique because of the hundreds of single factors that influence a person's reading. These factors include age, occupation, vocational demands, geographic location, availability of reading matter, community customs, the influence of close friends and family members, childhood experiences that support or discourage reading, the reader's sense of himself or herself as a reader—in short a whole series of environmental factors that interact with the individual's biological nature.

- A relationship exists between a reader's interest in and enjoyment of a text, the reader's estimate of the text's difficulty, and the reader's proficiency in reading it.

- People read with their experience and their emotions. "What a reader gets out of a passage depends, in large measure, on what he brings to the passage."

- "An individual's reading pattern has a central core or radix which, more or less, determines its nature."

Of equal significance as a groundbreaking, pioneering study of reading is Philip Ennis's *Adult Book Reading in the United States* (1965). Ennis combined qualitative and quantitative methods. One section analyses eighteen lengthy, tape-recorded interviews with readers, and another presents responses to the National Opinion Research Center (NORC) Amalgam Survey of June 1965 administered to a national sample of some 1,500 respondents. Ennis was particularly interested in explaining "the processes of making and keeping the book-reading audience" (33). The first problem he confronts is how to define what is meant by a reader. He says, "we might say that there are two major components in defining a reader: an objective measure of his book reading, whereby we can establish the threshold of being 'in' or 'out' of the category, and the person's own definition of himself as someone who reads books" (40). Ennis concluded, as have many subsequent studies, that the most accurate test of a reader was to ask about the number of books read in a given period (e.g., the last six months), the amount of time spent reading, and the number of books in the home.

Ennis wanted to understand the processes involved in making and keeping the book-reading audience. Hence he considered magazine and newspaper reading only insofar as they functioned as stepping-stones to book reading. In particular, Ennis was interested in finding "the various combinations of experiences in childhood and in school with those in adult life that hold people within the reading habit, lead them into it in later life, and prevent them from slipping out of it" (33). By correlating survey respondents' answers to whether they were book readers in childhood and whether they were currently book readers, Ennis produced a four-cell matrix of regular readers (those who read books both in childhood and currently), deserters (those who used to read books but stopped), late starters, and nonreaders of books. Table 4.2 shows the distribution of readers from the 1,466 subjects who responded to the NORC Amalgam survey. Not unexpectedly, childhood book readers were more likely than non–book readers to be current readers. However, it is interesting that 15 percent of the respondents took up book reading as adults, having not read books as children.

Table 4.2

Relationship between early reading and current reading.

		Early Reading		
		Yes	No	
Current	Yes	35%	15%	49%
Reading	No	24%	27%	51%
		58%	42%	

100% = 1,466.
(NORC Amalgam, 1965 reported in Ennis, 1965, 34)

By the early 1970s, so much reading research had been done internationally on readers and reading that synthesis and integration was needed. In the article "Books and Readers as a Subject of Research in Europe and America," a respected German authority on reading research, Heinz Steinberg, attempted to build a bridge across divides that separate Europe from North America, one language from another, and booksellers from librarians. Reporting on European research, he said:

> European cultural pride was shocked by the first results of book market research. "One household in three has no books," or "Country people read absolutely nothing"—headings such as these could be found in newspapers at the beginning of the sixties. Many intellectuals were at that time carried along by a surge of cultural pessimism and they found such headlines comforting. The masses—so prophesied these cultural pessimists—were every year reading less and less, and young people in particular preferred to play football or watch television instead of reading a good book. Yet, more, not less, books have been produced, bought and issued on loan all over the world than at any time previously. (Steinberg 1972, 747)

The year 1978 was a banner year in North America for large-scale national surveys of book reading, borrowing and purchasing. The Book Industry Study Group (BISG) commissioned the market research company Yankelovich, Skelly and White to undertake a study of adult reading in the United States. The objectives of the BISG study were to distinguish readers from nonreaders, to identify the types of materials read, and to find out why people read what they do. For the quantitative phase of the study, 1,450 in-depth, one-hour interviews were conducted in 165 U.S. cities, with randomly chosen Americans, aged sixteen and over. The sorting "in" or "out" question used in this study was whether a respondent had read any book, any magazine, and any newspaper in the past six months. Only 6 percent of the BISG sample said they had *not* read any format in the past six months, whereas 94 percent had read at least a newspaper. Thirty-nine percent read only newspapers and/or magazines and were labeled non–book readers. Fifty-five percent were book readers, defined as such because they reported having read at least one book in the past six months.

The reading of formats was cumulative. Some readers read only newspapers and/or magazines and not books. But there is almost no one (2 percent of the population) who reads books exclusively and does not also read newspapers and magazines. Book readers were the best educated of the three groups and more likely to report having had some college education. However, because of differences in sizes of the groups, the book reader market actually consisted of a majority (57 percent) with high school education or less.

Summarizing the 1978 BISG study, the principle investigators said, "In general, we find that reading for pleasure, a pattern of consistently heavy reading, and a view of books as best able to satisfy a number of reading 'motivations' were those factors linked with heavy reading and with a commitment to books in particular" (McEvoy and Vincent 1980, 137). Book readers differed substantially from non–book readers in their major reasons for reading as seen in Table

4.3 (data from the 1984 BISG study are also included). The main difference between book readers and people who read only newspapers and/or magazines is that the former were far more likely to report that they read for pleasure.

Table 4.3.

Major reasons for reading.

	Book Readers (%)	Non–Book Readers (%)
1978		
For general knowledge	76	59
For pleasure	**74**	**29**
To relax	51	26
For specific knowledge on work/career	39	13
As a time-filler	21	21
For spiritual/religious reasons	22	10
As an escape	23	6
To fulfill educational requirements	24	2
1984		
For general knowledge	82	82
For pleasure	**86**	**55**
For spiritual/ religious reasons	31	24
Work or career reasons	35	20
Reading to a child	31	18
As an escape	25	7
To fulfill educational requirements	32	12

From Book Industry Study Group 1978 and 1984.

Not to be outdone by the book industry, in the same year as the BISG study the American Library Association commissioned the Gallup Organization to undertake a large-scale national study reported in *Book Reading and Library Usage* (1978). Gallup conducted 1,515 telephone interviews with a representative national sample of adult Americans to find out who reads books, what book they read last, where they obtained the last book, frequency of visiting a public library, what they used the library for, and satisfaction with library services. Not unexpectedly, "heavy" readers were more likely to be women, from eighteen to thirty-four years of age, and with some college education (Gallup 1978, 14). About half of all respondents (51 percent) had visited a public library in the last year, including 9 percent who visit the library every two weeks (22). Among all respondents, the most widely used library services reported were borrowing books (38 percent), using reference materials (28 percent), and reading newspapers or magazines (25 percent) (Gallup 1978, 27). As evident in Table 4.4, there was no difference in the types of books read between book readers in general and library visitors.

Table 4.4.

Type of book last read.

	Book Readers (%)	Library Visitors (%)
Novel	50	50
Biography	8	8
How-to-do-something	7	7
Other nonfiction	27	29
Don't know, No answer	8	5

From Gallup 1978, 12.

Also in 1978, Statistics Canada conducted a survey of adult reading habits as part of a program of gathering cultural statistics. These data were the basis of several analytic reports, notably Ken Watson's *Leisure Reading Habits* (1980) and James Lorimer's "The Readership and Distribution of Books in Canada" (1981). Lorimer reported that the single most important factor influencing adult book reading is level of education, but he offered a qualification: "books are by no means the exclusive preserve of the highly educated. More than 50 percent of the Canadian population are book readers at every educational level beyond grade 8" (Lorimer 1981, 5).

The Statistics Canada survey offered its respondents an entirely different list of options for reasons why they read books for leisure than was provided by the BISG study described earlier. Watson notes, "It is striking that two research teams with such similar interests would have designed such different lists of potential reasons! The only items which are almost the same are 'general information' (Canadian) and 'for general knowledge' (American). Thirty percent of the Canadian population checked this item, and 65 percent of the American population. It is difficult to believe that there is a real difference in motivation between the two populations of this magnitude" (Watson 1980, 27).

For an international comparison, we could look at *Reading the Situation* (Book Marketing Ltd. 2000), a study commissioned by the Library and Information Commission in the United Kingdom to examine the reading habits and attitudes of adults and children in Britain at the end of the century. This study took a broad view of what it meant by reading, asking adults and children if they read comics, graphic novels, magazines, the Internet as well as/instead of books. It used a postal survey sent to a nationally representative sample of households in Britain. This study found a clear distinction between men and women with respect to the social aspects of reading:

> Men are far less likely to discuss the books that they read, to recommend them and to act on recommendations. They are less inclined to trust the judgement of their peers when choosing books to read, preferring to take the advice of "experts" (i.e. as found in reviews), or to use their own judgement. This relates to the fact that they tend to be more

cautious about book choice, and less willing to try a book or author that they aren't sure they'll like.

For women, a recommendation from a friend, relation or colleague is one of the chief sources of guidance for choosing books to read. They are far less concerned than men about making a wrong choice and don't mind giving up on a book if they find they aren't enjoying it. (Book Marketing Ltd. 2000, 11)

It must be acknowledged that these questionnaire data on "Who reads what and why?" are only roughly comparable because studies ask different questions and define differently what counts as being a reader. As noted earlier, reading studies typically use an "in or out" sorting question to determine whether the survey respondent is a reader (or a book reader) or not. Then they correlate reading with demographic variables such as sex, age, education, occupation, family income, and place of residence. Because studies vary in their operational definitions of a "reader," variation in the size of the reading population is an artifact of the question asked. So much depends on the kind of material counted and the time period specified. Some studies are interested only in voluntary reading done by choice ("excluding reading done for work or study"), whereas other studies count all kinds of reading, including work-related reading. Findings also vary depending on whether the sorting question used is "Are you currently reading a book?" or "Have you read a book recently?" or "Have you read a book in the past six months?" or "Have you read a book in the past year?" As Ennis (1965, 6), noted, "It became clear during the course of the interviews . . . that there was a wide range of calendar time contained in the notion of 'recently.' "

The 1978 Gallup study asked if the respondent had read "any kind of a book all the way through or part of the way through" in the past year and found that 75 percent of adult Americans were readers. However, in 1978, the Book Industry Study Group, which defined book readers as people who read at least one book in the past six months, found that 55 percent were book readers. The "all the way through or part of the way through" qualification is an attempt to address a methodological problem, but it has the effect of expanding who gets counted as being a book reader.

The problem is that, without guidance, questionnaire respondents vary dramatically in what they count as "reading a book," with some people counting it only if they read the whole book from cover to cover and other people counting it when they consult a reference book or cook book. Similarly definitions of categories such as "heavy readers" or "frequent readers" vary from one study to the next. Heavy readers in the 1978 BISG study are those who have read ten or more books in the past six months, whereas in the 2004 NEA study, they have read eight or more books in the past year. In the U.K. study *Reading the Situation*, a heavy reader was someone who spent more than 11 hours a week reading books (Book Marketing Ltd. 2000, 31).

Caution is therefore advised in interpreting these readership surveys. There is the question of whether we can take at face value what people say on surveys designed to elicit information about reading patterns and amount of reading. How accurate are people's memories, and how likely are they to tell the truth, even if they could remember it? Because book reading tends to be a socially approved activity in comparison with, say, watching television or playing pool, we might expect that questionnaire respondents would overreport their reading and book purchasing and underreport the amount of time they spend watching TV.

However, Philip Ennis (1965, 40) found that whatever exaggeration happened was canceled out by people's tendency to forget. Using a research technique that first asked people to report how many books they had read in the past six months and then check this estimate by looking at their book collection and consulting with family, Ennis (1965, 41) concludes, "it appears that the error of estimating book reading is to report fewer books than were actually read, on the average 30 per cent fewer." On the other hand, James Lorimer notes that when people are asked to report the number of hours spent on leisure-time activities during the previous week, they tend to round up to the nearest hour, a practice that inflates average reading times (Lorimer 1983, 64). And, as Heinz Steinberg notes, international comparisons are particularly problematic. He claims that for the average American a book is a tool, a means of study and entertainment, but the average German reverences books as a symbol of culture and therefore is more apt to overreport book reading on surveys (Steinberg 1972, 746).

Efforts to use survey methods to get at reasons for reading or not reading have produced findings that are predictable, but not very helpful. For example, in the Australia Council for the Arts study (Guldberg 1990), "lack of time" was the most common reason given by the one in six adults in Australia who said they never buy or borrow books (given by 45 percent of this group). However, because these nonreaders have less education and are less likely to have professional jobs, "lack of time" is possibly a polite way of saying that book reading has a low claim on discretionary time. That is, I won't have time to read until after I have knitted an Afghan rug, washed the car, and reorganized the sock drawer. Avid readers, on the other hand, *make* time for reading.

Despite justified skepticism about the accuracy of any particular number for the percentage of the population that reads books, the accumulation of demographic research conducted over seventy-five years demonstrates one thing beyond question. Although there is nothing magic about the book format in itself, choosing to read books for leisure means having the literacy skills effortlessly to make sense of extended text. "Reading books" turns out to be a useful proxy for a lot of other things that are considered socially desirable: engagement with the world, being in the know, the ability to use texts to satisfy one's active curiosity about the world and one's place in it, access to the specialized literacies that are associated with professional careers that pay the highest salaries, and the possession of social capital and status associated with education.

Case 16: Finding Time to Read

When Catherine Ross interviewed ten women following a meeting of their book discussion group, this is what they said about how they made the times and places to read. (For more on this reading group, see section 4.9.)

Ross: *Some avid readers have told me that they can fit reading into their lives whenever they have a few minutes, waiting in a lineup, on the bus, whatever.*

— That's right.

— I always take a book with me everywhere I go.

— I have a neighbor who says, "Oh, I don't have time to read." And I say, how can anyone not have time to read? How about between 11:00 and 11:30 at night? She says, "Oh I go exercising and I go running and I do this." And I think, "Why?" [laughter]

— But I don't want to read if I'm going to be constantly interrupted. I'm not like my sister who walks around reading a book, which is very rude—she's visiting my place but she's reading. I don't want to be interrupted, especially if I really like the book. I don't like to think that a kid's going to come in and want something and I'm going to have to answer. I would prefer, for a good book, to be on my own.

— I like going to the hairdresser because then I can read magazines I'd never read. It's like an interruption when they come and tell you you're ready to come out of the hairdryer.

— There was a cartoon of Crankshaft the other day where he's in the doctor's office reading. The nurse says, "Do you have an appointment?" He says, "No, I just came to read." [laughter]

— I know that's why I read in bed, to not be interrupted. I will read when I know I'll be interrupted, but once you get in bed you know you're not going to be interrupted.

Comments

Avid readers can fit reading into the busy flow of their lives by seizing moments to read—between 11:00 and 11:30 at night or under the dryer at the hairdressers. However, they agree that the ideal time for reading is uninterrupted time, as we shall see in part of section 4.2, "Places for Reading."

Research Tells Us

Philip Ennis (1965, 11–12) found that reading, if anything, was even more complex than Ruth Strang had reported. He came to the following conclusions:

1. While there was enormous diversity in the books read by readers, "the diversity of reading interests should not be construed as a cacophony of books. . . . In most cases, in fact, the person's reading had immediate and obvious relevance to his life."

2. "People read about what they want to believe and tend to select books that are in some way familiar."

3. "People reject or block out vast areas of books" on grounds that resisted probing or analysis, such as, "I'm not interested in fiction at all. I don't know why. It just can't sustain my interest at all."

What Libraries Can Do

1. Keep in mind the importance of accessibility, and make it easy and convenient for people to find reading materials of all kinds, not just books. Ruth Strang concluded in *Explorations in Reading Patterns* (1942) that "accessibility is the most important of the environmental factors influencing reading." In *The Library's Public* (1949) Bernard Berelson found that "accessibility of reading resources" was one of the two major correlates of reading and library use (the other was the educational level of the user).

To Read More

Cole, John Y., and Carol S. Gold, eds. 1979. *Reading in America: Selected Findings of the Book Industry Study Group's 1978 Study.* Washington, DC: Library of Congress.

This book summarizes the findings of the 1978 BISG study and includes a synopsis of a discussion of the BISG report by participants at a conference held by the Library of Congress in 1979. These seminar participants were skeptical about the study's conclusion that only 6 percent of Americans were "nonreaders." "Most seminar participants thought that this figure was low, primarily because people tend to overstate or exaggerate socially acceptable behavior such as reading" (73). Participants found the BISG study useful, among other reasons, for the way it added "to the growing body of evidence demonstrating that 'television is not the enemy' " (73–74).

References

Australia Council for the Arts. 2001. *National Survey of Reading, Buying & Borrowing Books.* Available as a pdf at http://www.ozco.gov.au/arts_resources/publications/ a_national_survey_of_reading,_buying_and_borrowing_books/ (accessed October 15, 2005).

Berelson, Bernard. 1949. *The Library's Public: A Report of the Public Library Inquiry.* New York: Columbia University.

Book Industry Study Group. 1978. *The 1978 Consumer Research Study on Reading and Book Purchasing.* New York: Yankelovich, Skelly and White.

Book Industry Study Group. 1984. *1983 Consumer Research Study on Reading and Book Purchasing: Focus on Adults.* New York: Book Industry Study Group.

Book Marketing Limited. 2000. *Reading the Situation: Book Reading, Buying and Borrowing Habits in Britain.* London: Library and Information Commission.

Cole, John Y., and Carol S. Gold, eds. 1979. *Reading in America: Selected Findings of the Book Industry Study Group's 1978 Study.* Washington, DC: Library of Congress.

Creative Research Group. 1987. *Literacy in Canada.* Research report prepared for Southam News. Ottawa, Canada.

Duxbury, Nancy. 1995. *The Reading and Purchasing Public: The Market for Trade Books in English Canada 1991.* Toronto: Association of Canadian Publishers.

Ennis, Philip H. 1965. *Adult Book Reading in the United States: A Preliminary Report.* National Opinion Research Center Report, no. 105. Chicago: National Opinion Research Center.

European Commission. 2002. Europeans' Participation in Cultural Activities: A Eurobarometer Survey carried out at the bequest of the European Commission, Eurostat. Available at http://www.readingeurope.org/observatory.nsf/InternationalSurveysB?OpenPage (accessed June 16, 2005).

Gallup Organization. 1978. *Book Reading and Library Usage: A Study of Habits and Perceptions.* Conducted for the American Library Association. Princeton, NJ: Gallup Organization.

Graves, Frank L. 1992. *Reading in Canada, 1991.* Ottawa, ON: Ekos Research/Associates and Ministry of Supply and Services Canada.

Guldberg, Hans Hoegh. 1990. *Books—Who Reads Them? A Study of Borrowing and Buying in Australia.* Sydney: Australia Council for the Arts.

Hickson, Martha, ed. 1988. *The 1988 Gallup Report on Book Buying.* Princeton, NJ: Gallup Organization.

Karetzky, Stephen. 1982. *Reading Research and Librarianship: A History and Analysis.* Westport, CT: Greenwood Press.

Leigh, Robert D. 1950. *The Public Library in the United States.* The General Report of the Public Library Inquiry. New York: Columbia University Press.

Link, H. C., and H. A. Hopf. 1946. *People and Books: A Study of Reading and Book Buying Habits.* New York: Book Manufacturer's Institute.

Lorimer, James. 1981. "The Readership and Distribution of Books in Canada." A paper for presentation to the conference on Book Publishing and Public Policy, Ottawa.

Lorimer, James. 1983. *Book Reading in Canada: The Audience, the Marketplace and the Distribution System for Trade Books in English Canada.* Toronto: Association of Canadian Publishers.

Lynd, Robert S., and Helen M. Lynd. 1937. *Middletown in Transition: A Study in Cultural Conflict.* New York: Harcourt Brace & World.

McEvoy, George F., and Cynthia S. Vincent. 1980. *Journal of Communication* 30, no. 1: 134–52.

National Endowment for the Arts. 2004. *Reading at Risk: A Survey of Literary Reading in America.* Research Division Report #46. Available at http://www.nea.gov/news/news04/ReadingAtRisk.html. (accessed June 16, 2005).

Nielsen. A. C. 2001. *A National Survey of Reading, Buying and Borrowing Books for Pleasure.* Available at http://www.analysphere.com/29Oct01/publishing.htm (accessed June 16, 2005).

Steinberg, Heinz. 1972. "Books and Readers as a Subject of Research in Europe and America." *International Social Science Journal* 24, no. 4: 744–53.

Strang, Ruth. 1942. *Explorations in Reading Patterns.* Chicago: University of Chicago Press.

Waples, Douglas. [1937]. *People and Print: Social Aspects of Reading in the Depression.* Chicago: University of Chicago Press.

Waples, Douglas, Bernard Berelson, and Franklyn R. Bradshaw. 1940. *What Reading Does to People: A Summary of Evidence on the Social Effects of Reading and a Statement of Problems for Research.* Chicago: University of Chicago Press.

Waples, Douglas, and Ralph W. Tyler. 1931. *What People Want to Read About: A Study of Group Interests and a Survey of Problems in Adult Reading.* Chicago: American Library Association and the University of Chicago Press.

Watson, Kenneth. 1980. *Leisure Reading Habits: A Survey of the Leisure Reading Habits of Canadian Adults.* Ottawa: Infoscan.

4.2. The Reading Experience

In the end, large national surveys can go only so far. It seems a little flat to be told by a major national survey based on 16,000 respondents that for 28 percent of Canadians the main reason why they read books for leisure is "Always have read" (Watson 1980, 26). There is something about the experience of reading itself that eludes checklists and multiple choice questionnaires. Survey research can't, for example, explain why avid readers panic at the thought of being without something to read. We have to go beyond statistical averages and turn to case studies of real readers reading. The best sources are studies based on accounts of individual readers: intensive interviews with readers; autobiographical accounts in which people, often writers or celebrities, reflect on books that have influenced them; and confessional memoirs of bibliomania and book obsession.

A good place to begin is Lynne Sharon Schwartz's engaging book *Ruined by Reading: A Life in Books* (1996). For avid readers, Schwartz's meditation on the experience of reading will be a starting point for their own reflections.

Schwartz's loving discussion of reading ranges over such topics as the voluptuous pleasure of reading late at night when immersion in the experience can be prolonged and uninterrupted ("sometimes at the peak of intoxicating pleasures, I am visited by a panic: the phone or doorbell will ring, someone will need me or demand I do something," p. 30); the worry over forgetting what has been read; not finishing books or throwing books out; possession ("There were some books I wanted to possess even more intimately than by reading. I would clutch them to my heart and long to break through the chest wall, making them part of me," p. 67; visualization ("Some readers may run their own private films as each page turns, but I seem to have only spotty fleeting images, a floaty gown, a sofa, a grand ballroom, or a patch of landscape," p. 77).

Schwartz's book reminds us that a complete account of the experience of reading needs to take into account myriad factors that aren't covered by an account of the demographic correlates of reading. Similarly valuable are collections of self-reports of readers who reflect on their own experiences reading. Nadine Rosenthal's *Speaking of Reading* (1995) is a collection of interviews with readers, both ordinary and well known, organized under themes such as "Literature Readers," "Frustrated Readers," "Voracious Readers," "Those Learning to Read as Adults," and "Information Readers." Rosenthal describes herself as a frustrated reader until well into adulthood when her life was transformed by a friend who became a reading mentor. Eventually becoming a tutor and literacy instructor helping nonreading adults, Rosenthal got interested in how reading affects people's lives.

Carlsen and Sherrill's *Voices of Readers* (1988) is another valuable source of self-reports by readers. To engage teachers-in-training in thinking about the experience of books and reading, Robert Carlsen asked students to write a "reading autobiography" in which they reflected on their experience of learning to read. This book is a selection of statements from the thousands of reading autobiographies collected from the 1950s to the 1980s, organized by themes such as learning to read, reading aloud, places for reading, what books do for readers, sources for books, and libraries and librarians.

More specialized collections of self-reports focus on the very particular kinds of reading that produce award-winning authors. Diane Osen's *The Book That Changed My Life* (2002) is based on interviews with fifteen National Book Award winners and finalists, including Don DeLillo, E. L. Doctorow, Cynthia Ozick, and Grace Paley. At the end of each interview is a list of ten or so books that shaped the author's life as a writer. For example, novelist Diane Johnson lists, among others, Jane Austen's *Pride and Prejudice* and Angus Wilson's *Anglo Saxon Attitudes*; nonfiction author Barry Lopez lists Herman Melville's *Moby Dick* and John Steinbeck's *The Grapes of Wrath*.

To celebrate the bicentenary of the bookseller W H Smith, in *The Pleasure of Reading* (1992) British author Antonia Fraser asked forty writers including Doris Lessing, Brian Moore, John Fowles, and Jan Morris to provide a short essay on their own pleasure of reading followed by a short section on "My favourite books." Similarly, in *Everybody's Favorites* (1997), Arlene Perly Rae distills responses from 150 well-known Canadian writers, artists, performers, politicians, and athletes who responded to her invitation to "Think of a special book you read as a child or teenager, a book that woke you up, stirred your soul or changed your life. A book you love." So Alice Munro's response is a reflection on the impact of her childhood reading of L. M. Montgomery's *Emily of New Moon:* "In this book, as in all the books I've loved, there's so much going on behind, or beyond, the proper story. There's life spreading out behind the story—the book's life—and we see it out of the corner of the eye" (Rae 1997, 94–95). Poet Dennis Lee reported that when he thinks back to his childhood years "of passionate reading, to their hungry joy, the flash I get is not of a particular book. What I remember is a discovery I made when I was—how old? . . . The discovery was: *There were books that came in series*" (Rae 1997, 125).

Here are some of the repeated themes that emerge from these self-reports by readers.

Effortlessness

Reading is like breathing, many avid readers say. Perhaps the most important point to make about the experience of pleasurable reading is that skillful readers speed through stretches of text with apparent effortlessness (Adams 1990, 17). For these readers, the act of reading itself can become transparent. The mediating role of words on the page drops from consciousness as the reader feels drawn effortlessly into the world of the text. Ockert, one of the interviewees quoted in Victor Nell's *Lost in a Book* (1988, 290), says, "The more interesting it gets, the more you get the feeling you're not reading any more, you're not reading words, you're not reading sentences, it's as if you are completely living inside the situation." Nell summarizes and elaborates, "You've sunk through the pages of the book [Ockert shows agreement] and you find yourself in the world on the other side of the book, as if you walk through a mirror or something, as if you are there and you are participating" (Nell 1988, 290). Nell's book, discussed in more detail in section 4.4, uses the research methods of cognitive psychology to study reading for pleasure and focuses in particular on the sense that skilled readers have of being entranced or absorbed into the world of the book.

At the other pole from this effortless reading where the words disappear is the difficulty reported by novice readers of "getting into" a book. This is the painful word-by-word struggle of the frustrated reader who sounds out the consonants, blends the vowels, but can't quite catch the sense. Fluent readers can recover this experience of puzzling over opaque black-and-white markings on a page when they read in a second language. In Nadine Rosenthal's *Speaking of Reading*, an interesting chapter, "Frustrated Readers," includes eleven accounts by adult readers who "are able to read, but can't seem to concentrate long enough for their minds to engage with the words to create meaning" (Rosenthal 1995, 25). For examples, see the case study in this section of the "Frustrated Reader."

Joy

Some people call it deep enjoyment; some call it joy. Mihaly Csikszentimihalyi, the psychologist who studies states of "optimal experience," calls it *flow*. This is a condition of total involvement with life, in which people feel creative and engaged—the way they do when engaged in the effortless reading described earlier. " 'Flow' is the way people describe their state of mind when consciousness is harmoniously ordered, and they want to pursue whatever they are doing for its own sake" (Csikszentimihalyi 1990, 6).

Csikszentimihalyi and his research team have collected data from thousands of individuals in all walks of life and in many countries around the world. His goal is to get people to describe how it feels to be effortlessly engaged in activities so enjoyable that nothing else seems to matter and everyday concerns disappear. It turns out that an almost identical experience of flow can be achieved from many, many kinds of apparently unrelated activities such as long-distance running, sewing, having sex, swarming around in motorcycle gangs, dancing, or gardening.

These are experiences of the body in flow, but there are also flow experiences of the mind. According to Csikszentimihalyi (1990, 117), "Among the many intellectual pursuits available, reading is currently perhaps the most often mentioned flow activity around the world." For both physical and mental activities, the felicitous conditions for producing flow are alike: there must be a component of skill involved; concentration on the activity is so complete that one is totally absorbed with no attention left over for distracting anxieties; there have to be rules, a goal, and a way of obtaining feedback; one acts with an effortless involvement and has a sense of control over one's actions; concern for the self disappears; and the sense of the duration of time is altered (Csikszentimihalyi 1990, 49-67).

Perhaps because reading for pleasure satisfies so many—all?—of these conditions, it is for many avid readers one of the chief ways in which they regulate their mood. When a negative emotion such as anger, anxiety, or fear threaten to disorder consciousness, readers report that they deliberately choose to read a book that will improve their mood.

Surrendering to the Book

In describing their reading experience, readers sometimes talk about their relationship to the text in terms either of surrender or of mastery. In some cases, they see themselves seduced, enthralled, caught up in a magic spell. At such times, they feel overpowered by the text and unable—or perhaps unwilling—to maintain a critical distance. Some readers report that this experience of being enthralled occurred most powerfully in childhood but remains an important element in adult reading, especially a first reading. The phenomenological critic Georges Poulet (1980, 43) describes himself as delivered, "bound hand and foot, to the omnipotence of fiction." He says, "I become the prey of language. There is no escaping this takeover." To describe what happens when he reads a book, Poulet uses metaphors of captivity: he writes of "the strange invasion of my person by the thoughts of another" (44) and refers to the takeover of his thought stream as "dispossession" (45) by a "usurper" or an "annexation" of his consciousness by another (47).

This is the pole of readerly compliance in which the reader is submissive to the text. The receptive reader feels caught up in the events of the story and may speak of a sense of being "right there" or of "identifying with" the fictional characters. In Carlsen and Sherrill's *Voices of Readers* (1988, 61), one person recalled a vivid sense in childhood of identifying with the characters in the first reader: "But in that first Reader, oh so vividly, I remember the story of the little red hen—and I *was* that hen: the story of the little girl who made the porridge that ran over into and filled the streets—and I *was* that little girl."

Avid readers report that when reading is especially pleasurable, it is as if they have fallen under a spell. They describe themselves as oblivious of their immediate physical surroundings as they enter the world of the story. Asked to distinguish a "good read" from a "bad read," Betty in Ross's study said, "In a good read, I sit down and find a half hour has gone by and I was unaware that it had gone by." In her reading diary, *So Many Books, So Little Time,* Sara Nelson (2003) describes the experience of falling in love with a book: "For me, the feeling comes in a rush: I'm reading along and suddenly a word or phrase or scene enlarges before my eyes and soon everything around me is just so much fuzzy background. The phone can ring, the toast can burn, the child can call out, but to me they're all in a distant dream" (33).

At the opposite pole from obedient reading, the reader is critically detached from the text, observing coolly from a distance. This is the stance of the critic or student who feels called on to provide an assessment or analysis of the text. It can also happen when the reader resists the text or finds it alien. In such a case, the colonization of a large part of our thought stream by another sensibility can seem uncomfortable or even sinister. As noted in section 1.6, this refusal to read the text on its own terms has attracted the attention of critics such as Judith Fetterley, who coined the term "the resisting reader."

Readers sometimes report conversions from compliant to resistant reading when they reread a text that had enthralled them once in childhood, but at the later reading they notice racist or sexist overtones not detected earlier. Some readers report feeling guilty about submitting too easily to the text, whatever its kind. Carlsen and Sherrill (1988, 54) include this statement from one self-critical reader, who reported reading two completely opposed studies of D. H. Lawrence and admiring and agreeing with both while reading them: "The weakness that disturbs me most seriously is my inability to read critically. I tend to accept the printed word as divine revelation. . . . It was only later that I began to wonder why it is that I shy away from the forming of opinions of my own. As I read, I read too passively; I read without a fight."

Critics have weighed in on the question of the ideal stance that the reader *should* take with respect to the book and usually advocate a Goldilocks, "not-too-hot, not-too-cold, but just right" relationship. In *The Company We Keep,* Wayne Booth (1988, 139–40), notes, "For more than a century now we have been exhorted to resist identifying with art works; we are advised instead to maintain some sort of 'aesthetic distance.' What is forgotten in such warnings . . . is that even when we resist a story, even when we view it dispassionately, it immerses us in 'the thoughts of another,' unless we simply stop listening." Booth's conclusion is: "I serve myself best, as reader, when I both honor an author's offering for what it is, in its full 'otherness' from me, and take an active critical stance against what seem to me its errors or excesses. We are pursuing here an ethics of self-culture in narrative, an ethics that entails both surrender and refusal" (Booth 1988, 136).

The Emotional Dimension of Reading

Reading is not a matter of mind only. The emotional dimension of reading is there from the beginning. For children who become successful readers, reading is associated with a sense of pride and competency. The three-year-old who opens a picture book, recites from memory a much-repeated story, and declares, "I readed it" is praised and celebrated by family members. For such children, memories of reading closely connect the experience of story with family scenes of comfort and caring. There is often a strong sensory dimension to these memories—reading is associated with the bedtime story, the parent's voice, snuggling into a lap, or curling up in a comfortable chair. The voice is so important that Carlsen and Sherrill's book has a section, "Literature and the Human Voice," in which readers recall the pleasurable experience of hearing books read aloud by fathers and mothers, sisters, grandmothers, and teachers: "I would live for the moments at night when my brother and I would be snuggled in my mother's arms, traveling into the land of princesses and dragons and fairies, just by closing our eyes and listening to my mother's smooth, convincing voice" (Carlsen and Sherrill 1988, 41).

Books themselves can be friends and comforters, always to be relied on in hard times. The award-winning children's author Katherine Paterson acknowledged in an interview with Diane Osen that she had grown up in a Chinese missionary family and moved fifteen times by the time she was fifteen. Paterson said, "Reading was where I could always find friends. I learned to trust books, and to love books and to find a great deal of comfort from books when I was quite young" (Osen 2002, 158). Similarly, in Ross's study, Shelley (student, age twenty-six) said that she had grown up feeling "like an outsider because I grew up in a poor family . . . Plus, in the military, you move around every three years. Like it's really traumatic, because every time you move, it's like everyone you've ever met in your life has just died." The one constant in her life was a small group of books such as *Anne of Green Gables* and *Little House on the*

Prairie that came with her and that she reread over and over: "I think they were a constant in a world where I didn't have very many constants."

For many avid readers, the experience of reading itself is an area of competency as well as independence. Children get a sense of achievement as they experience themselves as successful readers. As adolescents and adults, readers say to themselves, "There may be lots of areas where I'm not successful, but I'm reading these challenging books, so I must be quite smart really." For Jane (student, age twenty-two), reading is a private pleasure and sphere of independence. She says, "Reading has always been something I could do on my own and do it for me. Whereas a lot of things I've done in my life have been done for other people. Nobody can take these [experiences] from me. Even if dozens and dozens of people have read this same book, my experience of reading it is mine. It's something I can hold on to, something that can't be taken away from me."

In contrast, when frustrated readers think of reading, they don't think of the pleasure of story or the consolation of friends or the sense of competence, but rather of the anxiety of anticipated failure. They recall the humiliation of being called upon in school to read aloud and being laughed at or reproved for errors. Some examples: "I was always afraid and ashamed of my poor oral reading"; "Reading period was always a frightening experience for me" (Carlsen and Sherrill 1988, 34); "I remember my first grade classroom. . . . The image is so clear because my friends were laughing at me and I wanted to cry—I was reading out loud in a circle of students and I could not pronounce some of the words. . . . I was a public failure" (Rosenthal 1995, 30).

Living in a Chosen World

"If I have one life to live, I want to live it as a Cazlett," said one reviewer of Elizabeth Jane Howard's trilogy about the Cazlett family in England around the time of the second World War. When a reader chooses a book, she is choosing to enter a world and live there for a given period of time. Said one of the readers quoted by Carlsen and Sherrill, "I simply opened a book and shut myself in a different world" (1988, 51). Similarly a focus group participant in Toyne and Usherwood's study said, "I go completely into it, and become one of the characters and I have to stop myself from talking like that character [especially if it's something like Jane Austen]. . . . I move into another world when I read fiction particularly. I just get completely absorbed and I'm there and I'm involved and I'm feeling all of the emotions and everything else" (2001, 32).

In Ross's study, Elizabeth (doctoral student in English, age thirty-five) used the image of translation to describe the relationship between her everyday world and the fictional world. She likes books, she said, in which the translation between worlds is easy: "Some things are easier to translate than others. Perhaps that's why I say I can't read a book that pushes me too far away from the central characters. If the author is continuously expecting me to dislike or feel alienated from the characters, then I can't satisfactorily read the book, because the experience of reading that I like is to get soaked in the material. There is kind of a translation that may be why I always responded well to books about little girls growing up. The translation was very easy there."

Readers report being reluctant to leave the fictional world, carrying the book characters in their minds alongside whatever else is going on in their everyday world, and being anxious to get back to the world of the book. In this way, reading is interwoven into the texture of their lives, not separate from it. In Ross's study, Tina (youth support worker, age twenty-five) said with respect to Alice Walker's books, "I read a book of hers and it will stay with me; I'll be mulling it in my mind as I do the dishes."

Sometimes, but not always, the fictional world is attractive because it is more expansive or more intense or otherwise different than the reader's own life. Another reader in Ross's study, Sarah (library assistant, age forty) said, "I like the idea of being transported, moved into a world that's different from the everyday one." Charles (program coordinator, age twenty-three) commented on the favorable payoff from the investment involved in reading authors such as J. R. R. Tolkien or Stephen R. Donaldson: "Their worlds often span several books, so when you immerse yourself in the world of Stephen R. Donaldson, you know you're going to be in that world for a long time. So that makes you invest yourself quite a bit into that world because you know it's something you can be in and enjoy and walk around in for quite some time."

Sometimes this theme of choosing a world is described by researchers— and less often by the readers themselves—as "escape." As noted in section 4.1, about one-quarter of the respondents in the BISG surveys claimed to read "as an escape." In Ross's study, about 20 percent of avid readers talked about reading for escape, and they used the term in two ways: one disparaging and the other neutral or positive. In Toyne and Usherwood's *Checking the Books,* reading for escape was usually the first answer provided by focus group participants in answer to a question about what contribution reading imaginative literature makes to their lives. Toyne and Usherwood wonder if this reason is given so often because it comes as a ready-made answer and is easy to articulate (2001, 26).

Used pejoratively, "escapist reading" refers to the kind of reading *other* people do in a popular genre that they themselves personally dislike or it refers to undemanding reading they do themselves when they are feeling fragile or exhausted. In these cases, escapist books are understood to be works of formulaic fiction that require that the reader do minimum work to make sense of the text—Harlequin romances, westerns, detective stories, melodramas of the rich and famous, and the like. Time spent with escapist books, as defined in this first way, is sometimes considered time wasted—time better spent confronting and not escaping from life (see section 4.4, Better Than Life).

In contrast, there is a second meaning given to the term "escapist reading" that has to do with the nature of the experience that the reader chooses. Here the emphasis is not on what is being left behind but on the world that the reader is entering. As Craig (retired skilled tradesman, age sixty-seven) in Ross's study put it, "If I'm going to escape, well then let's escape to where I want to go. I want to acquire some knowledge about different times and different things—to know what happens in Iceland, in early England, between the stars. If you are going on a trip, that is escapism. But you will pick the place where you want to go, whether that place is Banff Springs or Las Vegas." Diane (social worker, age thirty-seven) talked about the sense of adventure that as an adolescent she loved in novels and that later she imitated in her own life, "doing terrible things, which were most uncomfortable and not generally thought of as fun, but I thought they were just *wonderful*":

> Do you remember [Conrad's] *Youth?* He runs away to sea and loves the adventure. Everything's *wonderful*. He's going to Bangkok, and he goes, "Oh, Bangkok! Just the sound of the name!" Before they get to Bangkok, they have all sorts of problems—storms—and at one point the ship blows up. And he says, "The ship blows up and my hair was singed and my eyebrows were burned right off and it was WONDERFUL!" I identified with that. I really liked that.

Readers talk about wanting to prolong the time that they can spend in the chosen world and their sense of loss when the book is over and they have to leave the fictional world. In Ross's study, Zoe (student, age twenty-two) said, "I know with books that I really really know that I'm going to enjoy. . . I read really slowly—it may take me ten minutes to read a couple of pages . . . making it last as long as possible." Ivor (graduate student, age twenty-six) said that "coming to the end of a book is a very jarring, sometimes a heart-rending experience, because I have to come back again. And it's not because I don't like this world particularly. . . . So yes, quite regularly I read, and am very sad when I come to the end. Not because people die, although that saddens me, but because I have to go back again. I have to leave that world behind; but I find another one."

Places for Reading

It is notable that in self-reports many readers talk about the importance of the physical place where they read. There is a difference between the places where avid readers *can* read because they read anywhere—on a subway, in a doctor's waiting room, in the airport waiting for the plane to be called—and places where they *prefer* to read. In this latter category, readers often talk with enthusiasm about reading in secluded, enclosed spaces where they are unlikely to be found and interrupted—like Jane Eyre reading in her double retirement behind the red curtains. Adults most often report their pleasure of reading in bed or in a favorite cozy armchair. In Carlsen and Sherrill's study (1988, 51–52), readers recalled favorite childhood reading spaces, including an "overstuffed red velvet chair," a "reading corner" created in an upstairs room of an old farmhouse, reading "behind the fireplace, next to the woodpile," and in "the seclusion of the haymow or the attic." Sometimes the reading experience is stolen or snatched (under the basement stairs, behind the closet door, under the dining room table, in the bathtub, under the bed covers by flashlight).

Not infrequently, readers report the association of pleasurable reading with food, as in this example, "My father built a seat in an apple tree in the orchard, and I can remember spending hours each summer sitting in this leafy bower, reading and munching crabapples or harvest apples" (Carlsen and Sherrill 1988, 52). In Ross's study, Ivor (graduate student, age twenty-six) said, "I love finding a little restaurant or cafe where they're really understanding about people who just come in and drink coffee and read all day." Similarly Madeline (student, age twenty-two) said that she could read anywhere—on a subway or wherever— but when she thought of the ideal reading scenario it was: "My cookies here, my cup of coffee here, preferably a couch but a good armchair will suffice with a blanket. Winter is better than summer. The whole 'curling up with a book'—a common phrase because that's what people do. It's a snugly kind of . . . that's ideal."

Delight in Language

"I read good fiction slowly because I want to savor the words," says Robert MacNeil, author of *Wordstruck,* in Rosenthal's collection of self-reports from readers (Rosenthal 1995, 8). For a significant proportion of avid readers, part of the pleasure of reading is their delight in language. For example, 20 percent of participants in Toyne and Usherwood's focus groups spontaneously mention the aesthetic pleasure of appreciating language skillfully used (2001, 34). When readers talk about their fascination with language, they sometimes report making lists of rare words encountered in reading or marking passages where language has been used with particular grace.

As Margaret Meek notes, "One of the distinguishing features of habitual readers and writers is their curiosity about language. They enjoy it. They use it with feeling and flair when they talk, tell jokes, invent word games and do crossword puzzles" (Meek 1991, 54). In Ross's interviews with readers, Jean (teacher librarian, age forty-four) describes how she marks passages to reread: "I like books where I can savor a section; I'll mark them and then I'll go back; I won't re-read the whole book, but I will read passages. In *Running in the Family,* [Michael Ondaatje] describes being in the house during the rain in Sri Lanka and listening to the sounds of the rain. I guess he was sitting at the table in Vancouver playing a tape of the rain and trying to describe it, and I found it marvelous. . . . I like to look at how someone uses language skillfully."

Not infrequently, the reader's love affair with language is the impetus that turns them into writers. When successful romance writers are interviewed, for example, they often say that they started writing the kinds of stories that they loved to read (Falk 1982). They have made the leap from consumer to producer.

Case 17: The Frustrated Reader

Here is Alexis, an elementary school teacher who came late to the pleasures of reading: "As a child I was not a good reader. I didn't understand what I read, and I found that in order to understand I had to read *so slowly* that I lost the flow. It was like pulling teeth—one word at a time. Because I had to read certain things to accomplish certain assignments, I found reading quite a chore." In a similar vein, Nadine Rosenthal's *Speaking of Reading* provides a rich set of accounts from people she calls "frustrated readers":

Janice: When I do read, I hate to read fast; I read one word at a time. I don't skip anything because I'm afraid I'll miss something (29).

Rich: Sometimes I still have difficulty comprehending what I'm reading . . . so I'll have to read it over and over. . . . The real issue is that I hit an internal mechanism that says, "By God, I'm not going to be able to understand this. I've gone through it two and three times, and I'm not going to try to decipher it anymore, it's just too frustrating." The adolescent is rekindled in me, and I just bail out (33).

Kevin: Reading is a waste of time for me unless I understand the book, which is rare. I guess people who read all the time must get something out of it that I just haven't experienced. . . . I ask myself, "What have I just read?" and I know nothing about what I just read. I might have read six pages and I know nothing (36).

George: I know that reading is important, but I'm still not doing anything to help myself. I should read, but I don't. I just don't know why not. . . . I can't seem to find that motivation in reading (44).

Nancy: I feel that my eyes stutter—I'm not able to see the words fast enough, smooth enough. . . . As a reader, I can't get the information in, in a fluid, effortless way. I start books, yet very seldom do I finish them (45).

Titus: I want to read, but I start and then I get lost and have to go back. I get stuck or lost or forget what I just read. I have to read things over and over. Sometimes I read and get stuck on all the words I don't know. Or I read the paragraph real slow to try to remember what I just read, but I can't . . . I get frustrated; it just drags on and on (49).

Comments

Avid readers think of reading as a reward—after the vacuuming is done or the report is written then they can go back to their book. Describing the romance readers in her study, Janice Radway (1984, 91) said, "This theme of romance reading as a special gift a woman gives herself dominated most of the interviews."

In contrast, frustrated readers find it almost incomprehensible that reading could be considered a treat. The imagery used by these frustrated readers shows that they regard reading as a chore or punishment: "one word at a time," "decipher," "my eyes stutter," "lost," and "stuck on all the words I don't know." Whereas confident readers may choose to read certain passages slowly to savor the language and prolong the pleasurable experience, frustrated readers approach reading as a painful task of decoding, letter by letter and word by word. With attention focused on sounds and letters, these readers have trouble making sense of what they read or remembering it. So they start all over again and sometimes they just give up.

What Libraries Can Do

1. Help readers experience success in reading by matching books to their level of reading ability. Unlike schools, where beginners are evaluated and judged on their reading, libraries can encourage readers in a context of low anxiety. Frustrated readers need to be given the experience of success.

To Read More

Meek, Margaret. 1988. *How Texts Teach What Readers Learn*. South Woodchester, England: Thimble Press.

Meek uses mostly children's books such as Pat Hutchins's *Rosie's Walk,* John Burningham's *Mr. Gumpy's Outing,* Janet and Allan Ahlberg's *The Jolly Postman,* and Ted Hughes's *The Iron Man* as a sort of workshop to make the case that readers give themselves private lessons in reading through their interactions with texts. She says, "The most important single lesson that children learn from texts is *the nature and variety of written discourse,* the different ways that language lets a writer tell, and the many and different ways a reader reads" (21).

Woolf, Virginia. 1932/1960. "How Should One Read a Book?" *The Second Common Reader*. New York: Harcourt, Brace, and World.

Virginia Woolf describes two aspects of respectful reading—initially a receptive openness to "the fast flocking of innumerable impressions" followed by a second stage of judging and comparing (242–3). She advises: "Do not dictate to your author; try to become him. Be his fellow-worker and accomplice. If you hang back, and reserve and criticise at first, you are preventing yourself from getting the fullest possible value from what you read" (235); "We must pass judgment upon these multitudinous impressions; we must make of these fleeting shapes one that is hard and lasting. But not directly. Wait for the dust of reading to settle. . . . Then suddenly without our willing it . . . the book will return, but differently. . . . We see the shape from start to finish; it is a barn, a pig-sty, or a cathedral. . . . [W]e are no longer the friends of the writer, but his judges; and just as we cannot be too sympathetic as friends, so as judges we cannot be too severe" (242).

References

Adams, Marilyn Jager. 1990. *Beginning to Read: Thinking and Learning about Print. A Summary*. Urbana: University of Illinois at Urbana-Champagne, Center for the Study of Reading.

Booth, Wayne C. 1988. *The Company We Keep: An Ethics of Fiction*. Berkeley: University of California Press.

Carlsen, G. Robert, and Anne Sherrill. 1988. *Voices of Readers: How We Came to Love Books*. Urbana, IL: National Council of Teachers of English.

Csikszentimihalyi, Mihaly. 1990. *Flow: The Psychology of Optimal Experience*. New York: HarperCollins.

Falk, Kathryn. 1992. *Love's Leading Ladies: Who's Who in the World of Romance*. New York: Pinnacle Books.

Fraser, Antonia, ed. 1992. *The Pleasure of Reading*. London: Bloomsbury.

Meek Margaret. 1991. *On Being Literate*. London: Bodley Head.

Nell, Victor. 1988. *Lost in a Book: The Psychology of Reading for Pleasure*. New Haven and London: Yale University Press.

Nelson, Sara. 2003. *So Many Books, So Little Time: A Year of Passionate Reading*. New York: Berkley Books.

Osen, Diane, ed. 2002. *The Book That Changed My Life: Interviews with National Book Award Winners and Finalists*. New York: The Modern Library.

Poulet, Georges. 1980. "Criticism and the Experience of Interiority." In *Reader-Response Criticism: From Formalism to Post-Structuralism*, 41–49. Edited by Jane P. Tompkins. Baltimore and London: Johns Hopkins University Press.

Radway, Janice. 1984. *Reading the Romance: Women, Patriarchy and Popular Literature*. Chapel Hill, NC: University of North Carolina Press.

Rae, Arlene Perly. 1997. *Everybody's Favourites: Canadians Talk about Books That Changed Their Lives*. Toronto: Viking.

Rosenthal, Nadine. 1995. *Speaking of Reading*. Portsmouth, NH: Heinemann.

Schwartz, Lynne Sharon. 1996. *Ruined by Reading: A Life in Books*. Boston: Beacon Press.

Toyne, Jackie, and Bob Usherwood. 2001. *Checking the Books: The Value and Impact of Public Library Book Reading.* Sheffield, England: Department of Information Studies, The University of Sheffield. Available at http://cplis.shef.ac.uk/ checkingthebooks.pdf (accessed June 16, 2005).

Watson, Kenneth. 1980. *Leisure Reading Habits: A Survey of the Leisure Reading Habits of Canadian Adults with Some International Comparisons.* Ottawa: Department of the Secretary of State.

4.3. What Role Does Reading Play in the Life of the Reader?

Avid readers say that reading gives them something that can't be experienced any other way. This value goes beyond the instrumental. Certainly they agree that by reading a lot they improve their level of literacy, increase their vocabulary, become better writers, and, as a result, do better at school and in their careers. But all this seems incidental. Committed readers are apt to say that reading is part of their identity. In answer to a question about the importance of pleasure reading in their lives, different readers in Ross's study said the following:

- For me to read is to live.

- Reading for me is almost a necessity.

- If I were stuck on a desert island without books, I would go crazy.

- My freedom to read is absolutely sacred.

- Reading becomes like eating and sleeping—I have to do it. I'd go nuts if I couldn't do it.

- It's a passion. I can't deny it.

- My panic is to be in the house without anything to read. That makes me just absolutely, totally panic stricken. I can't live without reading. Blindness probably scares me more than anything.

The direct question, "Why do you read?" can be hard for avid readers to answer because reading is so much a part of who they are. This response from one of the most committed readers in Ross's study illustrates the problem:

> That is very difficult. I wish I could say, "I read because of this" or "reading is important because of this." But I can't, because there are so many reasons that it's important. It's like that terror of losing my arms or losing my eyesight. I can't say that I read as an escape, because I don't. It may sound as though I read as an escape—all this talk about going to another world—but it's not really escaping because I'm always fully prepared to come back. Why do I read? I read to learn. Probably if I had to say why I read that would be it. I read to learn. Which is

not to say that I only read books of a strictly educational nature. But, whenever I read, I feel as though I'm assimilating what I read into this—almost like a one-man folk memory. Oh, this is so hard! Reading is, you see, just so huge to me—so huge that it's so hard to quantify it and say "this is true" and "this is not true." (Ivor, graduate student, age twenty-six)

The fear of blindness comes up a lot when avid readers talk about reading. One of the "habitual readers" in Rosenthal's collection of self-reports recalls an old *Twilight Zone* episode of a passionate reader who finds himself the sole survivor of a nuclear explosion. He goes to the library but then falls asleep and breaks his coke-bottle glasses. The reader's summary: "He has been robbed of reading, which is my own ultimate nightmare" (Rosenthal 1995, 104). In Ross's study, talk of blindness was a common response to the question, "What would it be like if for one reason or another you were unable to read?" Interviewees tended to assume that their not reading implied some catastrophic event—either their own blindness or a *Fahrenheit 451* world of thought control. The typical reaction was initially a horrified statement that the situation was unthinkable. The response was often, "I can't imagine it. Reading is so much a part of my life." As one person put it, "I wouldn't be me. I wouldn't be the person I am if I didn't read or wasn't able to read. It frightens me to think that something like reading can create you or at least influence who you are so much, because if I wasn't able to read I wouldn't be me. It frightens me, so I don't even want to consider it as an option."

When encouraged to say more about life without reading, interviewees said that life would be "empty," "boring," "very suffocating," "an intellectual wasteland," "very limited," "a prison." Not to be able to read would be "very terrible," "very upsetting," "awful," "catastrophic," "unimaginably horrible," "worse then not being able to have sex," "like not being able to see color." Interestingly, Toyne and Usherwood's study adopted the question from Ross's study ("What would it be like if . . . you couldn't read?") and got the same alarmed responses from readers in the UK—talk of blindness and suggestions of methods of coping such as memorizing texts or writing one's own texts. Then came panicky statements that the loss would be "devastating," "a huge gap," "like dementia, I would be dying," "it would be suicide, it would be like murder" (Toyne and Usherwood 2001, 47–48).

So what exactly is this crucial role that reading plays in the lives of committed readers? Despite the difficulty of disentangling the woven skein of reasons, researchers are naturally keen to get answers to the "Why read?" question. In Toyne and Usherwood's study, Chapter 3, "The Significance of Anybody Reading Anything," provides a typology of reasons why people say they read "imaginative literature" (2001, 25–52). This typology is based on discussions held with twenty-nine focus groups of both users and nonusers of libraries, located in nine public libraries. Analyzing answers to the prompt, "What contribution, if any, does the reading of imaginative literature bring to your life?" Toyne and

Usherwood came up with the following categories, illustrated in each case with statements from readers:

- Escapism (Relaxation; Opportunity to abandon the here and now)

- Means of escape (Escape into other worlds; Escape through association; Escape through aesthetic pleasure)

- Reading for instruction (Practical knowledge; Literary skills; Lessons about the world; Reliability of instruction)

- Self development (Personal insight; Insight into the "other")

- Location of reading in people's lives (Reading as bodily function; Exercise the imagination; Reading as identity).

Different studies of the reading experience have typically reported similar reasons or variants thereof. Qualitative studies done with real readers are the best sources for understanding how readers themselves value leisure reading—for example, the following:

- Gordon Sabine and Patricia Sabine's "Books that Made the Difference" project (1983), sponsored by the Center for the Book in the Library of Congress

- Janice Radway's *Reading the Romance* (1984), an ethnographic investigation to understand romance reading from the perspective of the readers who love the genre

- Joseph Gold's *Read for Your Life* (1990) based on his clinical work using books in family therapy

- Wendy Simond's *Women and Self-Help Culture* (1992), which contains a valuable chapter, "How and Why Women Read Self-help Books," reporting interviews with thirty women

- Nadine Rosenthal's *Speaking of Reading* (1995), which is a distillation of interviews with readers, some famous and some not

- Jim Burke's *I Hear America Reading* (1999), which is based on the more than four hundred letters sent to him in response to his letter to the editor of the *San Francisco Chronicle* asking for people's experiences with books

- Catherine Ross's "Finding without Seeking" (1999), which reports what readers say about encountering helpful information in the context of reading for pleasure

- *Reading the Situation* (Book Marketing Ltd. 2000), a U.K. study having the goal of understanding consumers' views of the value of book-borrowing

- "Reading Lives," a Web site sponsored by the Essex Libraries system in the United Kingdom, which posts personal testimonials from readers, mostly authors and librarians, about the importance of reading in their lives (askchris.essexcc.gov.uk/Adult/Readinglives.asp)

- Toyne and Usherwood's *Checking the Books* (2001), which investigates the contribution that library access to fiction and other imaginative literature makes to individual and social well-being

- Juris Dilevko and Lisa Gottlieb's *Reading and the Reference Librarian* (2004), which focuses more specifically on the leisure reading of academic librarians and the value of that reading in their personal and professional lives.

Over and over, in these studies based on self-reports, readers say: Books give me comfort; make me feel better about myself; reassure me that I am normal and not a freak because characters in books have feelings like mine; and provide confirmation that others have gone through similar experiences and survived. Books are a way of recharging my batteries and helping me keep my life in balance when day-to-day pressures are intense. Books help me clarify my feelings; change my way of thinking about things; help me think through problems in my own life; help me make a decision; and give me the strength and courage to make some major changes in my own life. They give me a sense of mastery and control; give me courage to fight on; make me think that if the hero(ine) can overcome obstacles, then so can I; give me the hope to rebuild my life; and help me accept things I can't change. They broaden my horizons; provide a window onto other lives and other societies; and put me in touch with a larger, more spacious world. In short, reading is like the patent medicines advertised in nineteenth-century religious magazines: it will do anything you want it to do. It will stimulate or calm down; provide confrontation with life's problems or escape from them; provide a form of engagement with the world or a retreat from it.

People interviewed for the "Books That Made the Difference" (1983) project provided concrete examples of being helped by reading. Readers variously said that *The Keys of the Kingdom* "gave me the comfort I needed" when my mother was dying of cancer (28); *The Heart Is a Lonely Hunter* made me realize I wasn't alone in my feelings (37); *The Island of the Blue Dolphins* "made me realize that even when you are all alone, you still can make it" (47); Thomas Wolfe "gave me a sense of recognition of myself" (39); *The Hobbit* "showed me you can overcome your handicaps and be whatever you want to be" (43); *Our Lady of the Flowers* "opened to me my homosexual self. . . . It validated those feelings of love which before the book I could not admit" (72).

Joseph Gold has written two books to explain why leisure reading has this beneficial effect. As an English professor turned bibliotherapist and family counselor, he has become convinced that fiction is not just entertainment—it changes people's lives and transforms how they think and feel. In *Read for Your Life* (1990), he made the case that people, especially women, use reading as a way to cope with stress and to achieve distance from and insight into their world. In *The Story Species* (2002), he advances his argument by drawing on the findings of neuroscience to argue that storying is a survival tool for the human species.

Reading as a Preferred Way of Finding Out

From research summarized in sections 1.3 and 4.1, we know that avid readers differ substantially from nonbook readers—that is, those who say that they have *not* read a book in the previous six months. Experiencing reading as hard work, nonbook readers limit their reading to newspapers or to newspapers and magazines and do not automatically turn to reading as the preferred way of finding out. Avid readers, on the other hand, have a history of successful interactions with books that typically started in childhood. They find it easy and natural to turn to texts as a favored source of information. They use their own life experience to make sense of texts and conversely use texts to make sense of life in a wide variety of situations.

For avid readers, there is authority in the printed word. In Ross's study, Stella (librarian, age forty-nine) said, "If I find something happening in my life, a high point or particularly low point, my first trip is generally to the library to see if I can read something about it. . . . And if I wanted to learn to do embroidery, I'd probably first find a book about it as opposed to asking somebody how to do it." Similarly Diane (social worker, age thirty-seven) said:

> I always turn to books for any questions, and I always have. [If a doctor said I had a mysterious disease], I'd go and get a book on it. . . . Part of how I would accept it would be to read everything there was on it. . . . I'd do that with anything that I'd see as a problem. I'd start reading everything I can get on it. I'll start reading a bunch of books around the area and I don't stop reading until I've somehow been reassured. . . . I think it must have something to do with mastery. Until I've got hold of all the information possible, I feel out of control.

An element in this authority conveyed by print is the reader's ability to go back to the same words over and over, as Wendy Simonds notes. Commenting on the security to be found in the printed word, Simonds quotes from two of her interviewees who were readers of self-help books: Lauren said the book captures knowledge and "holds it still, like a photograph." Bonnie reported on the value to her of reading "grief books" after her mother's death: "[S]eeing that in print is more comforting than having other people tell it to me verbally. It seems more real. Also, I can go back to it" (Simonds 1992, 26–27).

The Right Book at the Right Time

One of the mysteries of reading is the unpredictability of the connection a book will make with a particular reader at a particular time. Even with specifically targeted books such as self-help books, as Wendy Simonds (1992, 6) has shown in her study of thirty female readers, "What readers come away with depends on their reading both of the books and of their own situations." Similarly Oprah book club readers may expect an Oprah book to feature a strong woman who faces adversity and survives, but just how they will connect with a particular Oprah choice is often idiosyncratic.

With less targeted books, the connection is much harder to predict. In Osen's *The Book That Changed My Life*, author Cynthia Ozick recalled being seventeen and reading Henry James's "The Beast in the Jungle" in a story anthology that her brother had brought home from the library. She says, "Reading it, I felt it to be the story of my own life—which was strange, since it's about an elderly gentleman who suddenly discovers that he has wasted his years" (Osen 2002, 123). In such cases, a book may be experienced at first reading with the force of a strike by lightening. In other cases, a person may read something that remains black marks on a page; then at a later reading the words spring to life and speak directly to the life of the reader. Commenting on this phenomenon, Philip Davis (1992, 44) notes that when this later reading matters so intensely, "the fact that it didn't matter before is another part of the amazement of its mattering now. What has changed?"

The answer seems to be that when the right match is made between reader and story, readers use the text to create a story about themselves. They read themselves into the story and then read the story into their lives, which then becomes a part of them. Because the range of tellable stories is unlimited, readers who dip their net often enough into the ocean of narrative are almost certain to encounter the particular story they need to hear (Ross 1999). In Ross's study of avid readers, Nathan (English professor and novelist, age fifty) recalled powerful books he read in adolescence that resonated with his own ideas of struggling against the system and rebelliousness: "I wasn't ready for these books; they overpowered me with the sense that they were coded to tap into my own experiences. They were secretly about me."

Opening a Door

When readers talk about the value of reading in their lives, they often say they value the way books open up a new perspective, make them see things differently, offer an enlarged set of possibilities, or give their lives an increased sense of spaciousness. They may use the metaphor of an "awakening" or refer to books that were a "mind-opener" or that "opened my eyes" to a new perspective or "opened a door" on a new reality.

Reading, said various readers in Ross's study, "gives you a much greater internal world"; "It gives you a larger understanding of the world and just more ideas in general"; it provides "insight into somebody whose life has been very different from my own"; it "has made me more open to other possibilities, other ways of living." In Rosenthal's book, Chilean author Isabel Allende is quoted as saying, "Reading is like looking through several windows which open to an infinite landscape. . . . For me life without reading would be like being in prison, it would be as if my spirit were in a straitjacket; life would be a very dark and narrow place" (Rosenthal 1995, 3).

In contrast to the narrow prison of being trapped entirely in one's own life, reading is said to offer almost limitless possibilities for trying on roles, living other lives vicariously, and experiencing other times and other cultures. In Ross's study, Marie (social worker, age thirty-four) said, "[An important book] heightens or increases or expands your own feeling about yourself and your place in the world. So it enlarges your range of possibilities." A large part of that sense of expanded consciousness is the insight that reading gives into other people's lives. Toyne and Usherwood record the statements of one man who said that reading books by women helped him understand "life from a woman's point of view" and the statements of two people who said respectively that reading Toni Morrison's *Beloved* "opened my eyes to just how different our belief systems are" and "makes me want to wince" when reading Morrison's compelling account of black struggle (2001, 44). Through reading stories, readers can augment their own experience, as Joseph Gold (2002, 61) points out in *The Story Species:* "Reading Literature constitutes a very efficient behaviour for acquiring experience. It is of course relatively risk-free and energy saving."

Discovery of Identity

Norman N. Holland claims that readers make sense of texts in terms of their own "identity themes." Arguing in *5 Readers Reading* that there are more differences in the way five different readers read the same text than in the way that the same reader reads different texts, Holland says that "a reader responds to a literary work by assimilating it to his own psychological processes" (Holland 1975, 209). In this scenario, the reader's identity is fixed prior to reading and determines the way the reader interprets texts. Other accounts of reading emphasize instead the circularity of reading and life: each affects the other and in turn is affected by the other. That is to say, the reader responds intensely to a particular book that matches something in the reader's life right then, but the book, once read, becomes an agent of change.

Readers say that reading about other lives helps them try out possible roles or helps them give shape to inarticulate feelings or yearnings. Isabel Allende reported, "After I read the feminist authors from North America, I could finally find words for the anger that I had all my life" (Rosenthal, 1995, 3). Susan, another reader quoted by Rosenthal (1995, 165–7), provides a compelling account of how, following her divorce, she "had the odd feeling that my feet didn't touch the ground any more, that I was disintegrating, vanishing." Deciding that she needed to reintegrate the lost parts of herself, she deliberately turned to reading as a way to heal her spirit and discover who she really is: "Reading for insight is a continuing theme in my life."

Readers may use the term "identify with" to describe their relationship to one or more fictional characters. But the identifications can shift from one reading to another or within a single reading, and in any case are unpredictable and idiosyncratic. In Ross's study, Andrea (biologist and master of library science student, age thirty-eight) talked about the way her childhood identification with masked heroes chimed with her own sense of hidden, unrecognized strength:

> I enjoyed Zorro and books like *The Scarlet Pimpernel* too. You see, that's how I want to see myself. I'm sure that's how I want to see myself. That on the outside I'm just an ordinary housewife . . . but underneath I'm a wild romantic or a person who's capable of just amazing things. . . . I have a sense of a part of myself being hidden. The idea of being important but hidden—the world not quite realizing your true role—is a strengthening theme in a way. . . . Circumstances dictate that it's necessary for your real identity to be hidden. I think that gives me strength to cope.

Models and Blueprints

Readers frequently claim that books provide models, examples to follow, or rules to live by. Readers report that reading changes their beliefs, attitudes, or pictures of the world, which in turn alters the way they choose to live their lives after the book is closed. In notable contrast to literary critics who deconstruct the notion of character and admire the distanced contemplation of the aesthetic object, many readers say that they look for characters whose lives offer models for living.

Commenting on Book-of-the-Month Club (BOMC) editors who make their selections on behalf of middle-class readers, Radway (1989, 275) notes that these editors look for books that provide "suggestions, models, and directions about how to live." According to Radway (1989, 276), the editors demanded from the stories chosen as BOMC selections that readers be able "to map the insights gained from the experience of reading onto the terrain of their own lives."

Here are some examples of this successful mapping. In Ross's study, Marie (social worker, age thirty-four) said, "*The Color Purple* had a very big impact on me in that it really helped give me the courage to make some major changes in my own life that I was quivering and hesitant about acting on." Samantha (doctoral student in English, age twenty-eight) spoke of the way L. M. Montgomery's *The Blue Castle* became a model for her when she was a shy adolescent:

That book was an inspiration to me in my own life. It was one of several books that I really love that focus on a really shy, retiring, disliked person, who is not accepted in her society but who then manages to completely change her situation, manages to completely change herself. *Rebecca* by Daphne Du Maurier would be another one. *Jane of Lantern Hill* by L. M. Montgomery would be another example of that kind of a Cinderella story where there's that development of the person's personality, where they learn to stand up for themselves. I feel as if reading books like *The Blue Castle* just gave me a kind of blueprint for my life. One of the things in that book and in *Jane of Lantern Hill* is that the heroine changes herself by getting herself out of the location that she's in, where people have assumptions about her, going to a new environment where she can be herself and reinvent herself and then take that [change] back home again.

Connection with Others/Awareness of Not Being Alone

In readers' talk about reading, a recurring theme is the ugly duckling story. This is the story about a person who feels very different from everyone else in the immediate environment but then, through reading, becomes connected to kindred spirits. This role for reading is particularly valued by people who feel stigmatized by their differences. In Ross's study, Diane (social worker, age thirty-seven) said, "For years I thought that there was something wrong with me . . . that I wasn't a very feminine person. Something was wrong; something was very wrong. And still the sense that something is wrong with me is there, but it's not nearly so strong as it used to be. The books continue to provide reassurance that if something is wrong with me, I wasn't the only one." Similarly Irene (social scientist, age twenty-nine) said that reading Kate Millett's *Flying* when she was twenty-one helped her understand her own sexuality: "I felt I could identify with her in it. I read it a number of times. She had to come to grips with her lesbianism. The book helped me do the same thing. . . . Before that I felt pretty alone. But I didn't realize that anyone wrote about how they felt."

Truus (librarian, age forty) said that after her daughter was born with Down syndrome, she looked for books written by parents of children with chronic conditions: "Sometimes . . . you think that you're the only person in the world who ever felt this way. And then you can go out, pick up a book, start to read it and go, 'That's me!' That is somebody else who is doing the same thing and felt the same way and maybe I'm not so . . . alone. It's a way of reconnecting."

Reassurance, Comfort, and Consolation

Critics typically value reading that shatters preconceptions and dazzles with the new. They are apt to quote with approval Kafka's comments on reading written in a letter to a friend at age nineteen: "I think we ought to read only the kind of books that wound and stab us. If the book we're reading doesn't wake us up with a blow on the head, what are we reading it for? . . . A book must be the axe for the frozen sea inside us" (quoted in Josipovici 1997, 171).

General readers, however, may feel that being chopped open by an axe is a welcome novelty at nineteen but less attractive at a later stage of life, when, for example, they have just lost a job or have a child with an incurable illness. At such times, readers say they look for reassurance, comfort, consolation, confirmation of the self, or inner strength and the courage to go on. Reading can then be valued because it reinforces the familiar, supports current values, or confirms what is already believed.

Particularly when ill or in a stressful situation, some readers reread books, especially childhood favorites that they may refer to as "friends" (Ross 1994). For readers wanting comfort, repetition can be a valued element of the reading experience, whether the repetition is the result of rereading a trusted book or the result of reading in a genre such as the detective story or romance where each book is a variant of the same story. As Wendy Simonds (1992, 26) notes in her study of female readers of self-help books, even in the case of nonfiction repetition can a virtue and not a flaw: "The readers I interviewed were unanimous in their recognition that self-help books were repetitive, and thus secure. Reading could be a ritual of self-reassurance where repetition was *desired*."

Case 18: Plugged in, in a Very Grand Way

Sarah is one of the most committed readers in Ross's study. A forty-year-old library assistant and master of library science student, Sarah reflected on the variety of reasons why reading has been important to her.

Sarah: Books became increasingly more important through my childhood and my adolescence. I had a really desperately unhappy childhood and adolescence and, when I got to be in my teens, books became a place for me to go. They became a way of escape. They also became a way of establishing a certain self-esteem that I wouldn't have had otherwise. I could read, so I couldn't be all that stupid. I read big thick books, so I must be really, essentially, a smart person. And even at that age I recognized the value of having that control over language. I realized that books contributed to that and I loved language. I loved the way that words were used. So even though I had no other accomplishments, books were sort of like a lifeline for me. They provided me a place to go to be away from my situation. And they also provided me with a sense of self-respect. I really feel that they sustained me.

Interviewer: Can you discuss how your reading has affected other parts of your life?

Sarah: I would have to refer back to what I said earlier on about it being a lifeline, of being sustaining and helping me having a sense of self-worth, and self-respect and feeling not so alone. I was always very isolated. I know reading is a solitary activity and you think of someone who reads as an introvert because they're not socializing, but I never felt that way. I always felt that books were a connection with humanity and not just with my little world. My world was very narrow because it was a small town, which was at the end of the earth. But I was connected, I felt, to the whole universe when I was sitting there reading. I was connected to all of history. I was connected to great minds and wonderful thoughts all of humanity. I was . . . plugged in, in a very grand way.

Comments

This passage illustrates the difficulty with the flat statement, "reading is an escape." Here Sarah starts off with escape—books as a getaway from unhappy surroundings—but soon interweaves contrasting themes of engagement. For Sarah, reading is associated with self-respect, empowerment, control over language, and a connection with all humanity. Critics often set up polarities and value only the first element of the dyad: facing up to life versus escape; encountering the new versus repeating the familiar; shattering versus confirming expectations and values; opening doors versus returning home. Readers are more apt to say they value *both* elements in the dyad to different degrees at different times in their lives. The confounding variable for critics who value books that seize us by the throat and shatter our complacencies is that such effects are unpredictable and depend on what the reader chooses to take from the book—as in Samantha's account, quoted earlier, of the transformative power she found in reading *The Blue Castle*.

To Read More

Booth, Wayne C. 1988. *The Company We Keep: An Ethics of Fiction*. Berkeley: University of California Press.

> Distinguished rhetorician and professor of English, Wayne Booth investigates the somewhat unfashionable question of what effects, for good or ill, a literary work has on its readers. For him, an ethics of fiction encompasses both the responsibilities of the tellers of tales and the responsibilities of the listeners or readers. Using the metaphor of books as friends, he suggests a number of ways that reading friends can vary: the *quantity* of invitations they offer us; the degree of *responsibility* they grant to us; the degree of *intimacy* they offer us; the *intensity* of the engagement they expect from us; the coherence of the proffered world; the *distance* between their worlds and ours; and the *range of kinds* of activities invited (180–1).

Gold, Joseph. 2002. *The Story Species: Our Life-Literature Connection*. Markham, ON: Fitzhenry and Whiteside.

> Gold's argument is that the ability to read literature is a human adaptive behavior, currently under siege. Writing out of his experience as a family therapist, Gold claims that stories have healing power by helping human beings find balance. Reading other people's stories allows people to step outside of their own story long enough to decide what they want to change about it (126). A person who is trapped in the same disabling story— for example, "My parents didn't love me" or "I must be a bad person, or else this abuse would not have happened to me"—can rewrite the story by grafting into it new experience derived from literature. Stories represented in other media are not considered to have the same healing effect. Agreeing with Neil Postman, Gold argues that moving from the print world to the electronic world has the potential to put at risk the best survival tool that human culture has yet invented: literature. He sees a pychomachia shaping up between "Lits" and "Bits," comparable to the cosmic struggle of God and Satan fighting over humankind in *Paradise Lost* (145).

Radway, Janice. 1984. *Reading the Romance: Women, Patriarchy and Popular Literature*. Chapel Hill: University of North Carolina Press.

> This ethnographic study of romance readers examines the complex satisfactions of romance reading from the insider perspective of the readers who enjoy the genre. She says, "The theme of romance reading as a special gift a woman gives herself dominated most of the interviews" (92). The women in her study do the emotional work of providing support and validation for their husbands and children but to get their own needs met they turn to romance fiction, which are "chronicles of female triumph" (54).

References

Book Marketing Limited. 2000. *Reading the Situation: Book Reading, Buying and Borrowing Habits in Britain*. London: Library and Information Commission.

Booth, Wayne C. 1988. *The Company We Keep: An Ethics of Fiction*. Berkeley: University of California Press.

Burke, Jim. 1999. *I Hear America Reading: Why We Read, What We Read*. Portsmouth, NH: Heinemann.

Carlsen, G. Robert, and Anne Sherrill. 1988. *Voices of Readers: How We Come to Love Books*. Urbana, Illinois: National Council of Teachers of English.

Davis, Philip. 1992. *The Experience of Reading*. London and New York: Routledge.

Dilevko, Juris, and Lisa Gottlieb. 2004. *Reading and the Reference Librarian: The Importance to Library Service of Staff Reading Habits*. Jefferson, NC: McFarland.

Gold, Joseph. 1990. *Read for Your Life: Literature as a Life Support System*. Markham, ON: Fitzhenry and Whiteside.

Gold, Joseph. 2002. *The Story Species: Our Life-Literature Connection*. Markham, ON: Fitzhenry and Whiteside.

Holland, Norman N. 1975. *5 Readers Reading*. New Haven, CT: Yale University Press.

Josipovici, Gabriel. 1997. "Thirty-three Variations on a Theme of Graham Greene." In *Real Voices on Reading*, 165–72. Edited by Philip Davis. London: Macmillan.

Osen, Diane, ed. 2002. *The Book That Changed My Life: Interviews with National Book Award Winners and Finalists*. New York: Modern Library.

Radway, Janice A. 1989. "The Book-of-the-Month Club and the General Reader: The Uses of 'Serious Fiction.' " In *Reading in America*, 259–84. Edited by Cathy N. Davidson. Baltimore and London: Johns Hopkins University Press.

Radway, Janice. 2002. "Girls, Reading and Narrative Gleaning: Crafting Repertoires for Self-fashioning within Everyday Life." In *Narrative Impact: Social and Cognitive Foundations*, 183–204. Edited by Melanie C. Green et al. Mahwah, NJ: Lawrence Erlbaum.

Rosenthal, Nadine. 1995. *Speaking of Reading*. Portsmouth, NH: Heinemann.

Ross, Catherine Sheldrick. 1994. "Readers Reading L. M. Montgomery." In *Harvesting Thistles: The Textual Garden of L. M. Montgomery*, 23–35. Edited by Mary H. Rubio. Guelph, ON: Canadian Children's Literature.

Ross, Catherine Sheldrick. 1999. "Finding without Seeking: The Information Encounter in the Context of Reading for Pleasure." *Information Processing & Management* no. 35: 783–99.

Sabine, Gordon, and Patricia Sabine. 1983. *Books That Made the Difference*. Hamden, CT: Library Professional Publications.

Simonds, Wendy. 1992. *Women and Self-help Culture: Reading between the Lines*. New Brunswick, NJ: Rutgers University Press.

Toyne, Jackie, and Bob Usherwood. 2001. *Checking the Books: The Value and Impact of Public Library Book Reading*. Sheffield, England: Department of Information Studies, The University of Sheffield. Available at http://cplis.shef.ac.uk/checkingthebooks.pdf (accessed June 16, 2005).

4.4. Better than Life

In 1995, the Rec.arts.books newsgroup pursued a thread, somewhat tongue-in-cheek, under the subject header, "My Name is Jan and I am a Bookaholic." Various contributors commented on the "classic warning signs of literary addiction," among them: "There is no floor space left and you sometimes buy books you already have" and "You are unable to walk through a mall without stopping at a bookstore." Eventually Sandra from Washington helpfully reposted a list of the twenty-five tell-tale signs of confirmed book addiction, which had been originally posted in 1993, lifted from Tom Raabe's *Biblioholism: The Literary Addiction* (1991). The list included such indicators as:

> When a stranger walks into your house or apartment, are his or her first words usually a comment about your books?

> If someone asks you for a reading list of the twenty most influential books you've ever read, do you happen to have such a list on your person? (Rec.arts.book, 17 January 1995)

The danger, of course, is that somehow books can come to seem "Better than life." This phrase comes from David Homel's translated title of Daniel Pennac's (1994) book on the love of reading, a best seller published in France as *Comme un Roman* (published in 1992). Pennac's book is actually about how the love of reading originates in childhood and how sometimes, as in the case of his own son, it gets lost during adolescence. However, the title points to a theme that frequently arises in the context of the love of reading: bibliomania and whether books and reading can be *too* enjoyable, *too* seductive, so that they compete with life. In an ironic reference to this theme, the homepage of the HarperCollins UK site dedicated to reading groups (readinggroups.co.uk) prominently features a quotation from Logan Pearsall Smith, "People say that life is the thing, but I prefer reading."

The novelist A. S. Byatt, in an essay titled "The Irreplaceable Importance of Reading," confesses, "I used to be very worried about reading and all my early novels were about some kind of conflict between life and art. I now think that the fear that reading eats up life is just wrong. Nobody can spend enough of their life actually reading not also to live. Reading is just a real as any other things we do and insofar as it gives us a vocabulary for discussing moral, political and human issues, it is very useful for our daily life" (Byatt 1992, 17).

Nevertheless, many book lovers have the guilty feeling that reading is *too* pleasurable—taking their attention away from other claims on it such as housework or real-life relationships. Rosenthal's collection of accounts by readers includes a section titled "Habitual Readers," containing confessionals from self-identified compulsive readers who said things like, "I thought of books as real life, and of everything else as wan imitation" and "I'm convinced that, although reading is socially acceptable, it is an addiction. . . . There are times when

I read too much and I use it to hide out" (Rosenthal 1995, 100, 108). Jean (teacher librarian, age forty-four), one of the readers in Ross's study, said, "I hate to say that reading is everything, but I think sometimes it's more important than people, and that scares me. It is; it's everything. If I don't have a book, I'm bare. I feel like there's something lacking in my life."

The classic case of the seductive pull of the imaginative world is the four Bronte children who, growing up in an isolated Haworth parsonage, amused themselves by dreaming into existence a secret world more vivid, passionate, and intense than the everyday life around them. They invented the kingdoms of Glass Town and later Angria and Gondol, worlds stirred by imperial conquest, rebellion, and civil war and peopled by Byronic seducers, mad rejected heroines, cast-off children, and dark doubles locked in bitter rivalry. According to Charlotte's biographer Fanny Ratchford (1964), the worlds the children created were so brightly embroidered that thereafter real life could never measure up. As Charlotte Bronte put it in a poem, "We wove a web in childhood / A web of sunny air." This poem is quoted as an epigraph in A. S. Byatt's early novel *The Game* (1967), which is about two sisters, Julia and Cassandra, whose childhood game of an invented imaginative world dominates their adult life. Julia asks, "Don't you feel shut out of something?" "The question was disingenuous. Julia knew that Cassandra, in her draughty college, felt like Charlotte Bronte, cut off from Branwell and Zamorna, like Emily, silently pining for another world" (Byatt 1967, 101).

It may be that readers feel guilty because they are aware of the resentment of nonreaders, who see books as at best a competitor for the reader's time and at worst a source of dangerous ideas and subversive values. In Philip Ennis's study (1965, 39), one interviewee, Mrs. Kruger, reports poignantly on how her reading has produced a clash of values between her and her husband: "Ours is a mixed marriage; I am a reader and my husband is not." The nonreader feels excluded because the reader is lavishing attention and regard on someone else—characters in a book. The reader has escaped from the room, leaving only the physical shell behind, and can be seen to laugh and weep over unseen rivals. Metaphors used to describe the deeply pleasurable experience of reading point to this sense of living in another world: "lost in a book," "transported," "caught up in," "immersed," "entranced," "enthralled." In a book chapter titled "The Reader's Altered State of Consciousness," Brian Sturm (2001) surveys the rather sparse research on the experience of entranced reading, connecting the latter with other tranced states such as hypnotic states and dreams.

Janice Radway's ethnographic study of romance readers casts additional light on this body-snatching theme, linking it to reading as escape. Radway quotes extensively from an interview with an informant Dorothy Evans, a bookstore employee with a regular clientele of romance readers who relied on her for advice. Dot explains why her husband would hit the ceiling when she came home with books she had bought: "Because I think men do feel threatened. They want their wife to be in the room with them. And I think my body is in the room but the rest of me is not (when I'm reading)" (Radway 1984, 87).

Radway was so struck by the defensiveness expressed by the women in her study—she calls them the Smithton readers—that she felt compelled to comment on it at some length. "Guilt seems to arise over three specific aspects of romance reading. The Smithton readers are most troubled by the quantity of time they devote to their books . . . [time] that otherwise would be devoted to children, house or husband" (1984, 103). They also worry about the amount of money they spend on books (although they note that their husbands and children don't feel comparable guilt about money spent on their own toys and gadgets). And third, they feel guilty about the pleasurable feelings and emotions engendered in the act of romance reading, all the more because they are aware of critics' dismissive evaluation of these books as soft-core pornography. The feelings engendered by reading "appear to be remarkably close to the erotic anticipation, excitement, and contentment prompted when any individual is the object of another's total attention" (105). The Smithton readers' guilt, says Radway, "is the understandable result of their socialization within a culture that continues to value work above leisure and play, both of which still seem to carry connotations of frivolousness for the Smithton women" (105).

In *Lost in a Book* (1988) Victor Nell himself is ambivalent about the phenomenon he studies—effortless absorption so deep that the reader seems to be entranced. Nell ends up dividing readers into two types: Type A readers who read to dull consciousness and keep it at bay and Type B readers who read to heighten consciousness, enlarge experience, live more intensely, and solve real-life problems (229). Type A readers, according to Nell, use books as a narcotic, a way of avoiding confronting the realities of their everyday lives. In fact, Type A readers are apparently reprehensible in a variety of ways. They read too fast, "swallowing great mouthfuls of text whole in order to hold consciousness at bay" (231); they don't remember what they read and therefore tend to reread the same books over and over; they "select highly formulaic material which best meets their needs for safety and predictability" (231); and they aren't even as good as Type B readers at achieving the desired trance experience because they read for absorption and are therefore less discriminating about the books they choose. In short, Nell recuperates Type B reading by distinguishing it from Type A reading and displacing onto the latter all the negative themes that are sometimes associated with reading generally.

The Oliviers, a South African family of four "ludic readers," are presented in Victor Nell's *Lost in a Book* as prototypical examples of Type A reading. In the spirit of fair play, Nell allows the Oliviers to speak for themselves in a complete transcript interview of his interview with the Olivier family provided in Appendix D of his book (Nell 1988, 288–97). The father Ockert Olivier is a clerical worker with a laboratory reading speed of 350 words per minute, who said he typically reads nine books a week, one each weekday and two on each day of the weekend. Describing his experience of reading, Ockert says, "You read and every time it's as if you change. You get into situations, you go back, for example, to a thousand years before Christ. . . . I can't imagine how [non-readers like the husband of his daughter Mary] keep themselves busy, fishing and so on every weekend in a little world sixty miles around Pretoria. That's all their world consists of. . . . If I had to be occupied with myself all day I'd go mad, crazy."

The mother Wendy Olivier is a university lecturer with a reading speed of 316 words per minute who reads twenty-five books a month. She responds to Nell's questioning with a spirited defense, "When you asked that question, you said, "Would your professor of English . . . consider what you read as trash? That doesn't mean *I* consider it trash when I read it, but they would have considered it trash because it's not all of very high literary quality. . . . The point is I don't think it's a waste of time because I don't think it's trash myself."

The older daughter, Mary, is a businesswoman with a reading speed of 921 words per minute who reads twenty-eight books a month. She says, "The people who consider our activity as useless, like for instance my husband, who doesn't like movies or reading anything but biographical studies . . . he obviously considers it a waste of time in the sense that you're not getting on and doing things [such as sailing and fishing]. You're in a fantasy world hiding yourself away from reality, which I don't really think is the case, but this is the sort of attitude that people seem to take to a great extent, that you're not getting on doing things that you ought to be doing."

The younger daughter Sanette is an office worker with a reading speed of 456 words per minute who reads eighteen books a month. She says, "When I read a book, it's the type of book—the type of world—I want to live in. I'm very fond of cowboy books. Now maybe . . . a love story is so near real life that when I want to escape, I don't want to escape into the same real world again. That's why I want to escape into a fiction world, a world that was."

The Olivier family provides for Nell a scene of reading in which to examine the theme of escapism. In his analysis, Nell adopts the perspective of Mary's fisherman husband, remarking, "There is pathos in both these readers [Ockert and Sanette], a gnawing uncertainty about the true value of the rich but shadowy world in which they have chosen to spend most of their leisure time. . . . This is the plight of the constitutionally hyperexcitable introvert, who often turns his or her back on the bright lights and loud voices of the 'real world' " (241).

It seems that reading is subject to criticism by its detractors because it takes up more than its proper share of a scarce resource, whether time, money or attention. The other scarce resource is space, which is taken up by the reading materials themselves. And it's not just reading that can become addictive, but also book buying and collecting. Hence it's not surprising that the drive for possession of books themselves comes in for its share of attention. In *Collecting: An Unruly Passion*, Werner Muensterberger considers the nature of collecting of all kinds, including the obsessive desire of the nineteenth-century Sir Thomas Phillipps, who just wanted "one copy of every book!" and became the largest collector ever known of old papers and documents. Most of the rooms of his

Middle Hill estate became unusable, packed as they were with crates of books and paper. And what drives this acquisitive passion for completeness? Walter Benjamin in "Unpacking My Library" uses terms such as "rebirth," and "renewal of existence": "To renew the old world—that is the collector's deepest desire when he is driven to acquire new things" (Benjamin 1999, 6).

Research Tells Us

In a theory that can be applied to book collecting and identity formation, R. W. Belk (1988) has identified the concept of the extended self to explain how people incorporate material possessions into their definitions of self. According to Belk, we invest ourselves into possessions that define " 'who I am,' 'who I have been,' 'who I am becoming' or would like to become. Hence 'who I think I am,' or 'who I would like to become.' "

Belk argues that "By keeping and caring for possessions, often over a long period of time, a person maintains a biographical record that lends permanence and continuity to an otherwise less stable existence." In other words, we use possessions to extend ourselves across time. And, says Belk, the more energy and emotion we invest into a particular possession, the more it becomes me and the more attached we become to it.

Case 19: Selfish to Read?

Debbie is a twenty-nine-year-old copy editor and journalism student interviewed in Ross's study of avid readers. She dips into five to eight books a week, with several on the go at the same time. Her tastes are eclectic, including detective fiction, travel writing, science, biography.

Interviewer: Do you think it's somehow selfish to read?

Debbie: I don't know. I don't think of it as selfish, but I think it can be something that sets up barriers between people. I know that if I'm in a room with nonreaders and I'm reading, they don't interrupt me. I mean, it's one of the reasons why I bring—and a lot of people bring—books when you're traveling on a train or a plane, because it's a sign that you're doing something important that shouldn't be interrupted. *You're reading.*

Interviewer: It's an intentional barrier between you and—

Debbie: Yeah, it's an intentional barrier. And sometimes even when you don't intend it to be, when you're with family or friends and you're just relaxing reading, they don't understand that you can just be relaxing and it's okay to interrupt you when you're reading. And so it becomes a barrier.

Interviewer: Do they take it as a insult?

Debbie: Some people do, yes. I think, it's interesting to me because, as I said, having grown up in a family of readers, I find it perfectly acceptable for people to sit in a room together and to have quiet and everyone to be reading something. Whereas I find people who don't read, they find it upsetting in some way if you're not chatting or watching television or doing some communal activity. And instead you're just choosing to be quiet and read by yourself. They think there must be something wrong.

Interviewer: That you must be bored . . . ?

Debbie: Yes, or that—I guess it comes to people who don't take as much pleasure as I do from reading, that they can't understand that you would choose to read rather than converse with someone or rather than watch television or listen to the radio.

Interviewer: And what do you think about them?

Debbie: Well, I'm always surprised when I enter a home where people don't read—there's obviously not books around or even magazines. I just think their lives must be so much emptier. And I find too that often it's a barrier in a different way, because it seems to me that people that do read a lot—even people who just read junky paperbacks all the time—tend to have a larger vocabulary, a larger understanding of the world, to have more ideas in general. So that if I'm with people who don't read at all, I think that they're lacking something.

Interviewer: It's not just that you don't have a common frame of reference; it's that they have a much smaller frame of reference?

Debbie: That's right. I think reading gives you a much greater internal world. And because you're imagining things as you read, you have a richer world. And people who don't read don't have that world. They're really missing out on something.

Interviewer: Is there any particular thing that you think reading has done for you as a person?

Debbie: Well, I suppose for one thing it gave me a career, a profession, since it interested me in working in journalism, which is what I do now. I also think—I don't know— it's a double-edged sword. We talked about the sociability factor before. I've been in situations where I've been on my own and read to avoid being lonely. And yet, again, perhaps that's kept me from forcing myself to go out and meet people and do things with people, because I have that option. I don't have to be with people to read. On the other hand it's immensely pleasurable. I suppose the most important thing it's done for me is give me great pleasure.

Interviewer: You see it as escapist? If you see it negatively at all, is that how you see it?

Debbie: Yes, I think that's probably its greatest danger. That rather than living life you could just read about it.

Comments

Interestingly, Debbie starts and finishes this discussion with a strong statement of the negative theme of reading as a substitution for life and a social barrier. But she also examines the opposite: the positive value of reading as offering a larger understanding of the world, a richer inner life, and a source of immense pleasure. It's a "double-edged sword."

To Read More

Basbanes, Nicholas A. 1995. *A Gentle Madness: Bibliophiles, Bibliomanes, and the Eternal Passion for Books*. New York: Holt.

A finalist for the National Book Critics Circle Award in nonfiction in 1995 and named a *New York Times* Notable Book, this historical tour through two thousand years of book obsession provides portraits of people whose obsessive drive to find a quarry book lead them to lose kingdoms, spend their entire estates, commit thefts and murders, and even marry. One such portrait is of Don Vincente, a former Spanish monk, who committed eight murders during the 1830s to cover up his book thefts. His excuse: "Every man must die sooner or later, but good books must be conserved" (34). Another was Stephen Carrie

Blumberg, a self-described "rescuer of the past" (2), who spent two decades stealing 23,600 books from 268 libraries in 45 American states and two Canadian provinces to establish the "Blumberg Collection" in a secret Nebraska warehouse.

Rabinowitz, Harold, and Rob Kaplan, eds. 1999. *A Passion for Books: A Book Lover's Treasury of Stories, Essays, Humor, Lore, and Lists on Collecting, Reading, Borrowing, Lending, Caring for, and Appreciating Books.* New York: Three Rivers Press.

Beginning with Walter Benjamin's "Unpacking my Library" and ending with two lists published seventy years apart of one hundred best English-language novels, this collection of sixty pieces is a treasury of material on book mania of all kinds and includes cautionary tales of fanatical book collectors such as Thomas Rawlinson who were driven out of their homes by their monstrously expanding libraries.

References

Belk, R. W. 1988. "Possessions and the Extended Self." *Journal of Consumer Research* 15: 139–68.

Byatt, A. S. 1967. *The Game.* London: Vintage.

Byatt, A. S. 1992. "The Irreplaceable Importance of Reading." In *Reading the Future: A Place for Literature in Public Libraries,* 15–18. Edited by Rachel Van Riel. London: Arts Council of Great Britain.

Ennis, Philip H. 1965. *Adult Book Reading in the United States: A Preliminary Report.* National Opinion Research Center Report, no. 105. Chicago: National Opinion Research Center.

Muensterberger, Werner. 1994. *Collecting: An Unruly Passion—Psychological Perspectives.* Princeton: Princeton University Press.

Nell, Victor. 1988. *Lost in a Book: The Psychology of Reading for Pleasure.* New Haven, CT, and London: Yale University Press.

Pennac, Daniel. 1994. *Better Than Life.* Translated by David Homel. Toronto: Coach House Press.

Raabe, Tom. 1991. *Biblioholism: The Literary Addiction.* Golden, CO: Fulcrum.

Radway, Janice. 1984. *Reading the Romance: Women, Patriarchy and Popular Literature.* Chapel Hill: University of North Carolina Press.

Ratchford, Fanny E. 1964. *The Brontes' Web of Childhood.* New York: Russell and Russell.

Rosenthal, Nadine. 1995. *Speaking of Reading.* Portsmouth, NH: Heinemann.

Sturm, Brian. 2001. "The Reader's Altered State of Consciousness." In *The Readers' Advisor's Companion,* 97–117. Edited by Kenneth D. Shearer and Robert Burgin. Englewood, CO: Libraries Unlimited.

Walter, Benjamin. 1999. "Unpacking My Library." In *A Passion for Books: A Book Lover's Treasury of Stories, Essays, Humor, Lore, and Lists on Collecting, Reading, Borrowing, Lending, Caring for, and Appreciating Books.* Edited by Harold Rabinowitz and Rob Kaplan. New York: Three Rivers Press.

4.5. Reading High and Low

In "Green Glass Beads," the South African novelist Doris Lessing (1997, 236) laments the decline of real reading and the disappearance of the "cultivated person" whose tastes were informed by the classics from Greece and Rome and who, in Britain at least, were "soaked in the most glorious prose ever written—the Bible." She says:

> The difference between then and now is that there used to be a consensus about what was good and what was bad literature. This is no longer true. . . . But now that people read less, they have lower standards, accept worse books, don't know how to judge them. And they have no defence against current silliness, such as that there is no difference between, let's say, *War and Peace* by Tolstoy and the latest romantic or even pornographic rubbish. (Lessing 1997, 237–8)

Doris Lessing's account of the decline of reading and lowering of standards is familiar, even comforting, having been restated so often. Typically the author and the intended audience for this kind of analysis are represented as secure in their own standards and tastes because the alleged decline is happening to *other* people, usually younger or less educated people who are thought to be easily led astray. Not surprisingly, the culprit that is usually alleged to have produced the lowering of standards is some new medium that reaches a broad audience. For example, *Barry Sanders's A Is for Ox: The Collapse of Literacy and the Rise of Violence in an Electronic Age* (1995) popularizes the argument of Neil Postman's *Technopoly: The Surrender of Culture to Technology* (1993) that television causes moral collapse and spiritual impoverishment.

Implicit in most of these accounts is an assumption about some natural hierarchy thought to exist among the different media or among the genres that are the content of a single medium. So on one hand, people who are anxious about the collapse of literary and cultural values tend to see a natural hierarchy with books at the top, film and television further down, and comic books and videogames at the very bottom. Within the medium of books, there is similarly thought to be a natural hierarchy with "quality books" at the top and "trash" at the bottom, although of course people will still argue about what constitutes quality. "Good literature" is what literate persons and opinion makers regard as worth reading at any given time. Views change, of course, as we are reminded by the notorious footnote in F. R. Leavis's *The Great Tradition* cautioning readers that among Dickens's novels only *Hard Times* repaid adult attention.

In *The Western Canon,* Harold Bloom (1994) claims that canonical books can be identified by the arresting effect they have on the reader: "When you read a canonical work for the first time you encounter a stranger, an uncanny startlement rather than a fulfillment of expectations" (Bloom 1994, 3). For Bloom, the canonical authors, par excellence, are Shakespeare and Dante, but he also includes among the canon such authors as Chaucer, Cervantes, Milton, and

Goethe from among the earlier writers and Proust, Joyce, Woolf, Kafka, Borges, and Beckett from among more recent exemplars of the so-called "Chaotic Age" of the nearer present. For the loss of standards and neglect of the canon, Bloom blames, among other things, multiculturalism, feminism, Marxism, cultural studies, and the New Historicism. Curiously, Bloom's book on the Western canon ends in a thirty-seven-page list of books of quality, which he seems to offer as fragments shored against the general ruin: "I turn to my list, hoping that literate survivors will find some authors and books among them that they have not yet encountered and will garner the rewards that only canonical literature affords" (Bloom 1994, 528).

The faith in lists is common. *Hints for Home Reading* (Sweetser 1880), a volume of home reference in the Putnam's Handy-Book Series concludes with four lists for household libraries: the first list of "500 volumes of the most essential books in the best inexpensive editions"; the second list "forming an additional library of 500 volumes, recommended as the next most desirable and important"; the third list "comprising about 1,000 volumes, which are recommended as the most desirable and important after the works specified in the two previous lists have been obtained"; and finally an austere list of only 50 volumes for more modest home libraries.

One reason for the popularity of lists is the reader's sense that there is just so much out there to be read and so little time to read it. And then there is the worry about reading the right stuff. A forerunner of present-day book clubs, "great books" reading groups, and the radio and television programs designed to help middlebrow readers distinguish good from inferior books was Charles W. Eliot's "Five-Foot Shelf of Books," also known as the Harvard Classics. According to Shelley Rubin, the appeal of such programs of reading guidance was the promise to alleviate the middle-class reader's social anxiety about appearing at a dinner party unable to discuss a classic book or the current best seller. She says, "The expansion of publishing, by making it more difficult to discern 'the best' amidst the mountains of volumes published, partially enhanced the stature of genteel critics" (Rubin 1992, 18). Feeling "adrift in uncharted waters," the American reader turned for "comfort and guidance" to cultural authorities (Rubin 1992, 27), chief among whom in the 1920s was Charles W. Eliot.

As president of Harvard, Eliot from time to time gave speeches in which he would wax enthusiastic about a five-foot shelf of books that would furnish a liberal education to anyone willing to devote fifteen minutes a day to reading them. When publisher P. F. Collier proposed that Collier and Son would publish such a collection, Eliot agreed to choose the books, write an editor's introduction, and lend his (and Harvard's) name to the project. In his introduction, he identified the goal of his reading program as the development of the "liberal frame of mind" that great books "enriched, refined, and fertilized."

Readers must have been reassured that this "liberal frame of mind" did not require monumental effort but could be managed handily in "fifteen minutes a day." Sales of the volumes, says Rubin, surpassed Collier's expectations, spurred on by advertisements in the 1920s and 1930s that linked the ownership of these volumes to business and social success. Rubin quotes Everett Dean Martin's description of a 1920s advertisement for the Harvard Classics featuring dinner guests seated at the table: "There are two men and a beautiful woman. She is talking to the man on her right, and is evidently fascinated by his brilliant conversation. The man on the left sits dumb and miserable and unnoticed; he cannot join in such sophisticated and scintillating discussion. We are informed that the poor man has neglected to read his fifteen minutes a day" (Martin, p. 14 quoted in Rubin, 29–30).

Another marketing scheme whose success similarly depended on middlebrow anxiety about getting access to high culture is the Book-of-the-Month Club (BOMC). Janice Radway's *A Feeling for Books* (1997) is a provocative, stimulating, and occasionally exasperating study of the Book-of-the-Month Club. She recounts how in 1916 Montreal-born Harry Scherman hit upon the promotional scheme of a "Library Package." In this scheme, a large box of chocolates was sold together with a small leather-bound book, one of fifteen Shakespearean plays collected in the Little Leather Library series. Convinced that there was a pent-up demand among ordinary Americans for "really good literature," Scherman was faced with a marketing dilemma: there is a limited supply of ready-made "classics," but the market for each new quality book has to be created one book at a time.

Scherman's solution was to sell the concept of "the best"—"an open-ended collection of new books, [that] because they were the best, were sure to become classics" (Radway 1997, 171). Beginning in 1926, the Book-of-the-Month Club owed its immediate success to three essential elements: the panel of expert judges, which originally included Henry Canby, Dorothy Canfield Fisher, William Allen White, Christopher Morley, and Heywood Broun, who did the choosing of "the best"; the negative option, which Scherman invented in 1927 after *The Heart of Emerson's Journals* was returned by the truckload; and the use of the post to deliver books automatically to the subscribers' door. As Radway summarized the successful formula, "Scherman proved adept at mobilizing the language and symbolism of individuality, choice and agency while simultaneously taking advantage of the economic benefits offered by the principles of automation" (192).

Radway is interested in the Book-of-the-Month-Club as a theorized site of struggle between competing literary professionals for the authority to define "the best" books. Scherman's application to book distribution of Fordist principles of speed, uniformity, and endless flow had the effect of opening up a middle ground of taste. The "scandal" of the Book-of-the-Month Club, in the eyes of its critics, was that it blurred the distinction between high and low taste by interpolating a suspect taste community who counterfeited elite taste without having the proper cultural mastery. We can see this same sense of reservation when elite readers dismiss as negligible the fact that millions of people were introduced to Toni Morrison's *Beloved* or Gabriel Garcia Marquez's *One Hundred Years of*

Solitude because they were Oprah choices. Well, they say huffily, they aren't reading them for the *right* reasons—and anyway, if these works can appeal to so many people, maybe they aren't really all that good after all. Not when compared with, say, Djuna Barnes's *Nightwood*, declared by T. S. Eliot to be the greatest novel of the twentieth century but hardly ever read. These views seem to be particularly attractive to people who regard mass culture or popular culture as an oxymoron.

Stanley Aronowitz has suggested that the anxiety over "mass culture" has been experienced most keenly by people who are just not very comfortable with the taste preferences of ordinary people. He traces the distinction between "high" and "low" culture to the gulf that in the late middle ages separated aristocratic and church culture from peasant culture. When power shifted to the new bourgeois class, a new "high" culture was constituted by the elite class and its intellectuals as a way of consolidating their cultural authority (Aronowitz 1993, 63). But in the age of mechanical reproduction, non-elites who previously had no time or money to acquire cultural products could now afford to satisfy their cultural tastes. No longer able to impose their own taste as the taken-for-granted aesthetic norm, elites worried about a Gresham's Law at work: bad cultural currency driving out good.

The edited collection *Mass Culture* (Rosenberg and White 1957) is a classic source that documents the presumed faults of so-called mass culture, as discerned by such cultural observers as Jose Ortega y Gasset, Dwight Macdonald, Leo Lowenthal, Clement Greenberg, Herbert Gans, Theodor Adorno, Marshall McLuhan, and Gilbert Seldes. In the introduction, Bernard Rosenberg makes it clear where he stands: "Never before have the sacred and the profane, the genuine and the specious, the exalted and the debased, been so thoroughly mixed that they are all but indistinguishable"; "At its worst, mass culture threatens not merely to cretinize our taste, but to brutalize our senses while paving the way to totalitarianism" (Rosenberg and White 1957, 5, 9). Although there is some variety in the perspectives presented, the collection as a whole is a good source of arguments against popular culture—arguments that have had a surprisingly long afterlife. Popular culture, so the story goes, has the following fatal flaws:

- It is not an art form at all but a manufactured commodity that is mass produced and cheap. Created by the entertainment industries and sold for profit, it is geared to the lowest common denominator, which prefers standardized forms over the disruptions of avant-garde art.

- It is a simulacrum of genuine art, imitating the real thing through parasitic and kitschy counterfeits that delude mass audiences into mistaking them for the original.

- It wins over its audience by spurious gratifications and emotional appeals that are harmful and often escapist.

- It creates a passive audience that is a sitting duck for the persuasive techniques of totalitarianism and the manipulations of advertising.

These arguments are very similar to the ones mobilized in the 1880s against popular fiction (see section 1.2) and are similarly open to challenge. The Rosenberg and White volume includes within itself a powerful critique by David Riesman of the volume's own dominant analysis. In comparing armchair research with fieldwork, Riesman (1957, 409) notes that it can be a convenient shortcut to understanding what popular culture does for people if you make yourself the relevant audience and consult only your own reactions:

> But the danger exists then of assuming that the *other* audience, the audience one does not converse with, is more passive, more manipulated, more vulgar in its taste, than may be the case. One can easily forget that things that strike the sophisticated person as trash may open new vistas for the unsophisticated; moreover, the very judgment of what is trash may be biased by one's own unsuspected limitations, for instance, by one's class position or academic vested interest.

So what in the final analysis are we to think about this construction of the passive, manipulated consumer of low culture? Mass culture critics characteristically take for granted a passive reader, helplessly bombarded by repetitious messages and images from soap operas, reality TV, movies, rap music, videogames, comic books, glamour magazines, pulp fiction, theme parks, and advertising.

But what if, instead of asking what media does to people conceptualized as a "mass," we asked what individual people do with media? In "Girls, Reading and Narrative Gleaning," Janice Radway (2002) takes aim against the girls-at-risk story constructed by what she calls the "alarmist narratives" depicting girl readers as "defenseless recipients of external, all-powerful cultural messages" (2002, 185). She tells a counter-story of girls or "grrrls" ransacking media for usable images, ideas, and concepts that they can use in their self-making.

Case 20: Respecting Readers

Samantha, a twenty-eight-year-old doctoral student in English, described herself as a reader who for many years has read "more ephemeral kinds of literature right alongside the great classics of great world literature." Asked what she would say to those critics who call Harlequins trash or devalue them as mass-produced fiction, she said:

> Well it *is* mass-produced fiction. But there needs to be a respect for the readers of Harlequin romances, and the fact that they *know* what they're reading. . . . I think that critics tend to assume that readers are not *aware*

of the discrepancy between the world of Harlequin romance and the world of real life. That is really an incredibly condescending assumption to make. . . . What Harlequins really have to offer is that you can set up a relationship between two characters that is really very interesting and you don't have to be constrained in any way by probability.

So one of the best Harlequins that I read was one where you have these identical twin sisters and the one identical twin is in love with her sister's fiancé. And then the one who's actually engaged to him takes off and elopes on the day of her wedding and leaves the groom stranded at the altar. So her twin sister, who is really in love with him, takes her place and goes on the honeymoon. Now this is preposterous and everybody *knows* it's preposterous, but that's the whole point—we're reading a Harlequin, we're not dealing with real life any more. And so you can actually think, well what would happen if you were on your twin sister's honeymoon, and you're with this man that you're madly in love with, but he keeps calling you by your sister's name?

That's the kind of interesting emotional situation that I enjoy spending a couple of hours fantasizing about. A lot of people would just pick that up and say, well this is trash; it's not realistic. Of course it's not realistic. It's not trying to be realistic; nobody thinks that it's realistic. But it is fun. Soap operas are fun in the same way—they're not governed by the same kind of criteria that other kinds of literature are. You have to take it on its own terms, and either enjoy it or not enjoy it, but not necessarily feel that if you don't enjoy something that you're in a position to look down on those who do.

Comments

When people differ in their tastes, who has the power to look down on whom? Until recently, there was an open season on romance readers, but now they are learning to fight back.

What Readers and Libraries Can Do

1. Jettison the distinction between popular culture and high culture. The evaluative baggage entailed in these terms becomes a stumbling block to recognizing the variations of quality that exist within any particular genre of popular culture.

2. Be skeptical when you encounter evaluations that rely on some a priori distinction between "spurious gratifications" and "genuine experience" or between "imitative simulacra" and "original art" in order to dismiss a whole category of popular culture that the evaluator doesn't like and about which he or she too often has little firsthand knowledge.

3. Take a good look at how popular materials are being treated in public libraries, especially types of books that historically have been denigrated. Is there anything about the way romance books or westerns are catalogued or shelved that could give readers the message that these genres are considered second-class citizens, barely tolerated? Are the romance lines kept separate on the shelf to match readers' preferences, or are the innocent white covers jumbled promiscuously with the more sensuous dark pink and red covers?

To Read More

Cawelti, John. 1976. *Adventure, Mystery and Romance: Formula Stories as Art and Popular Culture.* Chicago: University of Chicago Press.
    An influential pioneering study of formula stories as popular culture. Includes a discussion of the formulas of adventure, romance, mystery, and best-selling melodramas.

Frye, Northrop. 1976. *The Secular Scripture: A Study of the Structure of Romance.* Cambridge, MA: Harvard University Press.
    In this encyclopedic study, Frye examines the building blocks of story. He shows how certain design elements—birth mysteries, orphans, oracular prophecies, amnesia, light and dark heroines, twins and doubles, the young hero coming over the sea, father-daughter incest, shipwreck, disguise, the recognition scene, the vertical descent into a lower world, the upward bounce of the happy ending—how these elements are the basic elements of story. They can be found in both low art and high art from Greek comedy to Shakespeare to Dickens to popular genres such as the soap opera and the detective story. Says Frye, "Romance is the structural core of all fiction: being directly descended from folktale, it brings us closer than any other aspect of literature to the sense of fiction, considered as a whole, as . . . man's vision of his own life as a quest" (15).

Rosenberg, Betty, and Diana Tixier Herald. 1991. *Genreflecting: A Guide to Reading Interests in Genre Fiction.* 3rd ed. Englewood, CO: Libraries Unlimited.
    The third edition (although not the fifth) of this indispensable tool for readers' advisors contains a useful introductory chapter, "The Common Reader, Libraries, and Publishing," that summarizes changing attitudes to popular genres and provides suggestions for further reading. The authors say, "Genre fiction no doubt developed out of that childhood capacity for innocent enjoyment" (2).

Rubin, Joan Shelley. 1992. *The Making of Middlebrow Culture*. Chapel Hill: University of North Carolina Press.

> Providing historical perspective on culture, consumption and status, Rubin examines radio and television literature programs, book clubs and "great book" programs, and the Book-of-the-Month phenomenon.

Stevenson, Gordon. 1977. "Popular Culture and the Public Library." In *Advances in Librarianship*, 177–229. Vol. 7, edited by Melvin Voigt and Michael H. Harris. New York: Academic Press.

> This article remains an excellent overview of the controversy over popular culture as it relates to the public library. Stevenson notes that the typical procedure followed by critics of popular culture is to look at an exemplar and then "make extravagant deductions about what is or will be in the minds of people as a result of exposure to that message" (189). Stevenson notes the unique contribution made to the debate by Edward Shils at the Tamiment Institute seminar on "mass culture," whose proceedings were summarized in a monograph dubiously titled *Culture for the Millions?* (Jacobs 1961). "At the Tamiment Institute seminar he bluntly suggested that the real issue was *why* the participants did not like popular culture, and proposed it was because they disliked the working classes and the middle classes" (193).

To Read More on the Canon

von Hallberg, Robert, ed. 1984. *Canons*. Chicago: University of Chicago Press.

> A great deal of controversy has been generated on the literary canon—that group of texts considered to be particularly worthy of study—especially in the light of feminist attacks on it. Some provocative essays on this subject are collected here. Of particular interest is Barbara Herrnstein Smith's essay "Contingencies of Value," 5–40.

Tompkins, Jane. 1985. *Sensational Designs: The Cultural Work of American Fiction 1790–1860*. New York and Oxford: Oxford University Press.

> A persuasive study on canon-formation in nineteenth-century American studies.

References

Aronowitz, Stanley. 1993. *Roll Over Beethoven: The Return of Cultural Strife*. Hanover, CT, and London: Wesleyan University Press.

Bloom, Harold. 1994. *The Western Canon: The Books and School of the Ages*. New York: Harcourt Brace.

Jacobs, N., ed. 1961. *Culture for the Millions? Mass Media in Modern Society*. Princeton, NJ: Van Nostrand.

Lessing, Doris. 1997. "Green Glass Beads." In *Real Voices on Reading*, 236–44. Edited by Philip Davis. New York: St. Martin's Press.

Martin, Everett Dean. 1926. *Meaning of a Liberal Education*. New York: Norton.

National Endowment for the Arts. 2004. *Reading at Risk: A Survey of Literary Reading in America*. Research Division Report #46. Washington, DC. Available at www.nea.gov/news/news04/ReadingAtRisk.html.

Nell, Victor. 1988. *Lost in a Book: The Psychology of Reading for Pleasure.* New Haven and London: Yale University Press.

Postman, Neil. 1993. *Technopoly: The Surrender of Culture to Technology.* New York: Vintage.

Radway, Janice. 1989. "The Book of the Month Club and the General Reader." In *Reading in America: Literature and Social History,* 259–84. Edited by Cathy N. Davidson. Baltimore and London: Johns Hopkins University Press.

Radway, Janice A. 1997. *A Feeling for Books: The Book-of-the-Month Club, Literary Taste, and Middle-Class Desire.* Chapel Hill and London: University of North Carolina Press.

Radway, Janice A. 2002. "Girls, Reading and Narrative Gleaning: Crafting Repertoires for Self-fashioning within Everyday Life." In *Narrative Impact: Social and Cognitive Foundations,* 183–204. Edited by M. C. Green and J. J. Strange. Mahwah, NJ: Lawrence Erlbaum Associates.

Riesman, David. 1957. "Listening to Popular Music." In *Mass Culture: The Popular Arts in America,* 408–17. Edited by Bernard Rosenberg and David Manning White. New York: The Free Press.

Rosenberg, Bernard, and David Manning White, eds. 1957. *Mass Culture: The Popular Arts in America.* New York: The Free Press.

Rubin, Joan Shelley. 1992. *The Making of Middlebrow Culture.* Chapel Hill and London: University of North Carolina Press.

Sanders, Barry. 1995. *A Is for Ox: The Collapse of Literacy and the Rise of Violence in an Electronic Age.* New York: Vintage.

Stevenson, Gordon. 1977. "Popular Culture and the Public Library." In *Advances in Librarianship,* 177–229. Vol. 7, edited by Melvin Voigt and Michael H. Harris. New York: Academic Press.

Sweetser, M. F. 1880. "What the People Read." In *Hints for Home Reading: Putnam's Handy Book Series of Things Worth Knowing,* 5–14. Edited by Lyman Abbott. New York: G. P. Putnam's Sons.

4.6. Best Sellers, Prizes, Lists, and the Manufacture of Taste

With hundreds of thousands of trade books available in English, readers need ways to narrow down their choices to something manageable. At the same time, it is more profitable for booksellers to sell a large number of a single title than it is to sell a single copy of a large number of different books. The successful bringing together of a reader and a book is the end point of a series of complex factors, some having to do with choices that determine the supply and others having to do with choices made by individual readers. In this section, we look at the supply side. The book industry has developed sales strategies that work by focusing readers' attention on a select number of books: the best-seller list, the prize book, the book club previously discussed in section 4.5, and the genre book, discussed in section 4.7. In this section, we consider best sellers, prize-winning books, and the production of lists.

There are accounts of best sellers before 1850—largely lists of religious works, with titles by Sir Walter Scott, James Fenimore Cooper, and Charles Dickens appearing toward the end of that period. But the term "best seller," in North America at least, arises from a publishing context that depends on several converging developments: the expansion of book publishing in centers such as New York; the rise of a large middle class with the resources to buy books; the development of cheap paperbound reprint editions; and the creation of an infra-structure to transport books and sell them in local markets, eventually including book clubs that used the postal system to deliver books to areas not well served by bookstores. Laura Miller (2000) points out the difficulties in deciding what counts as a best seller. Frank Luther Mott required a best seller to have sales fig-ures equivalent to 1 percent of the total continental U.S. population for the de-cade in which it was published. For others, "making the list" means appearing on one of the many best-seller lists produced since the invention of the form in 1895—and especially appearing on the *New York Times* best-seller list.

Right from the beginning, best sellers have been tainted with the charge of being *too* popular. By the middle of the nineteenth century, sentimental domes-tic novels, mostly written by and for women, were becoming so popular that Nathaniel Hawthorne complained that "America is now wholly given over to a d—d mob of scribbling women" and concluded glumly that his own books had "no chance of success while the public taste is occupied with their trash" (Hart 1950, 93). What he objected to was the popularity of authors such as Maria Susanna Cummins, who wrote *The Lamplighter* (1854), Elizabeth Wetherell (aka Susan Warner), who wrote *The Wide, Wide World* (1850), and Mrs. E.D.E.N. Southworth, whose sixty or so novels included *Ishmael* (1864) and *Self-Raised* (1864), which sold more than 2 million copies each (Greene 1978–81, 35). Although Hawthorne professed to be mystified by the numerous editions of *The Lamplighter,* James Hart provides some clues as to the elements of the book's appeal: an orphan girl befriended, an old injury rectified, a birth mystery, overcoming of obstacles through Christian fortitude, the marriage of the orphan to her childhood sweetheart who has meanwhile become rich, and narration from a female perspective.

At the heart of all accounts of best sellers are the lists. For a present-day reader, one of the surprises of reading lists of best sellers from an earlier era is the sheer hetero-geneity of books represented, including the full range from light fiction to "serious literature." Some books have retained their popularity and achieved the canonical status conferred by being put on college syllabi, for example, Joel Chandler Harris's *Uncle Remus* (1881), Robert Louis Stevenson's *Treasure Island* (1883), Thomas Hardy's *The Mayor of Casterbridge* (1886), or Steven Crane's *The Red Badge of Courage* (1895). Others that were equally popular at the time are today almost unknown, unread, and unreadable such as John Hay's *The Bread-Winners* (1884) or Francis Marion Crawford's *A Cigarette-Maker's Romance* (1890). Although analysts of the best-seller phenomenon often point retrospectively to certain elements that account for popularity—religious or spiritual themes, tear-jerking emotional appeal, information and guidance, sensationalism and adventure, humor, sympathetic characters, happy endings, topical subject matter, congruence with readers' values and beliefs—there is nothing that all best sellers have in common except that they sell spectacularly well.

Looking only at the lists and analyzing the best-selling books themselves gives just one part of the story. To get a complete picture, we need to recognize that best-sellerdom takes place within a communications circuit that also includes authors, publishers, booksellers/libraries, and readers. Typically critics who write about best sellers pick one of these nodes in the communication circuit as the dominant force. Giving the nod to the reader, Hart claims "the popular author is always the one who expresses the people's minds and paraphrases what they consider their private feelings" (Hart 1950, 285). Elizabeth Long's interesting study of the theme of success in best-selling American novels likewise depends on the assumption that novels become best sellers "because they resonate with the values of their readers" (Long 1985, 26).

An opposed view is that the readers are powerless before the manipulations of commercial forces that have reshaped publishing, turning it from a gentlemen's literary club to a business that treats books just like any other commodity. An early and still interesting analysis of the economic forces that affect publishing and reading audiences alike is Q. D. Leavis's *Fiction and the Reading Public* (1931). She used a number of research methods including sending questionnaires to best-selling authors and analyzing selected novels from the glory days of the pre-nineteenth-century novel as written by Bunyan, Fielding, Richardson, and Swift to the dismal present. According to Leavis, the superiority of those early authors lay in the way they provide their readers with a succession of "shocks and jars": "The eighteenth century novelist is continually pulling up the reader, disappointing his expectations or refusing him the luxury of day-dreaming and not infrequently douching him with cold water" (Leavis 1932, 109). In her chapter "The Disintegration of the Reading Public," Q. D. Leavis (1932) blames the economics of mass-market publishing, cheap books, the Railway Library, and the serial publication of fiction for a decline that she thinks set in around the time of Dickens.

More recently, critics such as Whiteside in *The Blockbuster Complex* (1980) point to corporate acquisitions of publishing houses and the domination of the market by a few large, vertically integrated publishing companies; the increasing importance of subsidiary rights, including film and television rights, with the result that sales departments have a growing role in selecting which books get published; and the growth of bookstore chains such as B. Dalton and Waldenbooks that use sophisticated computerized systems to track sales and winnow out slow-moving books. According to Sorensen (2004, 6), for the first quarter of 2003, the top six publishing conglomerates accounted for more than 80 percent of unit sales in adult fiction. Studies that emphasize the corporate matrix of publishing usually end up concluding that the chase to sign up the next blockbuster homogenizes production and reduces the choices available to readers. From Adorno onward, culture critics have argued that multinational conglomerates use the rhetoric of "free choice" as a smoke screen to hide the fact that consumers are reduced to choosing among standardized, interchangeable products on the basis of insignificant differences.

Elizabeth Long (1985, 31) points out the equally plausible speculation that "high culture, which used to be seen as *the* culture, is now being dealt with in publishing as one specialized aspect of a less hierarchical and more fragmentary cultural totality" (see section 4.5 on the politics of high culture). We can see this pattern in the fragmentation of the best-seller list from a single list to many lists corresponding to different taste communities. The first list produced by *The Bookman* in 1895 included only fiction; after 1912 *Publishers Weekly* produced both fiction and nonfiction lists; now we have best-seller lists categorized by format (hardcover, paper), audience (children, adult), nonfiction topic area (business, self-help etc.), and fiction genres (literary fiction, romance, crime, etc.) The bookseller Barnes & Noble has a Web page called "What America's Reading," which goes beyond the Barnes & Noble weekly charts of best-selling fiction, nonfiction, children's, business, and self-help to include what is called the "Top 10 of Everything."

This Top 10 is a daily record of sales in more than three hundred book categories, based on six months of sales data. Instead of undifferentiated lists that rank all fiction or all nonfiction on a single scale of popularity, this device of the Top 10 of Everything clusters readers tastes according to genre and subject area so that readers can find popular choices in such heterogeneous categories as "sports biography," "home renovation & repair," "historical romance," "etiquette," "British cozies," "horror fiction," "ancient history," "alphabet books," "political theory and ideology," "canning and preserves," and "women's health." Janice Radway has observed that the Book-of-the-Month Club follows a similar practice of replacing a hierarchy of taste with horizontal categories, each with its own criteria of excellence: "Distinctions are made . . . within equivalent categories," notes Radway (1989, 266–67). In this value system, literary fiction doesn't trump cookbooks, leading high-culture supporters to lament what they see as a leveling down of taste.

Ostensibly, best-seller lists are simply a tool to track consumer behavior. However, there is good reason to think that the lists also *shape* behavior. Given the huge numbers of choices available, readers need a way to reduce overload (see section 4.7) and use the lists as a marker of quality. They may not have heard of the author or title themselves but have confidence that at least some of the many who bought the book did so on the basis of positive information about the book's quality. Then, too, some people want to read what everyone else is reading in order to be in the know about popular culture and be able to talk about it with others. Finally, once a book is on the list, bookstores display it prominently and provide discounts.

Research Tells Us

Economist Alan T. Sorensen analyzed detailed weekly data from Nielsen Bookscan for sales of hardcover fiction books to study the impact of best sellers on the diversity of what gets published. His research question was whether the best-seller phenomenon "steals" sales that would otherwise go to non-best-selling books or whether, au contraire, it expands the total numbers of books sold and increases demand for *all* books. If the former were the case, then publishers would reduce their lists, curtailing "product variety." However, Sorensen found the following:

- "[T]he market expansion effect of bestseller lists appears to dominate any business stealing from non-bestselling titles."

- "Bestseller lists appear to increase sales for both bestsellers and non-bestsellers in similar genres."

- Appearing on the best seller list has the most impact on sales of books by debut authors and no impact at all on sales by the top five—John Grisham, Tom Clancy, Danielle Steel, Michael Crichton, and Stephen King—who accounted in 1994 for 70 percent of total fiction sales.

Case 21: Reading the Right Things

Some readers in Ross's study of avid readers reported that they felt that they should be reading something different—less fiction or more classics—or that they should be reading more systematically. One way to keep anxiety at bay is to make lists of books to read and consult other people's lists. Here is what some readers said about their efforts at self-improvement in reading, some successful and some less so:

Anita: I was in sciences in my earlier years in university, and I had friends in the English program reading all these classics. I suddenly decided that I hadn't read any of the classics at all. So I kind of made this big project that I was going to read the classics. That didn't work out very well. . . . My latest thing is that I've decided that all I read is fiction, . . . so I started just in the past two years trying to read nonfiction stuff. My father and my oldest sister are both scientists and they read a lot of stuff like *The Dancing Wu-li Masters*. . . . Next on my list is *The Brief History of Time*. I just kind of had this feeling of inadequacy that I wasn't reading the right things. (master of library and information science student, age twenty-five)

Neil: Between the ages of thirteen and sixteen, I probably did more reading in those years than I have before or since. I read anything that I could get my hands on. In fact, I used to look at the bibliographies in books to see what else I could read. But I only wanted important books. I hated novels. I didn't like novels, unless they were important in some respect, unless they were famous. . . . I read to gain knowledge—to gain the insights of the Western world and what literature had to offer. . . . I enjoy getting something out of reading. I think that's what it is. I can never understand the people that say, "Yeah, I read the book, but I can't remember it." To me reading something *means* you are *understanding* it. If I couldn't understand something that I was reading, it would pointless. . . . Mortimer Alder wrote a book called *How to Read a Book*. One of the things that he pointed out is that a lot of people don't know how to read a book and that to really understand a book you have to read it at least twice, if not more times. He also provided an excellent bibliography of what he called the "Great Books," and that's where I got a lot of my information on which books to read. (chemical technician, age twenty-six)

Marsha: After I finished high school and before I started university, I always thought that I should read important books. And I sort of had an idea of what I though was an important book, because of the books we took in high school English classes. I decided that Penguins—because we had a lot of Penguins at home—Penguins were important books. So I used to go to the bookstore and look for Penguins. (student, age twenty-six)

Sarah: I remember at one stage I decided I was going to read the whole library, entirely, all the fiction. I never read nonfiction. I would start at the As and I would work down to the Zs and after a few months I realized I was never going to finish the As so I started to be more selective and it took me five years to reach the Ds. I never got past the Ds because then I read Dickens and Dostoevsky and I got held up on them [laughter] another five years. I remember one day I went in and I thought I can't stand this any longer I'm going to go right to the Zs and work backwards and see if I can meet myself in the middle but then I ran into Emile Zola in the Zs and it took me a year or so to read a couple of his. (library assistant, age forty)

Valery: About once a year, I'll feel that I should read Charles Dickens just because: Are we a complete person if we haven't read the classics? I find them a bit hard going. I find anything actually written before 1900 sort of hard going. (English as a second language teacher, age forty-seven)

What Libraries Can Do

1. Provide help to readers who want to read "the classics" or "important books" or "significant nonfiction" by providing lists of books that have a track record of appeal. A reader who wants to start reading classic books should probably not begin with *Ulysses* or *The Sound and the Fury*.

2. Create displays and booklists. Because publishers already do a good job of publicizing the current best seller, libraries can use displays and booklists to use the popularity of the best seller to draw attention to excellent books in the same genre that are not being hyped. This is the familiar read-alike strategy of "If you've read everything by John Grisham, you might like X." But of course you need to make sure that the recommended books really do have appeal factors similar to a John Grisham book.

To Read More on Best Sellers

Hackett, Alice Payne, and James Henry Burke. 1977. *80 Years of Best Sellers, 1895–1975*. NY: R. R. Bowker.

This is the last of Alice Payne Hackett's books on the best seller, each new book adding an additional decade of best sellers from the *Publishers Weekly* lists. Hackett attributes the invention of the best seller list to Harry Thurston Peck, who was a reviewer and later an editor of the literary magazine *The Bookman*, which in 1895 began to run a monthly list of best sellers, based on the numbers of books actually sold. Hackett and Burke include chapters on "The History of Best Sellers," "Best Sellers 1895–1975," and "Best Seller Subjects" as well as a bibliography of books and articles about best sellers.

Hart, James D. 1950. *The Popular Book: A History of America's Literary Taste.* New York: Oxford University Press.

This book remains a useful and readable survey of popular reading in America from the *Bay Psalm Book* printed in 1640 to Norman Mailer's *The Naked and the Dead* (1948) and Norman Vincent Peale's *Guide to Confident Living* (1948). It includes a chronological list of best-selling books.

Korda, Michael. 2001. *Making the List: A Cultural History of the American Best seller 1900–1999.* New York: Barnes & Noble.

An editor at Simon & Shuster for more than four decades, Korda takes a personal and chatty approach to the phenomenon of best sellers. Ten chapters, one for each decade, provide annual lists and reflections on the types of books that have proved popular over the years, many now almost totally unknown but some with staying power (e.g., Owen Wister's *The Virginian,* the number one fiction best seller in 1902 or *The Education of Henry Adams,* the top nonfiction best seller in 1919). Librarians will find this book useful in creating displays: What did people read one hundred years ago or fifty years ago or the year when such-and-such happened?

Mott, Frank L. 1947. *Golden Multitudes: The Story of Best Sellers in the United States.* New York: Macmillan; Reprint, New York: Bowker, 1960.

A pioneering work on the best-seller phenomenon that still makes interesting reading. Asking if there is a best-seller formula, Mott concludes that there are a variety of audiences, formats, and appeals that are at play, but that certain elements of popular appeal have persisted in all periods of best-seller history including "religion, sensationalism, information and guidance, adventure, democracy, humor, characterization, juvenile suitability, timeliness."

Todd, Richard. 1996. *Consuming Passions: The Booker Prize and Fiction in Britain Today.* London: Bloomsbury.

Todd discusses the Booker Prize—originally a marketing initiative by the UK agribusiness conglomerate Booker—as well as the Salman Rushdie affair and patterns of authorship in the past two decades.

References

Cawelti, John G. 1976. *Adventure, Mystery, Romance: Formula Stories as Art and Popular Culture.* Chicago: University of Chicago Press.

Greene, Suzanne Ellery. 1978–81. "Best Sellers." In *Handbook of American Popular Culture,* 31–50. 3 vols. Edited by M. Thomas Inge. Westport, CT: Greenwood Press.

Hart, James D. 1950. *The Popular Book: A History of America's Literary Taste.* New York: Oxford University Press.

Leavis, Q. D. 1932. *Fiction and the Reading Public.* Reprint, London: Chatto and Windus, 1965.

Long, Elizabeth. 1985. *The American Dream and the Popular Novel.* Boston, London, and Melbourne: Routledge and Kegan Paul.

Miller, Laura J. 2000. "The Best-Seller List as Marketing Tool and Historical Fiction," *Book History* 3: 286–304.

Radway, Janice A. 1989. "The Book-of-the-Month Club and the General Reader: The Uses of 'Serious Fiction.' " In *Reading in America*, 259–84. Edited by Cathy N. Davidson. Baltimore and London: Johns Hopkins University Press.

Sorensen, Alan T. 2004. "Best Seller Lists and Product Variety: The Case of Book Sales." Stanford, CA: Graduate School of Business. Available at http://www.gsb.stanford.edu/news/research/mktg_bestseller.shtml (accessed June 16, 2005).

Whiteside, Thomas. 1981. *The Blockbuster Complex*. Middletown, CT: Wesleyan University Press.

4.7. How Do Adult Readers Choose Books to Read?

A question of interest to everyone in the book trade from booksellers to librarians is *how* do people choose books. Choices are of course constrained by gatekeeping decisions made all along the line by authors who decide what to write, by publishers who pick which books get published, and by booksellers and librarians who pick which books are available in bookstores and libraries. However, despite the view that the cultural industries hold all the chips and can use big advertising to control readers and manufacture taste, readers have a huge role to play in what actually gets read. Readers are unruly and unpredictable. Big-budget, would-be blockbusters often fall flat, despite large advertising budgets. So even taking into account the constraints that narrow choices, readers themselves have the final say when it comes to whether books actually get read as opposed to produced or sold. In this section, we look at the research that focuses on the processes of selection made by individual readers.

Although readers often say they will "read anything," this statement cannot be taken literally. The UK study of book reading and borrowing, *Reading the Situation* (Book Marketing Limited 2000, 145) reports that all of the readers in the qualitative part of the study qualified their "read anything" claim by specifying various categories they would *not* read. Men said they wouldn't read romantic fiction. Many, especially women, said they would not read nonfiction. Others said they would not read war stories or anything too violent, as in this example: "I don't like books which emphasize blood and gore—I don't like war books, or the sort of crime books which my son loves" (2000, 145). *Reading the Situation* (2000, 145–6) summarizes readers' strategies as follows:

> Most respondents . . . tend to stick mainly to a few preferred genres— and sometimes to a few preferred authors . . . [M]ost of the books they read will come from a fairly narrow band (in terms of all the books that they could read). This band can and does change over time, as new authors or new genres are tried and appreciated—and when an author's works are exhausted.

Ross found that avid readers differed from novice and frustrated readers in having a number of strategies that they used in combination to make selections. When talking about book choices, avid readers often mention categories such as the following: a favorite book or author I want to reread; a new book by a "trusted author"; a book by a new author I've heard about; a book in a favorite genre; something with certain characteristics such as a strong female central character or an Old West setting or an atmosphere of suspense; or something completely new, which I'll recognize when I see it. Moving from the beginning of this list to the end, readers find it progressively harder to get the books they want, especially in public libraries. Readers with specific authors and titles in mind can use the catalog or go directly to the shelf. But those who want books with a happy ending don't get much help from the catalog. They have to rely on browsing, a method which, especially for novice readers, often ends in failure.

Choosing enjoyable books to read is clearly a crucial element in the pleasure of the reading experience. Here are some of the themes that come up repeatedly in the literature on book selection and in statements from the readers themselves.

Choosing Enjoyable Books: Easy or Difficult?

Novice readers often find it hard to choose books they will enjoy. This is the "difficulty-getting-into-it" problem. As with any learned skill, a task that an old hand finds easy can be daunting for a novice. Deborah Goodall (1989, 96) reported that one-third of returned library books in her study were not enjoyed or not finished. Typical reasons given by readers in Goodall's study (1989, 96) for not finishing a book were: " 'it wasn't what I expected,' 'it didn't appeal to me,' 'couldn't get into it really,' 'too detailed,' 'a bit boring.' " Similarly Jennings and Sear studied fiction choices by Kent Library users and found that two-thirds described having some difficulty in choosing fiction (reported in Goodall 1989, 28). When these Kent Library borrowers were asked how much they had enjoyed the returned books, the findings were as follows: 60 percent of the three hundred returned books were enjoyed; 22 percent were considered OK; and 18 percent were not enjoyed or were unfinished (reported in Goodall 1989, 95).

As could be expected, the more the readers know in advance about the book, author, or genre, the more likely they are to enjoy the chosen book. Inexperienced readers are handicapped because they know much less in advance and are less able to predict. In Ross's study, Barbara (speech language pathologist, age twenty-eight) complained, "The last three times I went to the library, I have taken out five books and I've returned them unread. I start the first page and then I know. . . . I've just been in a kind of dead end lately." Amelia (housewife, age forty-five) expressed similar trouble finding satisfying books. She is a former nonreader, who started reading for pleasure after her marriage. The first book she read for enjoyment was Steven King's *The Shining*. After this, she went on to read other horror novels, including the Halloween series and Anne Rice. Her main strategy for choosing books had been by author and genre, but at the time of the interview she had exhausted her small stock of known authors and had difficulty in finding new books of interest:

> [Disgusted] I go to the library and, like, stand there for hours. So I end up picking just at random. I pick some books up, bring them home, and end up taking them all back. You read the first couple pages, and then the author *goes on and on about some medal,* or, you know, describing [something at length]. . . . It's just so boring and you don't really get any excitement out of it.

There is a lot of substitutability among books that readers will consider acceptable, but only within a certain range. Amelia wants some real excitement of the kind she found in Steven King and Anne Rice and can't be fobbed off with books that unfold slowly and are filled with description.

Does Browsing Work?

David Spiller's (1980, 245) study of fiction borrowing indicates that browsing is a component of almost every book selection transaction. When he asked five hundred borrowers in four different British libraries how they usually went about choosing novels to borrow, this is what they said:

Author only	11 percent
Authors/some browsing	22 percent
Equal authors/browsing	36 percent
Browsing/some authors	20 percent
Browsing only	11 percent

His impression was that "most respondents had a small list of 'favourite' authors, long since exhausted, and were anxious to discover new names. A handful of respondents carried about with them notebooks full of authors' names; the majority carried something between five to ten names in their heads, and if these drew a blank on their first shelf search they resorted to browsing" (247).

Deborah Goodall's (1989) thorough overview of the research on browsing lends support to the view that for many readers browsing is a last resort that doesn't work. She has reviewed the empirical research on browsing generally and has summarized in detail eight UK studies of pleasure reading and public libraries. In most of these studies, the term "browsing" is used for what readers do when they don't have a specific author or title in mind and are looking at what's available on the shelves or on display in the hope of finding *something* they will enjoy. Willard and Teece (1983) interviewed 226 public library visitors to a suburban library in Sydney, Australia, and found that almost 50 percent had come to the library to browse. Noting that access to fiction materials has been set up to accommodate users who know specific authors and titles, these researchers described public libraries as "browser-unfriendly," a situation made worse by the fact that "dissatisfied patrons had not asked for help in finding material before giving up" (quoted in Goodall 1989, 19).

In a similar vein, Goodall summarizes a UK study by Totterdell and Bird (1976) that drew attention to how frequently both library users and non-users "mentioned the problem of choosing or finding a book." Totterdell and Bird stated that this problem is "the significant reason for people not using libraries and not coming back to libraries." They say bluntly that this situation is the fault of the library, not the user: "it is not good enough to point out that a great amount of money and time is spent selectively stocking one's branches and therefore insist, ostrich-like, that if users cannot find a book they like, it is certainly their own fault" (quoted in Goodall 1989, 24).

Overload

A big problem for novice readers is the sheer numbers of books to choose from—what Sharon Baker (1986) has called "overload." Readers feel overwhelmed. Baker (1996, 132), who has published widely on the topic of browsing, quotes a visitor to a large public library as saying, "Using the library is a scary prospect. . . . It all seems so vast and overpowering." Similarly in Ross's study Geoff (funeral service director, age twenty-nine) observed, "Libraries are tough cases to crack as far as browsing is concerned because you can be overwhelmed by sheer wave numbers. Bookstores are easier to browse in because there is usually more limited number of books available." Anything that helps readers narrow down choices to something manageable for browsing is desirable. Goodall (1989, 70) summarizes research that has found that a very high percentage of borrowed fiction comes from the just-returned shelves. Other borrowers use the alphabet as an arbitrary system for narrowing down choices to a manageable subset—they may choose only authors whose names start with, say, A or P.

If it's hard to choose books for oneself, it's even harder to choose books for others. In the five studies that Goodall reviewed that dealt with borrowing for others, Goodall found that the prevalence of library users choosing fiction for others, usually in addition to themselves, ranged from 14 percent to 30 percent (Goodall 1989, 60).

Success Breeds Success

Successful choices are part of a self-reinforcing system that sustains the pleasure of reading itself, while disappointing choices kill the desire to read. In Ross's study, Marsha (student, age twenty-six) explained, "I think that's why I'm so careful about [choosing a book]. I don't just pick up any book and read it. Because if I get disappointed, then I get put off, and I get really mad. I get mad at myself for wasting my time."

According to the browsing studies summarized by Goodall, readers are more likely to enjoy books when they have chosen them on the basis of prior knowledge about the author or title. Browsers who choose a book cold because something about it looks "interesting" are much more likely to dislike the book or not finish reading it than people who "especially looked for books by an author," "browsed and recognized an author's name," or "looked for this genre" (Goodall 1989, 96). This means that inexperienced book selectors who don't have a store of books and authors in their heads and don't know much about genres are also the least likely, when browsing, to find books that interest them. This is a problem because, while practiced readers are willing to tolerate the occasional dud, novice readers give up, not just on the particular book but on reading in general. The successful choosers become more successful and the unsuccessful stop trying.

Sharon Baker claims that a significant part of the frustration of unsuccessful browsers stems from their lack of experience and their inability to read the clues provided:

> [They] find the *act* of browsing difficult in and of itself, since they don't know *what* to look for. These facts explain why, in one study, only 34 percent of browsers found it easy to choose fiction from the library's shelves. Forty-five percent felt it was "so-so," and 21 percent found it difficult. (Baker 1996, 129)

Reading the Situation (Book Marketing Limited 2000, 149) reports that there is a gender difference in readers' willingness to live with unsuccessful book choices. Male participants in the focus groups were much more cautious in their book selection, less prepared to try books on the off chance, and less willing to give up on a book they had started than women were. Women were also "far more likely than men to admit they [had] made the wrong selection of books in the past, and to accept that this is bound to happen."

Strategies for Successful Choice

Confident readers teach themselves strategies for choosing enjoyable books that less practiced readers may never discover. Being able to choose successfully is an important skill that is never directly taught but is learned by readers who teach themselves, beginning in childhood. Each book read contributes to the bulk of reading experience that enhances the reader's ability to choose another satisfying book. In Ross's study, avid readers said things such as, "I feel books. I get a feel for a book. I am sometimes wrong but rarely" or "I'm pretty good at telling what will work out. Maybe because of all these years of persisting through books." Jean (teacher-librarian, age forty-four) describes the process as intuitive and pleasurable in itself:

> I just choose from some inner stimulus. I don't know what prompts me to choose. . . . If I start to read plays and it's a satisfying experience, I will continue to take out some plays until I find some that make me feel a little jaded or disappointed and then I might stop. . . . And you read a really good book review and think, "I can't wait until I can read that book," and to me that's the whole aura of reading. Some of it is retrospective because you deliberate on what you have read; it's current because you're experiencing; and also it's anticipatory because you know what you want to read. (Ross 2001)

When interviewees in Ross's study (2001) were asked how they go about choosing a book to read for pleasure, these avid readers typically launched into an elaborate description, involving many interrelated considerations, often starting with their own mood at the time of reading and going on variously to how they find new authors or what clues they look for on the book itself. The systems they described for choosing books depended on considerable previous experience and knowledge of authors, publishers, cover art, and conventions for promoting books and sometimes depended on a social network of family or friends who recommended and lent books. This is the "behind the eyes" knowledge that the practiced reader can draw on when considering for selection or rejection any particular book that comes to hand. Ellen (retired librarian, age sixty-six) described how she would get ideas for new authors by looking at "Good Reading" lists: "If the lists contained a fair number of books that I had read and liked, they would probably contain others that I would read and, by association of them together, it would help me choose."

Past experiences with books and remembered information from reviews or from word of mouth are carried in the reader's head and available to be called on when the reader is browsing in a bookstore or library. To be alerted to the existence of new books that will provide the reading experience they want, committed readers typically put out antennae that scan their everyday environments for clues. They tuck away for future use in memory or on lists the names of books and authors mentioned in magazine and newspaper reviews; books given currency because they have been made into films or television productions; and authors and titles that come up in conversation. Jennings and Sear (1986, 22) asked Kent Library borrowers in their study if they brought a written list of desired authors or titles with them to the library and 31 percent said that they did.

Recommendations are important, but only from a trusted source whose tastes are known to be compatible, such as certain reviewers, family members and "friends that know my taste," selected bookstore staff and librarians, and more recently Internet acquaintances. *Reading the Situation* (Book Marketing Limited 2000, 147) reported that for "women, at any level of reading, the most common and trusted source of information about new authors is personal recommendation—and their circle of friends/relations/work colleagues is also probably the most common source of books to read." In contrast to women's reliance on a personal network, the men in this study were much less likely to talk about books at all, and many declared that they couldn't trust other people's recommendations because taste was so individualistic (2000, 148). Many readers are wary of overenthusiastic recommendations. They would rather take the reading suggestion, test it for themselves, and save it for the right time without a feeling of obligation to the recommender.

For each particular instance of choice, a single factor tends to be given precedence as an overriding consideration. For many, the bedrock is mood (Ross 2001). A reader might say that the major requirement is "nothing depressing or frightening," but she also wants to be "transported, moved into a world that's different from the everyday one." Another reader might be looking primarily for a mystery story, with the secondary requirement being the presence of a smart female detective. For others the size of the book is a key factor: "And the third thing I look at [after author and the description on the back cover] is the thickness. I will reject a book even if it's a book by an author that I know if it's a small, little book." In narrowing down choices, readers are strongly guided, as noted earlier, by what they *don't* want. They can quickly rule out whole categories ("nothing too long") and entire genres ("the psychological thriller") .

Known and Trusted Authors

Readers agree that choosing books by author is the most reliable method. When David Spiller (1980, 245) interviewed five hundred people who were returning fiction books to four British public libraries, 54 percent of the 1,265 novels returned were by known authors. Choosing books by author was similarly found to be a key strategy in Jenny Hartley's report of a UK study of 200 couples who kept reading diaries over a three-month period in February, March, and April 2002. This study, which was undertaken by the Book Marketing Ltd. for the Orange Prize, recruited couples in which both people were self-identified pleasure readers. Each reader logged a daily record of the timings for the materials read and the titles of the books read. Hartley (2003) reported, "A common pattern is to read more than one title by an author in close sequence. Authors favoured with this treatment include the romantic novelists (Emma Blair, Penny Jordan, Iris Gower), and also writers such as James Clavell, Leon Uris, Douglas Adams, Terry Pratchett, J.K. Rowling, and Bernard Cornwell."

Readers in Ross's study elaborated: "I would just look at the shelves—it is just hit and miss, but then if I found an author I liked, I would go back and read everything by that author"; "I follow authors that I like and I keep up with what they are writing"; "It's like finding a gold mine and following a vein when you find a good author like Salman Rushdie. Even though one book will be of lesser quality or lesser enjoyment, I will still read them"; "I'll walk along the shelves and authors will come past me in a sort of parade and I'll think, 'Oh, yes, I feel like a little bit of Atwood today' "; "an author string is a very common way for me to read"; "you have to trust your author. If you've read everything by your favorite author you have to try to re-produce the same satisfaction and enjoyment in another author"; "I choose primarily in terms of authors. I think first of authors and then, when I have exhausted those possibilities, I'll think of types. If a library has books divided into genres then that makes it easier for me." Some readers report a feeling akin to panic when they have read all the author's books: "When I come to the end of a supply of a given thing, I'll go, 'Oh my god, what am I going to do now?' " "If you've read everything by your favorite author, you have to try to reproduce the same satisfaction and enjoyment in another author," said another reader.

Genre

Genre is second only to the author in providing clues as to the kind of experience the reader can expect from a book. In fact, genre is often used in conjunction with author: "If I am looking for something light to read like a mystery novel, I will look at the authors—I have certain authors I like and if I see something I haven't read before." Once the reader starts to browse within a range of books, then the cover and the clues provided on the book itself become important. As Charles (program coordinator, age twenty-three) explained, "When you're as genre-specific as I guess I am, and read as voraciously as I do, you're looking for some quick identifiers on what's a good book. It'll take me ten minutes to go in [to the science fiction section], get five books, and leave because I'm just so familiar with the genre in general."

The most frequently mentioned "quick identifiers" are the cover, the blurb on the back, and the sample page. This finding is similar to the Book Industry Study Group survey result that 29 percent of readers indicated that the description or synopsis on the book jacket or cover was "very important" in making choices (BISG 1984, 133). Titles are also important—readers said they were drawn both to an unusual, catchy title (in the case of an unfamiliar book) and to a familiar title that they had heard about before. Charles stressed that "the cover actually does play a really important role in the choice" but was not an overriding factor: "If Margaret Weiss was wrapped in a brown paper bag, I'd still pick her book."

A problem beginning readers face is that it takes a long apprenticeship in reading to build up the depth of knowledge needed to interpret the cover information that provides these valuable clues to experienced readers. Series books such as Harlequins simplify the process of choice by highlighting genre, publisher, and cover in one easily identifiable logo.

Ease of Access

The likelihood of a reader's choosing a particular book can be regarded as a ratio of the degree of pleasure expected from the book divided by the degree of work needed to appropriate, physically and mentally, the book. Some readers said that they often read "books lying around" or they would "read what's around me" or "books I find at home." "I will not go out of my way to read this book," one reader said, but did in fact read it because the book came easily to hand. Conversely, readers reported being willing to put themselves on waiting lists, special order a book, or pay hard-cover prices to read a book that they expected to yield a high degree of pleasure. It follows that people who want to promote a particular book choice can either increase the reader's expectation of pleasure from a book or decrease the work needed for the reader to acquire the book.

Research Tells Us

Ross's analysis (2001) of almost two hundred open-ended interviews with readers suggests that a comprehensive model for the process of choosing a book to read for pleasure must include five related elements that come into play in concert with each other.

1. **Reading experience wanted: the "what mood am I in?" test**

   - Familiarity versus novelty

   - Safety versus risk

   - Easy versus challenging

   - Upbeat and positive versus hard-hitting, ironic, or critical

   - Do I want to be reassured/stimulated/frightened/amazed?

   - Do I want my beliefs and values to be confirmed or to be challenged by an uncomfortable but stimulating new perspective?

2. **Alerting sources that the reader uses to find out about new books**

   - Browsing in bookstores or libraries, including looking for genre labels, limiting searching to certain subject or genre areas, and monitoring displays of new books and "just returned" shelves

   - Recommendations from friends, coworkers, or family members

   - Reviews or advertisements in newspapers, magazines, Internet, radio, and television

   - Viewing dramatized productions of an authors' work in stage-plays, television, or films

   - "Literary log-rolling" (books highlighted by trusted, favored authors, either within their own books or on publicity blurbs, for example, "Pynchon writes jacket blurbs for DeLillo")

- Lists (prize-winning books; books made familiar on course curricula; lists of recommended books produced by libraries, literary critics, or other readers)

- Serendipity

3. **Elements of a book that readers take into account to match book choices to the reading experience desired**

- Subject (related to genre in fiction and to topic in nonfiction)

- Treatment (popular versus literary or serious style; conventional and familiar versus unpredictable; upbeat versus negative or pessimistic in tone)

- Characters depicted (e.g., presence of strong female characters or sympathetic characters or depressing characters; use of schematized black-and-white characterization; focus on one or two characters or dispersion of interest over many characters)

- Setting (the kind of world that the reader enters in reading the book)

- Ending (happy or sad; predictable or unexpected; resolved or open-ended)

- Physical size of the book ("thick books" versus "quick reads")

4. **Clues on the book itself used to determine the reading experience offered**

- Author

- Title

- Genre

- Sample page

- Cover

- Publisher

The more experienced the reader, the greater their ability to use these clues to make subtle discriminations about the anticipated reading experience.

5. **Cost in time or money involved for the reader in getting intellectual or physical access to a particular book**

- Intellectual access (previous knowledge of content or of literary conventions needed by the reader to make sense of the text)

- Physical access (time and work required before the reader can lay hands on the book itself)

• Length of time required or degree of cognitive and emotional commitment required by the book itself (easy, quick read versus long, demanding read)

Case 22: "I very rarely pick up a book that I've never heard of."

Marsha (student, age twenty-six) is a practiced reader in Ross's study. She described how she uses an array of cues in concert with each other when choosing books:

• previous experience with the author ("It's very safe to know that you've got an author that you like, and there are more books sitting there waiting. . . . I like the fact that LeCarre is still writing.")

• the reputation of the book ("I always thought I should read important books.")

• the reputation of the publisher ("I decided that Penguins . . . were important books.")

• recommendations of friends and family ("So it's important for someone to recommend a book. I very rarely pick up a book that I've never heard of.")

• clues provided by the packaging of the book itself ("I always read the blurbs on the back. I'm easily put off or become very cynical of something that's too glowing.")

Comments

Each instance of a reader's engagement with a particular book takes place within a personal context that includes the following: the reader's literary competencies derived from previous experiences reading books; the reader's preferences developed during a lifetime of reading; and events going on in the rest of the reader's life at any particular time, which in turn relate to the reader's mood and time available for reading. Practiced book choosers have all this information to draw on when making a selection at any given time.

To Read More on Choosing Books

Baker, Sharon. 1996. "A Decade's Worth of Research on Browsing Fiction Collections." In *Guiding the Reader to the Next Book*, 127–48. Edited by Kenneth D. Shearer. New York: Neal-Schuman.

> Having summarized the research on browsing fiction collections, Baker provides tips on how libraries can help users narrow their choices by creating smaller subsets from which to choose. Suggestions include the following: eye-level displays marked with a topical header, booklists prominently displayed just inside the library's front door, advertising the returned book shelves, physically separating books by genre, and spine stickers with logos indicating the book's genre or with a label that reads, "Recommended by a patron."

Ross, Catherine Sheldrick, and Mary Kay Chelton. 2001. "Reader's Advisory: Matching Mood and Material." *Library Journal* (February 1): 52–55.

> Provides concrete examples of how libraries can help users, especially novice users, find enjoyable books.

References

Baker, Sharon. 1986. "Overload, Browsers, and Selections." *Library and Information Science Research* 8 (October–December): 315–29.

Baker, Sharon. 1996. "A Decade's Worth of Research on Browsing Fiction Collections." In *Guiding the Reader to the Next Book*, 127–48. Edited by Kenneth D. Shearer. New York: Neal-Schuman.

Book Industry Study Group. 1984. *1983 Consumer Research Study on Reading and Book Purchasing: Focus on Adults*. New York: Book Industry Study Group.

Book Marketing Limited. 2000. *Reading the Situation: Book Reading, Buying and Borrowing Habits in Britain*. London: Library and Information Commission.

Goodall, Deborah. 1989. *Browsing in Public Libraries*. Occasional Paper No 1. Department of Library and Information Studies, Loughborough University of Technology.

Hartley, Jenny. 2003. "The Way We Read Now." *The Bookseller Magazine,* (April 11): 55.

Jennings, Barbara, and Lyn Sear. 1986. *How Readers Select Fiction*. Kent County Library Research and Development Report No 9. Kent County, England: Education Committee, Kent County Council.

Ross, Catherine Sheldrick. 2001. "Making Choices: What Readers Say about Choosing Books to Read for Pleasure." *Readers, Reading and Librarians*. Theme issue edited by Bill Katz. *The Acquisitions Librarian* 25: 5–21.

Spiller, David. 1980. "The Provision of Fiction for Public Libraries." *Journal of Librarianship* 12, no.4: 238–66.

Totterdell, B., and J. Bird. 1976. *The Effective Library. Report of the Hillingdom Project on Public Library Effectiveness*. London: London Library Association.

Willard, P., and V. Teece. 1983. "The Browser and the Library." *Public Library Quarterly* 4, no. 1: 55–63.

4.8. Advising Readers

Getting personal advice on reading matter is something readers both yearn for and dread. Reading is a very private act, and receiving advice from someone who wants to instruct, impose, or proselytize is unwelcome. On the other hand, avid readers are hungry for suggestions about new books and authors from people they trust. For that reason, they turn for help from friends and family members whose tastes are known to be similar to their own and they make use of book reviews and reading lists. Sometimes personal networks are inadequate, however, and readers have to look further afield for advice. As Francine Fialkoff, editor of *Library Journal*, has noted (Fialkoff 1998, 58), "All the surveys we've seen, conducted by librarians as well as non-librarians, indicate that there is virtually no service library users value more highly than the ability to match a book with a reader or to answer the question, 'What do I read next?' " Anyone—librarian, bookseller, teacher, friend—who helps readers identify the next book to read is a readers' advisor. Of course readers' advisory includes advice on both fiction and nonfiction.

Bookstores are ahead of many libraries in the readers' advisory area. They have a long tradition of what they call "hand-selling," which means putting a likely book right into the buyer's hand. Bookstores have also been quicker than libraries to recognize that organizing books by genres, providing good signage, creating attractive displays, and providing staff recommendations are all good ways to help readers find books they will want to buy and take home. And unlike library staff, bookstore staff members are never heard to say to customers, "Why are you wasting your time reading a Harlequin when you could be reading a *good* book like *Jane Eyre*?" Whether book advice happens in the context of a bookstore or library or in an informal exchange between friends or family members, the elements of successful advising are the same: respecting the readers' tastes and drawing on what you know about those tastes and the universe of books to make a successful match.

In public libraries, two elements are currently recognized in effective readers' advisory work: the behind-the-scenes work—sometimes called "passive strategies"—and the face-to-face interaction that librarians call the readers' advisory interview although users experience it as a conversation about books. So-called passive strategies include putting spine labels on books, shelving books into separated genre collections such as Mysteries or Science Fiction, creating bookmarks and annotated book lists, and setting up attractive displays that are constantly replenished. Research shows circulation increases when libraries adopt these strategies that Sharon Baker describes as helping browsers cope with overload (see section 4.7). Like the layout of the bookstore, the physical arrangement of the fiction collection itself should help readers choose books. When these strategies are pursued, the library itself becomes a prop for the readers' advisory conversation.

Readers' Advisory in Public Libraries

There have been three phases of readers' advisory (RA) work in public libraries in North America, which can be summarized as follows: 1) Don't ask, don't tell; 2) Uplifting the masses; and 3) Putting the reader in the driver's seat. Each phase can be illustrated by a book that embodies the spirit of the period: F. B. Perkins's *Public Libraries in the United States* (1876); Jennie Flexner's *A Readers' Advisory Service* (1934); and Joyce Saricks and Nancy Brown's *Reader's Advisory Service in the Public Library* (1989/97). As Bill Crowley (2004, 11) has pointed out, in 1876—the same momentous year when the American Library Association was founded and *Library Journal* was launched—opinion leader F. B. Perkins of the Boston Public Library was arguing *against* RA service. According to Perkins, it was "unreasonable" and an "undeserved annoyance" for library users to "plague the librarian by trying to make him pick out books" instead of choosing their own books (Perkins 1876, 428–9). Lazy readers should not expect busy librarians to do their work for them in the Boston Public Library.

By the 1920s, public libraries were ready to build on fifty years of professional experience by moving confidently to fill a social need for public education in the postwar years. According to Robert Ellis Lee (1966, 46), separate RA offices were established in the public libraries of Detroit and Cleveland in 1922, of Chicago and Milwaukee in 1923, and of Indianapolis in 1924. New full-time positions were created to staff the "Readers Bureaus" set up in major public libraries across the United States. Publicity for the New York Public Library (NYPL) service appeared under the heading, "THE BOOK That Leads You On" and asked, "Are you interested in systematic reading? Would you use a reading list made for you, based on what you have previously read?" Readers' advisory service during this period emphasized "reading with a purpose"—systematic reading on socially significant topics for purposes of self-improvement and self-education. The emphasis was on making the public library primarily an educational institution directed toward the diffusion of knowledge (Learned 1924).

Jennie Flexner's *A Readers' Advisory Service* (1934) explains how readers' advisors interviewed clients as the basis for drawing up individualized, annotated reading lists and then discussed the list with clients in follow-up interviews. These lists were designed to provide a variety of viewpoints on a serious topic such as economics, sociology, the life of Christ, or classical Greek drama, while leading the reader in orderly, consecutive steps from introductory works to more complex treatments. Margaret Munro recalled how, as a NYPL staff member, she was privileged to have a series of training conferences with Jennie Flexner in the Readers' Advisor's Office of the central library: "Booklover that I was, I came alive to the art of reading guidance as we talked and as I poured over the rich collection of bibliographies constructed for individual readers and read the correspondence guiding the inquirers to their use" (Munro 1986, 437).

But interviewing readers, creating personalized reading lists, and corresponding with individual readers was labor-intensive. So in 1925 the American Library Association issued its first bibliographic essay in a series called "Reading with a Purpose," designed to cut down on the work needed to create personalized lists for each individual reader. Each essay or "reading course" was prepared by a subject specialist and consisted of an introductory essay on the topic followed by descriptions of eight to twelve books arranged in the order in which they should be read to achieve a systematic understanding of the topic. According to Robert Ellis Lee (1966, 49–50), by 1933 when the series of sixty-seven reading courses finally ended, 850,000 copies of the "Reading with a Purpose" pamphlets had been sold.

Given the long-entrenched suspicion of fiction (see section 1.2 on the "fiction problem") and the postwar value assigned to adult education, it should not be supposed that reading with a purpose encompassed popular fiction read for pleasure. John Chancellor (1931, 138) urged readers' advisors to promote the library as a "people's university" and emphasized the importance of "consecutive reading." He said, "Let us emphasize *thoroughness* as much as we can, the getting of a whole and complete view. . . . Let us not just urge people to read—read haphazardly—but to 'read with a purpose,' a very apt slogan." The job of the readers' advisor was accordingly to stimulate purposeful, consecutive, developmental reading of "solid books." Unfortunately, as admitted by Virginia Bacon, adviser in Adult Education from Portland, Oregon, many individuals who showed up at the readers' advisors desk were "only vaguely or momentarily interested in study" and may have been drawn in by "the 'get wise easy' type of advertisement." Some had minds "made lazy by . . . easy victories over popular magazines, light fiction and moving pictures" (Bacon 1927, 317). Nevertheless, Bacon (1927, 318) said, "With us, as elsewhere, demand is already taxing our ability to give adequate service."

By the 1940s, this second phase of readers' advisory had lost momentum, and it was folded into adult services. The special job designation of the readers' advisor was phased out, not to reappear for another fifty years. Except in the area of children's services where librarians continued to act as suggesters of books, the emphasis shifted to information and information technology. When RA returned in the 1980s, it had transmogrified into a different creature. New thinking about popular culture and pleasure reading set the stage for another kind readers' advisory service in public libraries that put less emphasis on improvement and uplift and more emphasis on pleasure reading, less emphasis on nonfiction and more emphasis on genres of popular fiction (Balcom 1988; Ross 1991).

Readers' Advisory, New-Style

Bill Crowley (2004, 19) dates the contemporary revival of RA in North American public libraries from 1984, the year of the founding of the Adult Reading Round Table (ARRT) in the Chicago metropolitan area under the leadership of such RA advocates as Ted Balcom, Merle Jacob, and Joyce Saricks. The book by Joyce Saricks and Nancy Brown titled *Readers' Advisory Service in the Public Library* (1989) embodies the new approach to readers' advisory. Now in its third edition as updated by Joyce Saricks (2005), this indispensable guide stresses that readers' advisory service "is a patron-oriented library service for adult fiction readers" (Saricks and Brown 1997, 1). The emphasis throughout is on a knowledgeable, nonjudgmental approach that values all kinds of reading and takes the view that the reader, not the librarian, knows best what kind of reading experience is desired.

Contemporary RA service emphasizes the importance of knowing the appeal factors of the various popular genres of fiction and recognizes that people have a variety of purposes for reading. According to Saricks and Brown (1997, 107), the Downers Grove (Illinois) Public Library reassures readers by posting behind the service desk a sign saying, "Rosenberg's First Law of Reading: Never apologize for your reading tastes." Saricks says that this sign is often commented on by users and has been the starting point for many satisfying readers' advisory interviews.

In the United Kingdom, the effort to foster pleasure reading goes under the name "reader development" and includes readers' advisory, promotion, and outreach. Briony Train, coauthor of *Reading and Reader Development: The Pleasure of Reading* (2003, 31–33), notes that until recently in the United Kingdom, adult services librarians provided passive service to the fiction reader, whereas children's librarians, in contrast, took an active role in providing reading advice and in organizing programs to foster the enjoyment of reading. This situation changed, starting in the late 1980s and early 1990s, with a new emphasis on pleasure reading from a coalition of groups. In 1992, a conference *Reading the Future: A Place for Literature in Public Libraries* (Van Riel 1992) brought together publishers, booksellers, librarians, and arts administrators under the banner of promoting fiction reading. Delegates emphasized the need for a "large-scale change in library culture," including the "[n]eed to counter the move to make literature less important than information" in libraries (Van Riel 1992, 45).

Rachel Van Riel has been one of the leaders in reader development in Britain. She is the director of Opening the Book, a company she founded in 1991 to promote literature from the reader's point of view. On her "Opening the Book" Web site (http://www.openingthebook.com/; accessed June 16, 2005), Van Riel defines "reader development" as something that "sells the reading experience and what it can do for you, rather than selling individual books or writers." She says, "The best book in the world is quite simply the one you like the best." She emphasizes an egalitarian approach to reader development in contrast to projects that are explicitly targeted at social inclusion: "The problem with 'socially inclusive' reader development projects is that they inevitably proceed from a 'them' and 'us' attitude—'we' are bringing the benefits of reading to 'you' out there who need them. Reader development begins with an assumption of fundamental equality between readers—no one reader is more important than another—while celebrating the differences of individual reading experiences."

Putting the Emphasis on the Quality of the Reading Experience

The key factor that distinguishes this new-style readers' advisory or "reader development" is that both put emphasis not on the quality of the book but on the quality of the reading experience, as determined by the reader. The publication in 1982 of the first edition of Betty Rosenberg's *Genreflecting* was a precursor of this new reader-centered approach. As Diana Tixier Herald (2000, xiii) says in her Preface to the fifth edition, "This guide . . . is an attempt to help bring together readers and the books that will give them pleasure." *Genreflecting* was the first of what is now a sizable collection of professional reference tools that allows librarians to approach readers' advisory work in the same professional way that they would approach any reference question, using professional tools to find answers. No longer is there any reason for readers' advisors to limit their book suggestions to the scope of their own personal reading. As the readers' advisor talks to the reader about what kind of crime fiction (or romance or adventure or western or science fiction) she or he enjoys, the advisor can show the reader the relevant section in *Genreflecting* and use the categories provided to help narrow down, for example, whether the crime reader wants police procedurals, hard-boiled mysteries, or mysteries with an anthropological interest, or whether the romance reader wants contemporary romance, romantic suspense, historical romance, or Regency.

Genreflecting was followed by other tools designed to help readers' advisors answer the "What do I read next?" question. By 1996, professional tools for RA had expanded to the point that the American Library Association's Readers' Advisory Committee (1996) found it necessary to produce a bibliography of recommended tools. Some RA guides focus on particular age levels such as Diana Tixier Herald's *Teen Genreflecting* (1997). Others specialize in a particular genre such as Kristin Ramsdell's *Romance Fiction: A Guide to the Genre* (1999) and Nancy Pearl's *Now Read This: A Guide to Mainstream Fiction* (1999) or cover many genres published within a limited time period such as the annual *What Do I Read Next?* by Neil Barron et al (1990–). The electronic readers' advisory tool NoveList (http://www.epnet.com/public/novelist.asp) allows for retrieval from a database of more than 100,000 adult, young adult and children's titles, searchable by author, title, and subject. Internet-based sites are increasingly valuable resources for readers' advisors. The Downers Grove Public Library has taken a leadership role in becoming a gateway for electronic readers' advisory resources (http://www.webrary.org).

Genre guides that provide lists of authors and titles help with half of the job. The other half is to find out, through a conversation with the reader, what the reader thinks is a good book. Readers are often wary of advice, however well intentioned, when it seems that the advisor wants to sell a list of his or her own favorites, without finding out the reader's own tastes and preferences. When Ross sent library and information science students in an introductory reference course to a public library to ask for help in finding "some good books to read," one participant in this RA study commented on the tact needed in the RA process: "I will never forget how intimate and private this entirely professional and public exchange seemed to me, how vulnerable it made me feel." Another reader in Ross's RA study reported how unhelpful it was to be regaled with a list of the advisor's own favorite books:

> I was wondering if she were just going to show me her own favorite books, or would she ask more questions to gauge what I prefer to read. We arrived at the stacks. She said, "Oh, here's one by Anita Shreve. And here, this is a good one too. I enjoyed this one." She handed me *Where the Heart Is* by Billie Letts. "It's good if you like romance." She had handed the book to me without really asking whether I liked romance, which I don't. I said, "Well, actually, I'm not really into romance books. I prefer something a little deeper." She said, "OK, here's another Oprah book; it's a dark story" and handed me *Ellen Foster* by Kaye Gibbons. . . . She then said, "Do you like John Grisham? I really like his books." "No, not so much," I replied. "I prefer something with more colorful language, more on the literature side." She said, "Colleen McCullough would be good for you then. I enjoy her books."

Nor does it work to have a list of canonical "Good Books" and recommend these same good books to everyone. What counts is the reader's *experience* of the text. As we have seen in section 4.7, the term "good book" is relative. Effective readers' advisors discover readers' tastes by inviting them to talk about their own engagement with books or authors. For many avid readers, talking about books is an enjoyable experience in itself and an extension of the pleasurable reading experience. To initiate the conversation about the reader's experience, the readers' advisor may say, "Can you tell me about a book that you've really enjoyed?" followed possibly by, "What did you enjoy most about that book?" and "What do you feel in the mood for reading now?" This is the conversation about books that librarians call "the readers' advisory interview," an indispensable element in the process of matching book to reader (Ross, Nilsen, and Dewdney 2002, 162–75).

The features of preferred books that the reader chooses to talk about provide important clues about reading tastes (Smith 2000). Does the reader talk about fast-paced action or leisurely description? Does the reader emphasize a single strong character or the complex interweaving of many characters, perhaps through several generations? Is setting important, and if so what settings in time and place are preferred? Is the reader looking for something that is soothing and comforting or challenging and quirky? Are there types of books that the reader dislikes and *won't* read? As was noted in section 4.1, Philip Ennis discovered that "People reject or block out vast areas of books" (Ennis 1965, 11–12)—as, for example, the reader quoted above who is "not really into romance books" and prefers something "more on the literature side." In readers' advisory work, there is seldom a single right answer—there are usually many books that would suit the reader. But there are also many wrong answers—books that would *not* be appropriate for that particular reader.

Saricks and Brown (1997, 35–55) emphasize the importance for readers' advisors of learning how to identify what they call the book's "appeal factors"—pacing, characterization, storyline, and frame. The readers' advisor's job is to help narrow down choices to a manageable number of suggestions that match the reader's stated interests and tastes. Joyce Saricks (2001, 3) advocates that readers' advisors make suggestions rather than recommendations: "Learning to suggest, rather than to recommend, was another major breakthrough. . . . Recommending places us in the role of expert: Take this book; it is good for you. *Suggesting*, on the other hand, makes us partners with readers."

As expertise about new-style readers' advisory work is being developed in public libraries and shared on lists such as Fiction_L, the next step has been the sharing of best practices. Edited collections such as Kenneth Shearer's *Guiding the Reader to the Next Book* (1996), Bill Katz's *Readers, Reading and Librarians* (2001), Kenneth Shearer and Robert Burgin's *The Readers' Advisor's Companion* (2001) and Robert Burgin's *Nonfiction Readers' Advisory* (2004) provide insights about RA work distilled from practice and research.

Rachel Van Riel's Opening the Book Web site contains descriptions of a number of pioneering projects, including the following: reader-centered library design and layout; *whichbook.net*, a way of searching a database of books by allowing readers to specify the dimensions of a book that matter to them such as predictable/unpredictable, gentle/violent, happy/sad, no sex/sex, optimistic/bleak; and *word-of-mouth.org.uk*, which is a discussion board for readers to make recommendations within specific reader-centered categories. At word-of-mouth, in the "Indulgence" category of books read "purely for enjoyment," there are fifty mini-reviews posted by readers about beloved books, including Alice Sebold's *Lovely Bones,* Daphne du Maurier's *Jamaica Inn,* Penelope Lively's *The Photograph,* Roald Dahl's *The Twits,* Iain Pears' *The Instance of the Fingerpost,* Agatha Christie's *Peril at End House,* and Jake Arnott's *Truecrime.*

In view of this reaffirmation of the value of books and reading, public libraries now see themselves as the place for readers to come to get help in choosing pleasure reading. Many readers, on the other hand, are still unaware that readers' advisory is what libraries do. Said one reader in Ross's RA study, "It never occurred to me before to go to a library for help in finding pleasure reading material. I have usually gone to a large bookstore for advice. My vision of the library has been one where a person would go for other types of assistance, mainly in finding information regarding a subject." However, statistics (Clevinger 2004, 47) showing that between 2000 and 2003 American Public Library adult circulation has increased by 25 percent in absolute terms and by 13 percent per capita suggests a growing market for a well-executed matchmaking service between reader and book.

Research Tells Us

A presenter at the *Reading the Future* Conference held in York, England, in March 1992, John Sumsion drew on his experience with the Public Lending Right to summarize some interesting patterns relating to the circulation of books in public libraries in the United Kingdom.

- The proportion of published British books that are acquired by UK public libraries is about 5 to 10 percent.

- The top three categories of book circulation in UK public libraries were general fiction—20 percent; romance—15.6 percent; and mystery/crime/thrillers—15.6 percent.

- Twentieth-century poetry is acquired and found on shelves, but almost none of it circulates.

Sumsion concludes with recommendations for promotion: 1) use prize short lists for promotion; 2) promote new novelists by collecting and displaying reviews; 3) promote genres and types of fiction; and 4) do something about shelving to get over the anonymity of A–Z shelving.

Case 23: Tailor-Making the Pitch

Readers' advisory goes on informally all the time among people who love books and talk about them. Here is a description of readers' advisory between friends, as described by Rita, a fifty-five-year-old married homemaker in Ross's study of committed readers.

Interviewer: So you'll sort of "tailor-make" your "pitch," as it were, to the person you're [recommending a book to]?

Rita: [interrupting] Oh yeah. I mean there's no point . . . as a matter of fact, I have a friend, a Scottish woman that I know, who does not read murder mysteries, and her husband does. . . . Her husband said, "I tried to introduce her to one" and I said, "Well, what did you give her?" Well, he gave her an Elmore Leonard— I don't read him very much, he's kind of like a Mickey Spillane–type of thing—and I said, "Oh my God, that's the worst possible thing to have started her on!" So recently, when she went off to visit her mother in Victoria, I said to her,

"I'm going to give you something to read." And I gave her *The Scold's Bridle* by Minette Walters. Well, she was riveted by this book! She didn't know what a scold's bridle was, which is the contraption that, in medieval times, they used to clamp on the mouths of women who they thought were nags. . . . And the plot revolved around this medieval piece of equipment. She found the whole thing riveting! She called the other day and she said, "Do you have any more of that author?" and it made me feel so good!

Interviewer: You'd opened up a whole new avenue.

Rita: Yes! I'd opened up a whole avenue of something for somebody else. Now she, on the other hand, has been reading a lot about Tuscany—travel-type novels—factual, on Tuscany, because we're talking about maybe going, two couples. So she's given me the name of her author. And I'm going off to find something about that, so that could be a whole new avenue for me.

Comments

Rita's discussion of "tailor-making" her pitch underscores the importance of matching appeal factors of the book to the reader's interest. Effective matching goes beyond identifying genre. In this case, the match was successful because the readers' advisor picked a mystery that connected with her friend's interest in women's issues.

What Libraries Can Do

1. Recognize that knowledge about genres of fiction and their appeal is an important competency for public library staff (Smith 2000, 139). One good way to develop an understanding of appeal factors is to read five books in a new genre every year to get an understanding of the genre. This is the five-book challenge first issued by Ann Bouricius in her *Romance Readers' Advisory* (2000) and expanded by Joyce Saricks in *The Readers' Advisory Guide to Genre Fiction* (2001). For fifteen genres, Saricks suggests five authors and titles that are good starting points for exploring a genre. To diversify your background, start by reading in the genre that you have read the least and have always thought you don't like. The experience may surprise you.

2. Create a physical environment that says, in effect, "In this library, we care about your reading interests and want to help you find books that you would enjoy. We are the place to come not just for factual information, but for the delights of story." Libraries need to change the public's mental model of the library so that they see it as a place to get advice about books to read. Public libraries have a lot to learn from bookstores when it comes to creating a welcoming environment for readers. A good start is to provide comfortable chairs for reading near the fiction stacks. Readers' advisors need to be situated near the fiction collection so that they can be prepared to offer help. The professional RA tools such as the *Genreflecting* series are of interest to readers too and should be shelved where library users can find and use them. Clear and readable signs should advertise the existence of RA service by saying something like, "Wondering what to read next? Ask us for suggestions."

3. Forget the stereotypes about readers. Kim Kofmel's interview-based study of thirty-two self-identified readers of science fiction (SF) and fantasy indicates that SF readers are not just young, male, white computer geeks but span the spectrum (Kofmel 2004). Making assumptions about presumed reading tastes on the basis of age or gender—for example, imagining that an older female reader will prefer a Regency to a contemporary romance featuring explicit sex—is problematic.

To Read More on Readers' Advisory

Chelton, Mary K. 1999. "What We Know and Don't Know about Reading, Readers, and Readers' Advisory Services." *Public Libraries* 38, no. 1 (January/February): 42–47.
    Summarizes research on reading and readers and discusses the implications of this research for public libraries. Notes Chelton, "Librarians would also do well to pay more attention to how people read popular texts, rather than to what they read" (45).

Elkin, Judith, Briony Train, and Debbie Denham. 2003. *Reading and Reader Development: The Pleasure of Reading*. London: Facet.
    This book, which combines the authors' academic and practice-based knowledge in the area of reading for pleasure, broadly defined, provides a state-of-the-art summary of best practices in reader development in the United Kingdom and elsewhere. Denham's chapter, "Reading: A UK National Focus," provides a useful summary of national programs in Britain to promote reading such as the following: The National Year of Reading sponsored in 1998 by the National Literacy Trust; the National Reading Campaign, which funded projects that reached out to novice adult readers; and Reading Is Fundamental, which has distributed over 450,000 free books to more than 150,000 children and young people.

Herald, Diana Tixier. 2000. *Genreflecting: A Guide to Reading Interests in Genre Fiction*. 5th ed. Englewood, CO: Libraries Unlimited.

An invaluable guide that lists authors and books, grouped by genres, themes, and types. The companion *Genreflecting* Web site at http://genreflecting.com/ sponsored by Libraries Unlimited provides information on genres, a list of library information science faculty who teach readers' advisory courses, and an "Ask the Experts" service.

Saricks, Joyce G. 2001. *The Readers' Advisory Guide to Genre Fiction*. Chicago: American Library Association.

Written by one of the world's best readers' advisors, this invaluable resource provides an overview of fifteen genres, including "gentle reads," "women's lives and relationships," and "literary fiction" as well as science fiction, mysteries, romance, thrillers, historical fiction, westerns, and so on. Each chapter contains a discussion of the genre's appeal to readers, a section on key authors and subgenres, "Sure Bets," and suggestions of questions to ask in the readers' advisory interview.

Saricks, Joyce G. 2001. "The Best Tools for Advisors and How to Integrate Them into Successful Transactions." In *The Readers' Advisor's Companion*, 165–77. Edited by Kenneth D. Shearer and Robert Burgin. Englewood, CO: Libraries Unlimited.

Saricks provides an overview of electronic and print reference tools and explains how readers' advisors can use them "to create truly satisfying conversations about books with readers, setting up the long-term relationships on which readers' advisory thrives" (166).

References

American Library Association's Readers' Advisory Committee, Collection Development Section, RUSA. 1996. "Readers' advisory reference tools: A suggested list of fiction sources for all libraries." *RQ* 36, no. 2 (winter): 206–29.

Bacon, Virginia Cleaver. 1927. "Possibilities of Informal Education Under Library Guidance." *ALA Bulletin* 21: 317–19.

Balcom, Ted. 1988. "Rediscovering Readers' Advisory—and Its Rewards." *Illinois Libraries* 70, no. 9: 583–6.

Barron, Neil, Wayne Barton, Kristen Ramsdell, and Steven A. Stilwell. 1990–present. *What Do I Read Next? A Reader's Guide to Current Genre Fiction*. Detroit, MI: Gale Research.

Bouricius, Ann. 2000. *The Romance Readers' Advisory: The Librarian's Guide to Love in the Stacks*. Chicago: American Library Association.

Burgin, Robert, ed. 2004. *Nonfiction Readers' Advisory*. Westport, CT: Libraries Unlimited.

Chancellor, John. 1931. "Helping Readers with a Purpose." *ALA Bulletin* 25, no. 4 (April): 136–9.

Chelton, Mary K. 1993. "Read Any Good Books Lately? Helping Patrons Find What they Want." *Library Journal* (May 1): 33–37.

Clevinger, Charity L. 2004. "Public Library Circulation and Expenditures Increase in 2003." American Libraries 35, no. 10 (November): 47–48.

Crowley, Bill. 2004. "A History of Readers' Advisory Service in the Public Library." In *Nonfiction Readers' Advisory*, 3–29. Edited by Robert Burgin. Westport, CT: Libraries Unlimited.

Ennis, Philip H. 1965. *Adult Book Reading in the United States: A Preliminary Report.* (National Opinion Research Center Report, no. 105). Chicago: National Opinion Research Center.

Fialkoff, Francine. 1998. "New Twists on an Old Service." *Library Journal* 123 (October 15): 58.

Fiction_L Archive. Available at http://www. webrary.org/rs/flmenu.html (accessed June 16, 2005).

Flexner, Jennie. 1934. *A Readers' Advisory Service*. New York: American Association for Adult Education.

Herald, Diana Tixier. 2000. *Genreflecting: A Guide to Reading Interests in Genre Fiction.* 5th ed. Englewood, CO: Libraries Unlimited.

Herald, Diana Tixier. 1997. *Teen Genreflecting*. Englewood, CO: Libraries Unlimited.

Katz, Bill, ed. 2001. *Readers, Reading and Librarians*. New York: Haworth Press (published simultaneously as Vol. 25 of the journal *Acquisitions Librarian*).

Kofmel, Kim. 2004. "Sci-Fi 101." *Library Journal* (September 1).

Learned, William S. 1924. *The American Public Library and the Diffusion of Knowledge.* New York: Harcourt, Brace.

Lee, Robert Ellis. 1966. *Continuing Education for Adults through the American Public Library, 1833–1964.* Chicago: American Library Association.

Munro, Margaret E. 1986. "Vivid Colors of High Significance." *RQ* 25, no. 4 (Summer): 437–8.

Pearl, Nancy. 1999. *Now Read This: A Guide to Mainstream Fiction, 1978–1998.* Englewood, CO: Libraries Unlimited.

Perkins, F. B. 1876. *Public Libraries in the United States of America: Their History, Condition, and Management.* Washington, DC: Government Printing Office.

Ramsdell, Kristin. 1999. *Romance Fiction: A Guide to the Genre*. Englewood, CO: Libraries Unlimited.

Ross, Catherine Sheldrick. 1991. "Readers' Advisory Service: New Directions." *RQ* 30, no. 4: 503–18.

Ross, Catherine Sheldrick, Kirsti Nilsen, and Patricia Dewdney. 2002. *Conducting the Reference Interview*. New York: Neal-Schuman.

Saricks, Joyce G. 2001. *The Readers' Advisory Guide to Genre Fiction*. Chicago: American Library Association.

Saricks, Joyce G., and Nancy Brown. 1989. 2nd ed., 1997. 3rd ed., 2005. *Readers' Advisory Service in the Public Library.* Chicago and London: American Library Association.

Shearer, Kenneth D. 1996. *Guiding the Reader to the Next Book*. New York: Neal-Schuman.

Shearer, Kenneth D., and Robert Burgin, eds. 2001. *The Readers' Advisor's Companion*. Englewood, CO: Libraries Unlimited.

Smith, Duncan. 2000. "Talking with Readers: A Competency Based Approach to Readers' Advisory Service." *Reference & User Services Quarterly* 40, no. 2 (Winter): 135–42.

Sumsion, John. 1992. "Who Reads What in Libraries?" In *Reading the Future: A Place for Literature in Public Libraries*, 47–57. Edited by Rachel Van Riel. London: The Arts Council of Great Britain and Library Association Publishing.

Train, Briony. 2003. "Reader Development." In *Reading and Reader Development: The Pleasure of Reading*, 30–57. Edited by Judith Elkin, Briony Train, and Debbie Denham. London: Fawcett.

Van Riel, Rachel, ed. 1992. *Reading the Future: A Place for Literature in Public Libraries*. London: The Arts Council of Great Britain and Library Association Publishing.

Van Riel, Rachel. www. openingthebook.com/website (accessed June 16, 2005).

4.9. Reading as a Social Activity

Most of the research on reading has viewed it as a solitary activity. Often the reader is portrayed as an individual who withdraws from human society to become absorbed in a private world that others cannot share. As Christine Pawley (2002, 144) has said, "Despite recognition that reading is first and foremost a social act, the image of the lone reader still exercises a powerful hold on the imagination." She notes that even work such as Cavallo and Chartier's *History of Reading in the West* (1999), which calls for more attention to reading communities, reinscribes the idea of the young, female, isolated reader by reproducing on its dust jacket Jean Honoré Fragonard's famous painting *Young Girl Reading*. In this painting, a young eighteenth-century girl whose dress and surroundings identify her as a member of an affluent class is sitting alone, her attention engrossed by a tiny book that she holds in her right hand.

Nonreaders are familiar with this image of the solitary reader and sometimes complain about reading, which they see as antisocial—a selfish activity that excludes them, unlike watching television, which is seen as an experience that can be shared. Sometimes readers themselves use reading as a way to create privacy. Macon, the main character in Anne Tyler's *Accidental Tourist,* always carries a very thick book, *Miss McIntosh,* onto planes to deflect conversational overtures from seatmates. Other accounts of reading, such as Lynne Schwartz's *Ruined by Reading* (1996), emphasize the intoxicating pleasure of private, uninterrupted reading.

Histories of reading record how our sense of reading in the last two hundred years or so has been tied to the possibility of privacy—the ability to retreat to a private space of one's own in a dwelling place large enough for such spaces to be found. Jane Eyre, for example, creates a little hidden space for herself behind the red curtains where she can read in privacy. In the twentieth century, central heating and the electric light have made it possible for readers to leave the heat and light of the central hearth and go to separate bedrooms to read their own books. When Jim Trelease advises parents in the *Read-Aloud Handbook* (2001) that a bedside light is one of the crucial elements in making child readers, he wants to expand opportunities for the private kind of reading that happens before the light is turned off at bedtime. In short, when we think of the reader, we tend to think of one reader reading. Hence, when Italo Calvino starts off his wonderful book about reading with an image of the solitary, private reader, he is invoking an image that is widely recognized:

> You are about to begin reading Italo Calvino's new novel, *If on a winter's night a traveler.* Relax. Concentrate. Dispel every other thought. Let the world around you fade. Best to close the door; the TV is always on in the next room. Tell the others right away, "No, I don't want to watch TV!" . . . "I'm reading! I don't want to be disturbed." . . . Or if you prefer, don't say anything; just hope they'll leave you alone.

But that image of the solitary, secluded reader is changing. An activity once thought of as belonging to the private sphere has gone public with a bang. The phenomenon of the Oprah Winfrey Book Club, which burst on the scene in 1996, suddenly gave visibility to the phenomenon of communal reading. As Mary K. Chelton (2001, 31) notes, "When Oprah picks up a new hobby, so does a nation." In the past decade, a spate of books, Web pages, and newspaper articles have appeared to announce, and wonder at, the huge popularity of public readings by authors, online book discussion groups, and the face-to-face book discussions that are sometimes called book clubs in the United States and reading groups elsewhere else. No one knows exactly how many book clubs and reading groups there are, but the answer is clearly "a lot." Jenny Hartley begins her book *Reading Groups* (2001, vii), a report of a survey of 350 such groups in the United Kingdom, with the comment, "Reading groups are the success story of the past few years. . . . No one knows just how many there are; estimates run as high as 50,000 in Britain and 500,000 in America."

Of course, plenty of reading groups had been meeting all along to talk about books—eighteenth-century salons in Paris and nineteenth-century Women's Literary Clubs in North America are only the most well-publicized examples. The Chautauqua Literary and Scientific Circle, for example, enlisted members, mostly women, from small communities in New York, Pennsylvania, Ohio, Illinois, and Iowa who read together in discussion groups. Billing itself as the "oldest continuous book club in the United States," the Chautauqua Literary and Scientific Circle (CLSC) is still active. It was founded in 1878 as an educational experiment in distance learning to promote reading and study among people living in isolated communities. Chautauqua founder John H. Vincent set up a four-year home study course for which participants signed up and read twelve books a year. In the first year, the chosen books included J. R. Green's *A Short*

History of the English People, John Hurst's *Outline of Bible History*, and Henry Warren's *Studies of the Stars*. According to William Zinsser (1992, 147), by 1914, the program had enlisted half a million members in 12,000 circles. The entire CLSC Book List, 1878–2004 is available at www.chautauqua-inst. org/clsc.html.

Elizabeth Long (1986, 1993, 2003) was the first to study reading groups in any serious way. Her long-awaited *Book Clubs* (2003) is a fine-grained study of women's reading groups in Houston, Texas, from the nineteenth century to the present and their role in the everyday lives of women. Similarly, other historians of reading (Gregory 2001) began to see continuities between the contemporary phenomenon of women's reading groups and nineteenth-century women's clubs and literary societies whose members got together to educate themselves and incidentally acquire the organizational and public-speaking skills that allowed them to agitate for causes in the public sphere such as temperance and women's suffrage.

Until the 1990s, however, most group reading activity happened in the private sphere, was invisible to outsiders, and left no physical trace. Typically eight to twelve women would meet once a month for up to twenty-five years in the living rooms of group members, possibly keeping lists of the books they had read and sometimes preparing written reports on the books. Nobody outside of the group itself paid much attention. But now communal reading activity is leaving traces behind—for example, reading groups are posting on Internet sites information about themselves together with their reading lists.

Book club members are appearing on television shows to talk about their favorite books. TVO, the Ontario public broadcasting network, has a regular spot where book club members of all kinds—groups of high school students, work groups from the Cami auto plant, retired teachers—talk about and recommend their favorite books. In short, the reading group has made it big time into the media mainstream. The book club has variously become the setting for the British situation comedy series *The Reading Group,* for Elizabeth Noble's novel *The Reading Group* (2003), and, apparently soon, for a reality television program. Azar Nafisi's *Reading Lolita in Tehran* (2003), which became a *New York Times* number one best seller in its own right, demonstrates that the reading group is a global phenomenon.

Publishers, bookstores, and libraries have also recognized that catering to reading groups can be a good way to connect with readers and to promote books. Penguin Books and Orange Telecommunications have teamed up to sponsor the Penguin/Orange Reading Group Prize, which in 2004 attracted more than seven hundred entries from reading groups across the United Kingdom. The aim of the prize is "to find the reading group that demonstrated the most imaginative and diverse reading as a group." Barnes & Noble has a section of its site dedicated to Book Clubs and provides information on "How to Run a Reading Group" with links to reading group guides.

Enterprising bookstores and public libraries are beginning to promote themselves as important resources for reading groups. Bookstores may offer discounts to reading group members, provide meeting spaces, keep directories of reading groups, display book club selections, and offer help with choosing books. The impact goes beyond the members of the book club itself, because other customers use club selections as recommendations for their own reading. *The Secrets of the Ya-Ya Sisterhood,* which was displayed in the David-Kidd bookstore in Nashville, Tennessee, as the Women's Book Club March selection, sold 310 copies in two months while on display (Burns 1999). Not to be outdone by bookstores, the New York Public Library provides on its Web site listings of some thirty book discussion groups it runs in its branches, together with the list of books being discussed in the next year or so. In the United Kingdom, the Essex Libraries system has taken a pioneering role in reader development with funding from the DCMS/Wolfson Reader Development Programme. It supports more than two hundred "Booktalk" groups and produces a quarterly newsletter for readers and reading groups (askchris.essexcc.gov.uk/Adult/Booktalk.asp).

So what's going on? How did this apparently private pleasure turn into such a social activity? Here are some ways to approach the question.

The Social Infrastructure of Reading

As Elizabeth Long points out in *Book Clubs: Women and the Uses of Reading in Everyday Life* (2003), the social nature of reading is crucial, although rendered invisible by the "cultural hegemony of the solitary reader" (8). In fact, the ability to read is taught within a web of social relations and the practice of reading is sustained by conversations about books. Shelley (student, age twenty-six), an interviewee in Ross's reading study, said, "I'm really interested in what other people are reading. The way I probably pick up most of my reading is from people around me and what they are reading and I want to read it."

Typically children are introduced to the pleasure of reading through the bedtime story and through hearing stories read aloud; they learn to read in classrooms in the context of teacher-directed routines for teaching phonics and "word attack" skills or through whole-language experiences with sharing books. Long (2003, 8–11) refers to this as the "social infrastructure of reading." Once beginning readers have cracked the alphabetic code, they learn strategies of how to make sense of extended text in the context of what Stanley Fish has called "interpretive communities." Interpretive communities share a set of norms and procedures for making sense of texts. An interpretive community might be embodied in a literature class, a graduate seminar, or a long-established reading group but could also be derived from an imagined community of book reviewers, judges of literary awards, or other cultural authorities. Readers learn which kinds of texts are denigrated and which are valued by the culture at large. They know, for example, that romances and westerns are *not* valued; in contrast, reading Booker prizewinners confers prestige and cultural capital on the reader. As Elizabeth

Long (1993, 192) puts it, "collective and institutional processes shape reading practices by authoritatively defining what is worth reading and how to read it."

So learning how to read, what to read, and how to interpret it is socially mediated. But at the same time, reading itself is a means of engagement with the world, as was noted in section 1.3. Shelley, the reader referred to earlier, said "A lot of people think it means you're introverted [if you read]. But I'm an extremely extroverted person and I think that's why I read—because it really connects me with other people and what's in their minds. And that's why I like to read something that someone else is reading, because then it gives you something else to talk about and see if you got the same thing out of it that they got out of it. And, then, reading always relates to real life. I think reading has a lot to do with relating to real life and figuring out what's going on in life and what you want to do with your life. So [reading helps in] making sense of your life."

The report of the 1983 Book Industry Study Group (BISG 1984, 71–73) confirms this connection between reading and social engagement. The BISG study emphasizes that book readers are more active than non-book readers in a wide range of social and cultural activities and implies that reading mediates this engagement with the world: "Book readers are far more likely to socialize (59 percent) than non-book readers (41 percent) or nonreaders (33 percent). . . . Book readers as a group are simply more likely to participate in a whole range of activities than are non-book readers and nonreaders."

Imagined Communities of Readers

Benedict Anderson (1983/91) has coined the term "imagined community" to explain how people who have never met each other can feel part of the same nation state. In particular he was interested in the way that people reading books, newspapers, and novels could feel themselves part of a large group of invisible other readers who were simultaneously reading the same newspaper article or book. Readers have doubtless always been aware, when they read the morning newspaper or a best seller, that they are part of an imagined community of other co-readers. But recently there have been two widely publicized phenomena that have made explicit this theme of imagined communities of readers: Nancy Pearl's "One city, one book" program and Oprah's Book Club.

Nancy Pearl, executive director of the Washington Center for the Book at the Seattle Public Library and reader par excellence, invented the "One city, one book" idea in 1996. That's when she launched what came to be known as "If All of Seattle Read the Same Book." In an interview with the *Orlando Sentinel* held when she was in Orlando for the American Library Association conference in 2004, Nancy Pearl (2004) said that this initiative grew from three strong beliefs:

> I have three very strongly held beliefs about libraries and reading: (1) that libraries should introduce readers to books and authors they might not have read or found out about on their own; (2) that thoughtful discussion of a book can broaden and deepen a person's experience with a

work of literature; and (3) that book discussions—building a common vocabulary through talking about a book—builds a community of readers out of a disparate group of strangers.

By 2002, the American Booksellers Association *Bookselling This Week* reported that more than fifty cities, countries, or states had begun programs to encourage communities to read the same book at the same time and then discuss it at various venues.

The second phenomenon, Oprah's Book Club, has provided an enormous boost to reading. *Salon Books'* New York editorial director Laura Miller (2002) claimed that "Winfrey's book club represented a kind of supercharged word of mouth" that reached 7 million ears daily, an audience that trusted her recommendations because it feels it has a relationship with her. Miller challenges those guardians of elite taste such as Gavin McNett, also writing in *Salon Books,* who takes Oprah to task for recommending books that "play on base sentiment . . . reaffirm popular wisdom . . . and tell readers what they expect to hear" (McNett 1999). Unlike McNett who is offended by Oprah's enormous impact on reading and publishing, Miller recognizes that Oprah was influential because she "presented books first and foremost as a source of pleasure." Says Miller, "Simply put, she helped people who liked the kind of book that she liked find more of that kind of book."

When Oprah's Book Club returned to active status in June 2003 after a lapse of thirteen months, she announced that she would be focusing on classic works of literature. Her first three picks were John Steinbeck's *East of Eden,* Alan Paton's *Cry, The Beloved Country,* and Gabriel Garcia Marquez's *One Hundred Years of Solitude.* Following the announcement of Oprah's pick, Marquez's work of magical realism shot to the Number 1 spot on the Barnes and Noble Hourly Top 100.

In *Reading Oprah,* Cecilia Konchar Farr (2005) claims that Oprah's Book Club has changed the way that America reads. Farr's introductory chapter, "Oprah's Reading Revolution," (2005, 1) starts off with an epigraph from Toni Morrison that includes the following, "Reading is solitary, but that's not its only life. It should have a talking life, a discourse that follows." Farr emphasizes Oprah's role as a teacher of reading, not just "get[ting] American reading again," but teaching readers about the "talking life" of books.

Reading Groups

By the end of 2004, the Google Directory was listing some sixty sites for Reading Groups, including online discussion groups, weblogs of online book clubs, commercial sites such as the NYTimes.com Reading Group, Web pages for groups that meet face-to-face such as "Mostly, We Eat" and even a spoof site, "The Emily Chesley Reading Circle." With so many reading groups needing advice on how to choose appropriate books and how to run discussions, a number of guides have been published to fill the gap—for example, the *Bloomsbury*

Good Reading Guide (Rennison, 2004) and Rachel W. H. Jacobsohn's *The Reading Group Handbook* (1998)—some of which are described later in the suggestions for further reading. As reading lists are exchanged among book clubs, word-of-mouth has been given credit for catapulting previously little-known books such as David Gutterson's *Snow Falling on Cedars* into best sellers.

So what *are* reading groups like anyway? It turns out that reading groups attract people who share a love of book discussion but that they vary in many other respects. In the survey of 350 UK reading groups reported by Jenny Hartley (2001, 155), 69 percent were all-women groups; 27 percent were mixed male and female; and 4 percent were all men. Some groups are quite new, but others have been going for upward of twenty-five years or more. Most reading group members buy their own books, often following a paperback-only rule, but some borrow book group packs from libraries. Some meet in public spaces and are open to all comers—in the UK survey, 6 percent of groups reported meeting in libraries and 16 percent met in other public spaces such as pubs, bars, restaurants, fitness centers, or "a quiet corner of the Royal Festival Hall" and 80 percent met in members' homes (Hartley 2001, 10). Membership in private clubs is by invitation only, typically with new members recruited from friends of existing members. Private book clubs have other restrictions—to take a turn hosting the meeting, would-be members need a sizable home with a living room big enough to accommodate a dozen or so people.

Some well-to-do groups hire a professional reading group leader such as Rachel Jacobsohn, but most share the job of discussion leader among group members, each of whom takes a turn. Some groups treat the book discussion as if it were a well-structured graduate seminar, and others prefer casual, free-flowing conversation that wanders off the chosen book to other books and other topics. Some groups pick their books a whole year in advance, often at the last meeting of the year before breaking for the summer. Others prefer the flexibility of picking books as they go along. Eating and drinking is an important element for many reading groups. One long-time reading group member who had traveled three thousand miles to attend the twenty-fifth anniversary of her reading group advised, "Never have a feminist activity without food." Rachel Jacobsohn's *Reading Group Handbook* includes a whole chapter on food, but some reading group members warn against allowing refreshments to become so elaborate that preparing the food becomes a chore.

The ReadingGroupGuides.com Web site has posted group interviews with reading groups that conveys the diversity of ways of being a book group. For the group interviews, the reading group is invited to provide information on the following: the name/theme of the group, composition of the members, how and where the group meets, whether food is an aspect of meetings, who leads the discussions, how books are chosen, some titles of best picks, advice for other reading groups, and horror stories. Group names frequently capture something of the group identity, as suggested by the following selected examples:

Reading between the Wines—Thirteen women between the ages of twenty-six and forty-something who have been meeting once a month for six years and whose best book was Patricia Gaffney's *The Saving Graces* because they "read it at a time when we were all experiencing life changes of some sort and the book helped us form a bond."

The Bluestockings Book Club—a group with fifty-five members, all women, that meets once a month in the Barnes & Noble bookstore to discuss fiction and nonfiction that foregrounds women's experiences.

Beagle Books Men's Book Club—Eight to ten men who meet in a bookstore to discuss books written by men and for men and "have the best luck with books that are compact, to the point, and have depth."

China Dolls—Eight women who sell porcelain china.

The Monday Afternoon Book Club—composed of eleven women aged fifty and older who mostly "did not know each other before forming our club [in 2002] and now we have become friends."

Sistahs of Color Reading Group—Twenty-seven members ranging in age from twenty-five to early seventies who read African American fiction and nonfiction. Each member shares and discusses the book she is currently reading, and so in a typical meeting "you have been exposed to approximately twenty or more books."

Cantdecide—Nine women between the ages of fifty and sixty-five who have been meeting for twenty-five years to read books they "would not find if left to our own taste."

Sisters Sippin' Tea (SST) Literary Group—the Tulsa Chapter of the SST group, which has chapters across the United States, describes itself as "a sassy group of ladies, and our opinions and attitudes can get quite bold."

Women in Abu Dhabi—a group of eight to twelve expatriate women from around the world who are living in Abu Dhabi.

Girls Night Out of Rochester, New York—composed of three sets of mothers and daughters and ranging in age from sixteen to sixty.

The Inklings—Nine women and "one token man" who meet in a small library to talk about challenging books such as *Ulysses,* Dante's *Inferno,* and *The Canterbury Tales.*

Book Talk

Knowing how to talk about books is a learned skill. For some, the reading group is an extension of the graduate English seminar, where students learn to discuss the literary elements of tone, point of view, imagery, patterned language, and so on. To support this kind of learned literary talk, Rachel Jacobsohn's *The Reading Group Handbook* (1998, 225–32) includes as an appendix a "Glossary of Literary Terms." The glossary includes "terms, definitions, and examples . . . intended to enrich your discussion," from A to Z: allegory, allusion, ambiguity, anachronism, analogical, anticlimax, antihero, archetype, and so on up to verisimilitude and zeitgeist. In the nineteenth-century book clubs that Elizabeth Long (2003, 68) reports on, each woman took turns presenting a book at a meeting, spending long hours in advance preparing a report that analyzed the book as a literary artifact.

Contemporary reading groups tend to be more informal, with the discussion leader providing only a short introduction to the author and the book before initiating the discussion with an open question such as, "Well, what did you think about the book?" Nevertheless the concern remains for some that what they think about the book won't be the *right* things. Shelley (student, twenty-six), quoted earlier as loving to talk about books, said, "Yeah, I would love to join a book club." But she hasn't joined one so far because she is worried her book talk won't measure up: "I'm so afraid to join one because I'm afraid that the people in it would know a lot about books and be very well read. And the things I would have to say about them probably wouldn't sound too intelligent. I still have this really bad fear that when I read something, I don't understand it as much as other people." However, not every book club privileges an analytical discussion of the book itself. In her critical ethnography of a romance reading group, Linda Griffin (1999, 144, 160) describes how the group members she observed resisted attempts by a bookstore employee and would-be group discussion leader to have a focused discussion in "an orderly fashion," preferring instead to exchange books and provide brief recommendations ("What did you think of Barbara Delinsky's book?" "That was great." "I loved that one.").

Recognizing that some readers need the reassurance of learning a common language to talk about books, many publishers including Ballantine, Harcourt Brace, HarperCollins, Penguin, Random House, Signet, and Vintage have begun producing "reading guides." These guides consist minimally of lists of questions designed to foster good discussion, and sometimes they also include information about the author, prizes the book may have won, and excerpts from reviews. The ReadingGroupGuides.com site makes available in a single place more than 1,500 reading group guides that were contributed by each book's publisher. This site, which bills itself as "the online community for reading groups," provides a place for reading groups to register, transcripts of interviews with reading group spokespersons, and, of course, the reading group guides.

The questions provided in the reading group guides are clues to what the publishers think make a book discussible. The reading guide for Ann Pachett's *Bel Canto* provided on the HarperCollins readinggroups.co.uk site provides three questions about the book as "starting points," including "Do you think it's possible to fall in love with someone to whom you cannot speak directly?" and "What do you think of the novel's ending?" On the same site, the reading guide for Tracey Chevalier's *Girl with a Pearl Earring* asks, "In what ways have your perceptions of Vermeer's painting changed as a result of reading Chevalier's book?" The Bloomsbury.com/ReadersGroups Web site recommends that discussion leaders use a set of questions that "provide a framework for a focussed discussion"—either questions from reading group guides or generic questions such as:

- What is the story about?

- How does the story develop?

- What message is the author trying to get across?

- Who are the main characters? Do they change over the course of the book?

- How important is the author's use of language?

- Does the book have any relevance to your own experience?

- Does the book remind you of anything else you've read?

While paying attention to the literary elements of plot and character development, theme and language, these questions also validate readers in making connections between the fictional world and their own lives. The goal seems to be to create a discussion framework that strikes a good balance between literary analysis and personal discovery.

Elizabeth Long (2003, 145–6) notes that although reading groups defer to cultural authorities in their book choices, they tend to be more subversive in their actual discussions: "Participants talk about books with deep engagement, but very differently than literary professionals do, and they sometimes interpret characters and evaluate novels with marked disregard for critics' opinion. . . . [W]omen often expand on an opinion by discussing their personal reasons for making a certain interpretation, using the book for self-understanding and revelation of the self to other participants rather than for discovery of meaning within the book."

Reading groups that meet regularly for a long time with the same members gradually teach themselves a common language for talking about books. With each new book that they read, they develop a set of commonly shared literary experiences that can function as a reference point for a new book ("Well at least it's not as bad as *The Beans of Egypt, Maine!*"). In *Reading Lolita in Tehrah*, Azar Nafisi (2003, 21) illustrates the development of a commonly shared language of literary allusions with the example of "upsilamba," a made-up word from Nabokov's *Invitation to a Beheading* that the reading group came to associate with creativity and freedom: "*Upsilamba* became part of our increasing repository of coded words and expressions, a repository that grew over time until gradually we had created a secret language of our own."

Choosing Books

Just as readers who say that they "read anything" usually turn out to mean anything but *not* romances/war stories/nonfiction (see section 4.7), in the same way reading groups who say they read anything actually exclude whole categories such as plays, poetry, and avant-garde fiction (Poole 2000). Elizabeth Long (2003, 119) says, "groups usually do not deal with either end of the literary spectrum: most do not read poetry, plays or difficult postmodernist novels, and if they do, they will mention it proudly. At the other end, groups rarely even consider genre books to be part of the relevant literary universe." According to Long (2003, 118), "No mainstream group considers romances, for example, to be discussable." Similarly Jenny Hartley (2001, 63) reports that reading groups give poor ratings to genre books: "Crime fiction, courtroom dramas, and romantic fiction have been judged too lightweight, affording too little to discuss. 'We have joked about Elmore Leonard for years,' commented an American group on a bad choice." Rejecting this hierarchical positioning that devalues genre books, some reading groups do of course focus exclusively on mysteries or science fiction or romance, considering books in these genres to be discussable even if the cultural authorities might not count what they say as genuine discussion.

The majority of books chosen by reading groups are what booksellers call literary fiction leavened with a sprinkling of classics. For example, in its April 2004 poll, when the ReadingGroupGuides.com site asked, "Which of the following has your group read, or do you plan to read?" 1,129 voters responded. The top seven picks were as follows:

1. *The Secret Life of Bees* by Sue Monk Kidd

2. *The Da Vinci Code* by Dan Brown

3. *The Red Tent* by Anita Diamant

4. *The Girl with a Pearl Earring* by Tracy Chevalier

5. *The Lovely Bones* by Alice Sebold

6. *Bel Canto* by Ann Patchett

7. *Life of Pi* by Yann Martel

There is a consensus among the discussion group experts as well as among book club members themselves that a good book for a reading group has certain defined qualities, particularly "discussibility." After warning that "picking good books for your group can also be intimidating," the ReadingGroupGuides.com Web site advises, "You want the perfect book: one that's not too easy, not too hard, that will hold the interest of a diverse group of readers and will also inspire a lively discussion." So what kinds of books are considered discussible? The advice offered by the Women in Abu Dhabi reading group is this: "Don't confuse a book that is a 'good read' with one that will be good to discuss. The difficult books often yield the best discussions." One of the pleasures of the reading group discussion is the discovery that other people's experiences with a book can be dramatically different from your own. This means that the ideal book club book needs to be complex enough to support different responses and interpretations. Books don't have to be well liked, or liked by everyone, to sustain a good discussion. Jenny Hartley (2001, 80) reports one book group's response: "*Fugitive Pieces*: some loved it; others hated it. It provoked real debate."

The pattern of production of book discussion guides suggests the types of books that the publishers themselves consider to constitute the genre of the "reading group book." On the ReadingGroupGuides site, there is an alphabetical listing of the authors for whom reading group guides have been written. Looking just at authors with names beginning with A and B, we can see that the following authors have had guides written for at least three of their books: Isabel Allende, Maya Angelou, Kate Atkinson, Margaret Atwood, Elizabeth Berg, Chris Bohjalian, Frederick Busch, Octavia Butler, and A. S. Byatt. There seems to be close agreement between the group guide publishers and the reading groups themselves on what constitutes a good pick. In the UK survey of 350 reading groups reported by Jenny Hartley (2001, 152), the top-ten authors read by groups were as follows: Louis de Bernieres (read by eighty-three groups), Frank McCourt (read by seventy-one), Ian McEwan (sixty-eight), Arundhati Roy (fifty-eight), Margaret Atwood (fifty), Anne Tyler (forty-five), Beryl Bainbridge (forty-five), Kate Atkinson (forty-three), Sebastian Faulks (forty-one), and Charles Frazier (forty-one).

Certain books such as *Captain Corelli's Mandolin* and *Angela's Ashes* turn up repeatedly on lists of reading group picks because readers want to read what other people are reading and be part of a community of readers. But Jenny Hartley (2001, 66–67) points out that groups also want to have their own identity, which they confirm through individual choices. Of the 1,160 titles mentioned by the reading groups in the UK survey, 882 or 76 percent had been read by one group only.

Evidently reading group books can be best sellers, but not all best sellers are considered good reading group choices. Long (2003, 118) makes the case that the taken-for-granted assumptions about which books are worth discussing show that reading groups generally accept the cultural authority of arbiters of literary taste such as reviewers, awards committees and professors. In their advice to book club members, the ReadingGroupGuides site reinforces distinctions based on a hierarchy of taste: "Lists of award winners and nominees such as the Pulitzer Prize, the Mann-Booker Prize and the National Book Award can provide your group with many quality suggestions."

It's a plus for readers when their reading choices have the stamp of approval of what Bourdieu (1984) calls "professional valuers." But not all prizewinners make good reading group choices either. Books that distance the reader from all the characters are usually rejected. A question commonly asked in group reading guides goes something like, "Which of the characters did you most identify with or feel closest to?" If the answer is "none of them," then it's usually "game over" for that book. Jenny Hartley (2001, 132–3) says that there is a "striking consensus" in the comments made by reading groups that they put a high premium on "empathy, the core reading-group value. . . . The failure of reader-character empathy is what doomed Beryl Bainbridge's *Every Man for Himself,* the title itself so anti-group in its sentiments." Agreeing on the importance of empathetic characters, Elizabeth Long (2003, 153) says that participants' responses to characters "become a prism for the interrogation of self, other selves, and society beyond the text."

Reading Communities: What Makes Book Discussion Groups So Popular?

"The real, hidden subject of a book group discussion is the book group members themselves," Margaret Atwood is quoted as saying in the epigraph to Elizabeth Noble's novel *The Reading Group* (2003). Atwood's insight is the theme of Karen Joy Fowler's *The Jane Austen Book Club,* which is a novel about how readers engage with fiction. The five women and one man who are members of the "Central Valley/ River City all-Jane-Austen-all-the-time book club" meet to discuss the six Jane Austen novels but end up talking about themselves, each seeing the novels through the lens of her or his own life. In a successful reading group, the book and the group itself are almost equally balanced as draws. When book club members are asked what attracts them, they say, "the group of people" and "the talk about books" almost in the same breath.

When pressed further, reading group members say that being in a book club does the following:

- It gives status to the act of reading.

- It validates your spending time reading the books you enjoy and thus counters implied criticism of your reading tastes by nonreaders, husbands, and sometimes reading elites.

- It gets you out of the rut of your usual book choices and expands literary horizons by introducing you to new authors and unfamiliar genres you would never have read on your own.

- It provides helpful scaffolding in helping you stretch beyond your usual reading because you get a deeper understanding of the book when you talk with others about it.

- It gets you reading in a more reflective way.

- It provides an opportunity to compare your own interpretations with others, providing a diversity of perspectives and opinions.

- It's a supportive environment that gives you confidence in yourself as a reader and in your ability to learn.

- It's a way of learning about yourself and others.

- It provides a way of meeting a diverse group of new people who eventually become friends in the course of sharing booktalk and talk about their lives.

- And finally, the experience of meeting on a regular basis with an interesting group of fellow readers provides a high in itself. Club members talk of leaving the meeting with their minds racing, full of ideas sparked from the discussion.

Seasoned reading groups that have been meeting for many years talk about the evolution that happens as individuals who come together to discuss books come to know each other in the context of their reading. Initial meetings may be fairly stiff, but after a while members learn to trust each other and eventually risk self-disclosure. One avid reader, Nancy, who has belonged to two book groups for more than twelve years—one group for couples and one all-woman group—says that people are unprotected when talking about books: what they say "comes from the core" and they show you their "unshelled self." Therefore you can know longtime reading group members at a deeper level than is usually the case, Nancy thinks.

The "Hooked on Books Group" from Wickham Bishops, Essex, England, explains how this works. This group posted a statement about reading on the "Reading Lives" page of the Essex Libraries Web site:

> Funny how books have an extraordinary way of relating to an individual reader for one reason or another. This has become evident in the past year, our third as a reading group. A year in which we have had more than our share of personal adversities. On beginning we knew little of each other's lives nor did we know if we would "gel" as a group. I will give you an example of what I mean. One of our ladies (we are nine in all) is coping with a difficult illness in her family. A book by Rohinton Mistry *Family Matters* tells of a lovely man living in Bombay who suffers a debilitating illness which eventually forces him against his will to take up residence with a step-daughter. The minutiae of the family life and struggles this story conveyed enlightened us to a greater understanding of our friend's difficulties." (askchris.essexcc.gov.uk/Adult/Readinglives.asp)

Research Tells Us

Four doctoral theses have examined women's reading groups in four settings: Victoria, Australia (Howie 1998); Houston, Texas (Griffin 1999); St. Louis, Missouri (Gregory 2001); and Vancouver, British Columbia (Sedo 2004). Studying St. Louis women's Literary Societies in the late nineteenth and early twentieth centuries and comparing them with contemporary book clubs in St. Louis, Gregory says, "The evidence shows that book clubs have changed in their group structure, methods of accumulating cultural capital and the arbitration of taste, and in women's use of the clubs for affiliation, accommodation and resistance." However, some things have not changed. All four researchers found that women use book clubs to achieve social, intellectual, and spiritual growth. Howie found that the "ritual" of the book club provided a safe, women-only space for personal change and self-understanding. Sedo found that there is an interpretive community dimension to a reading group that unfolds over time among a community of learners. Additionally, in the romance reading group that Griffin studied, members also found validation through social interaction with other romance readers who shared their love of a genre that is widely stigmatized and denigrated.

What Libraries Can Do

1. Cater to reading groups. Make the local library the first place that reading group members look when they want a space to meet or suggestions for appropriate books to read or copies of the chosen book or background information on the book and its author.

2. Create an area in your library where you have assembled the tools to help people start a book club and then find suitable books for their group. This can be as simple as several shelves, with clear signage, that display books on book clubs. Because of the huge popularity of reading groups, many books have been published to cater to this audience.

Case 24: "After that first meeting, we never looked back."

On January 19, 1994, on a night of record-breaking cold, Catherine Ross went to the house where the January book discussion meeting was being held. The group had finished discussing its book (by Canadian author Michael Ignatieff) and was on to the wine-and-cheese and vegetable dip stage. Ten women were present, almost perfect attendance—impressive given the extreme cold of the evening. This group had been meeting regularly, ten times a year for six years. This account is a verbatim, unedited transcript of what was said. However it doesn't convey the dynamics of the group discussion, which was often a bit like a string quartet, where someone would start a thought and two or three would chime in to complete the thought, to agree, or qualify or extend the thought. As discussion leader, Ross's role was quite limited. Most of the discussion was carried in a free-flowing way, back and forth (and sometimes simultaneously), among the group members themselves.

Ross: *One of the things that interests me is this. What does being in a book club provide to its members that you wouldn't get by just reading the book at home?*

— Seven or eight people to discuss what you have thoroughly enjoyed or thoroughly hated gives you the chance to see if other people's viewpoints match yours.

— It's the sharing.

— I really like it because it's a different group of people than I usually come in contact with. I go to meetings at this or that organization, but I don't have a chance to sit down and just discuss ideas, or issues, or relationships. This is a group of people who are interested in finding out what makes people tick.

— We pull out different snippets from each book, favorite things.

— It brings the book alive again and makes you think about it all over again.

— This is just my second year. I've always read. I've read and read. But I've never discussed a book with anybody before. Sometimes I'd read a book and want to talk to somebody about it, but I never did. And now that I come here it's great, because everybody talks about the book.

— Out in the real world, there aren't very many readers out there. You say, "Have you read the latest Margaret Atwood?" and they look at you blankly. People don't have time or aren't interested. I'm like Sheila; I would read over anything else. If you went to my house during the day and I wasn't doing anything, I'd be sitting there reading. You feel like you're being caught. [laughter] "Oh, no, I wasn't on the couch reading. I was really vacuuming!"

— You feel guilty. But now I can say to my boyfriend, "I have to read this book for my book club." And it's just an excuse, isn't it? [laughter]

— One of the things it did for me was—I was an English major. So everything that I had read, I'd been taking it apart into pieces and analyzing it. I was really tired of doing that.

So it was really good to get back into reading just for enjoyment—I didn't have to write essays and I didn't have to figure out the workings of it. I could just read it to enjoy it. And I could still discuss it—I just wasn't discussing plots and themes. . .

— But you still do. [Everyone agrees, saying, "You do! You do!"]

— I do, but not in the same analytical way.

[People say variously at once: It's not as intense. No one's marking you. You're not right or wrong.]

— You get the same insights you might get in class.

— You get *more* insights. But there's no pressure.

— I had the opposite feeling, because I loved my classes and I missed it when I finished. So I thought, "Where can I get that again?"

— I was telling a long-standing, since-we-were-babies, friend, that I was joining a book club and she said, "You always do things that are so intelligent." [laughter]

— I think that's part of it. For me, I like reading a book and I like using my head to think about it and I like to relate it to my own experience and see how you relate the book to your own experience. It's an affirmative experience.

— The other thing is we have a comfortable group. People may not like it, but they're not going to say you're stupid for suggesting this book.

— We were not as open with each other the first year. The first few meetings were very subdued.

— I don't ever remember that. By the time I came in, everybody was talking. Everybody came in and you rolled up your shirtsleeves and got down to it.

— I remember the very first meeting that nobody said very much.

— And after that, we never looked back.

— Obviously now we feel comfortable with each other.

— Yes, we can agree to disagree, without feeling threatened.

— Yes, people don't get hurt, if we disagree.

— I always come away [from book club discussions] with my mind racing.

— That's right, I can hardly sleep. [laughter]

— Generally it's the wine that does this. [laughter]

— I think so. I agree with that. I've known these people for a long time, and yet people are always surprising me.

— In different ways. Like you go home after a meeting and you think "I've never thought about that before."

— But even just names of authors. That's not a minor thing. Like somebody giving you the name of an author where you can read five or six books. That's an amazing thing that I don't think I could get on my own.

Comments

In these reflections, a concatenation of reasons emerge for valuing the reading group experience: the sharing of different experiences and perspectives as each person reads the book in the context of her own life; the validation of reading—this is not just a selfish pleasure but a serious obligation—in the face of other people's demands on the reader's time; the exhilaration of debating new and challenging ideas in a comfortable, nonthreatening environment; the replication of the graduate seminar in a more relaxed setting; and the cachet of doing something seen to be "intelligent."

To Read More on Running a Reading Group

Balcom, Ted. 1992. *Book Discussions for Adults: A Leader's Guide.* Chicago and London: American Library Association.

A useful guide written by a leader in the promotion of books and readers' advisory in libraries.

Jacobsohn, Rachel W. 1998. *The Reading Group Handbook: Everything You Need to Know to Start Your Own Book Club.* Rev. ed. New York: Hyperion.

A professional reading group leader, Rachel Jacobsohn has drawn on more than twenty years of experience for this handbook, which includes tips in chapters such as "What Makes a Good Member" (conscientious people who come to the meeting having read the book and who can strike a happy medium in discussion between being too quiet and too talkative), "Rachel's Rules of Order" (no smoking, no lateness, no children, no pets), and "Food" (keep it simple or eat later). Includes suggested reading lists culled from reading groups around the country.

Laskin, David, and Holly Hughes. 1995. *The Reading Group Book: The Complete Guide to Starting and Sustaining a Reading Group.* New York: Penguin.

> Laskin and Hughes begin by asking, "Why do you want to start a club?" and "What kind of books do you want to read?" They cover all the basics for getting the most out of the group-reading experience and provide a section on "Troubleshooting" on how to cope with pitfalls. Includes a list of 250 good picks together with annotations on what makes these books good for generating provocative discussion.

Pearlman, Mickey. 1994. *What to Read: The Essential Guide for Reading Group Members and Other Book Lovers.* New York: HarperCollins.

> This is a book of lists—thirty-three annotated lists of books organized by categories such as "Family Feuds," "Southern Comfort," "Gay Writes," "Science Fiction by Women" and "la, la, la, It's Magic."

Rennison, Nick. 2004. *Bloomsbury Good Reading Guide*: *What to Read and What to Read Next*, 6th ed. London: Bloomsbury Press.

> Provides short articles on more than 350 major authors "from Margaret Atwood to Emile Zola," alphabetically arranged. Each article includes a "Read On" section that directs readers to other books with similar themes.

Saal, Rollene. 1995. *The New York Public Library Guide to Reading Groups.* New York: Crown.

> Drawing on the New York Public Library's experience over the years with hundreds of reading groups, Rollene Saal provides advice on getting a book club started, choosing appropriate books, and leading good discussions, including ways of dealing with problematic members such as the "Book Hog" and "Shy Tillie." Includes more than seventy pages of annotated lists of recommended titles.

To Read More on the Study Of Reading Groups and Book Clubs

Chelton, Mary K. 2001. "When Oprah Meets E-mail: Virtual Book Clubs." *Reference & User Services Quarterly* 41, no. 1 (fall): 31–36.

> Examines the differences between face-to-face and virtual book clubs with special emphasis on the role of libraries in supporting such groups. Provides lists of selected Web sites and books that are resources for reading groups.

Hartley, Jenny. 2001. *Reading Groups.* Oxford, England: Oxford University Press.

> Together with Sarah Turvey, Jenny Hartley surveyed 350 reading groups in England and reports what the readers told them about who belongs (69 percent are all-female groups), how groups choose what they read ("with difficulty"), how groups talk about books (the most successful discussions happen when there is a variety of interpretations and opinions about the book), and which books are chosen (an appendix includes nine reading lists and a menu).

Long, Elizabeth. 2003. *Book Clubs: Women and the Uses of Reading in Everyday Life.* Chicago: University of Chicago Press.

> Written by a sociologist who has studied reading groups for twenty years by recording their meetings and interviewing readers, this book focuses on seventy-seven women's book groups in Houston, Texas, and the reading practices of

women who often described their book club as a lifeline, a crucial form of connection with others, and a saving grace.

Nafisi, Azar. 2003. *Reading Lolita in Tehran: A Memoir in Books.* New York: Random House.

This nonfiction book tells how Azar Nafisi and seven of her former students met at her home in Tehran every Thursday to discuss forbidden works of Western literature such as *Pride and Prejudice*, *Daisy Miller* and *Lolita* in the context of their own lives. "There, in that living room, we rediscovered that we were also living, breathing human beings; and no matter how repressive the state became, no matter how intimidated and frightened we were, like Lolita we tried to escape and to create our own little pockets of freedom."

References

American Booksellers Association. 2002. "Following Seattle's Read: Citywide Book Clubs Sprout Up Throughout the US." *Bookselling This Week.* March 13, 2002. Available at http://news.bookweb.org/news/306.html (accessed December 4, 2004).

Anderson, Benedict. 1983. *Imagined Communities: Reflections on the Origins and Spread of Nationalism.* Revised edition, London and New York: Verso, 1991.

Balcom, Ted. 1992. *Book Discussions for Adults: A Leader's Guide.* Chicago: American Library Association.

Book Industry Study Group. 1984. *1983 Consumer Research on Reading and Book Purchasing. Focus on Adults.* New York: Market Facts.

Bourdieu, Pierre. 1984. *Distinction: A Social Critique of the Judgement of Taste.* Cambridge, MA: Harvard University Press.

Burns, Kelli S. 1999. "The Bookstore Reading Group: Members, Support, and Benefits." Submitted to the Qualitative Studies Division of the Association for Education in Journalism and Mass Communication (AEJMC) for the 1999 convention in New Orleans. Available at http://list.msu.edu/cgi-bin/wa?A2=ind9909e&L= aejmc&F=&S=&P=590 (accessed June 16, 2005).

Calvino, Italo. 1986. *If on a Winter's Night a Traveller.* Translated by William Weaver. Toronto: Lester & Orpen Dennys.

Cavallo, Guglielmo, and Roger Chartier, eds. 1999. *A History of Reading in the West.* Translated by Lydia G. Cochrane. Oxford, England: Polity.

Crowley, Bill. 2004. "A History of Readers' Advisory Service in the Public Library." In *Nonfiction Readers' Advisory*, 3–29. Edited by Robert Burgin. Westport, CT: Libraries Unlimited.

Farr, Cecilia Konchar. 2005. *Reading Oprah: How Oprah's Book Club Changed the Way America Reads.* Albany: State University of New York Press.

Fish, Stanley. 1980. *Is There a Text in This Class? The Authority of Interpretive Communities.* Cambridge, MA: Harvard University Press.

Fowler, Karen Joy. 2004. *The Jane Austen Book Club.* New York: Putnam.

Gregory, Patricia Lehan. 2001. "Women's Experience of Reading in St. Louis Book Clubs (Missouri)." Ph.D. diss., Saint Louis University, St. Louis, Missouri.

Griffin, Linda Coleman. 1999. "An Analysis of Meaning Creation through the Integration of Sociology and Literature: A Critical Ethnography of a Romance Reading Group." Ph.D. diss., University of Houston and Rice University, Texas.

Hartley, Jenny. 2001. *Reading Groups*. Oxford, England: Oxford University Press.

Howie, L. 1998. "Speaking Subjects: A Reading of Women's Book Groups." Unpublished Ph.D. thesis. Latrobe University, Bundora, Australia.

Jacobsohn, Rachel W. 1998. *The Reading Group Handbook: Everything You Need to Know to Start Your Own Book Club*. Rev. ed. New York: Hyperion.

Long, Elizabeth. 1986. "Women, Reading, and Cultural Authority: Some Implications of the Audience Perspective in Cultural Studies." *American Quarterly* 38, no. 4 (Autumn): 591–612.

Long, Elizabeth. 1993. "Textual Interpretation as Collective Action." In *The Ethnography of Reading*, 180–211. Edited by Jonathan Boyarin. Berkeley and Los Angeles: University of California Press.

Long, Elizabeth. 2003. *Book Clubs: Women and the Uses of Reading in Everyday Life*. Chicago and London: University of Chicago Press.

McNett, Gavin. 1999. "Reaching to the Converted." *Salon Books* (November 12). Available at http://www.salon.com/books/feature/1999/11/12/oprahcon/index.html (accessed June 15, 2005).

Miller, Laura. 1999. "Shopping for Community: The Transformation of the Bookstore into a Vital Community Institution." *Media, Culture and Society* 21: 385-407.

Miller, Laura. 2002. "After Oprah." *Salon Books* (April 18). Available at http://www.salon.com/books/feature/2002/04/18/oprah/?x (accessed June 15, 2005).

Noble, Elizabeth. 2003. *The Reading Group*. London: Hodder & Stoughton.

Pawley, Christine. 2002. "Seeking 'Significance': Actual Readers, Specific Reading Communities." *Book History* 5: 143–60.

Pearl, Nancy. 2004. "Five Questions with . . . Nancy Pearl, author." *Orlando Sentinel*, Sunday June 27, F2.

Poole, Marilyn. 2000. "Between the Covers: Women's Reading Groups." Sociological Sites/Sights. TASA 2000 Conference, December 6–8, 2000, pp. 1–9. Adelaide: Flinders University, South Australia.

Sedo, DeNel. 2004. "Badges of Wisdom: Reading Clubs in Canada." Ph.D. diss., Simon Fraser University, Vancouver, British Columbia.

Trelease, Jim. 2001. *The Read-Aloud Handbook*. London: Penguin.

Zinsser, William. 1992. *American Places: A Writer's Pilgrimage to 15 of This Country's Most Visited and Cherished Sites*. New York: HarperCollins.

In Conclusion:
Reading Becomes You

At the 2005 American Library Association midsummer conference in Chicago, I bought a packet of fifty bookmarks bearing the message, "Reading . . . It Becomes You." Of course it's a pun. Reading shows you off in a flattering light—just as wearing a becoming article of clothing does. But more important, reading enters into you and becomes you. You are what you read and through reading you discover who you are. All the stories, all the plots, all the words, all the fictional people, all the information about people, and places encountered in books—they settle into your memory, layer upon layer, to be drawn on later. One of the interviewees in Ross's study, Ivor, summed it up when he said, "whenever I read, I feel as though I'm assimilating what I read into this—almost like a one-man folk memory" (graduate student, age twenty-six).

Which is why we felt encouraged, just as we were finishing this book, by a new national study on reading for pleasure sponsored by Heritage Canada that surveyed a random sample of 1,963 Canadians, sixteen years of age and older. Unlike the 2004 National Endowment for the Arts (NEA) study *Reading at Risk,* which classified reading among the endangered species (see section 1.3 on Myths about Reading), the Canadian study *Reading and Buying Books for Pleasure* found pleasure reading holding its own among all age groups. In this survey, 87 percent of those polled said that they read at least one book a year and about half, or 54 percent, said that they read for pleasure almost every day. Heavy readers, who read more than fifty books a year, make up 13 percent of the Canadian population. Here are two prominent findings from the study (Heritage Canada 2005, 4) that tackle head-on the myth of the death of reading:

> Contrary to certain alarmist claims that there is a trend towards a lower reading rate in our society or that the Internet has had harmful effects on reading habits, this national survey has shown that reading for pleasure remains a solidly established and widespread habit with little or no change over the last fifteen years.

> Contrary to a widely held fear or belief, there is nothing to indicate that the incredible popularity of the Internet, video games, chatting over the Internet, and downloaded music has impinged on the rate of, and time devoted to, reading.

As we have seen, other myths about reading are yielding to new research-based insights. We know that our understanding of what reading is and what it means to read needs to be expanded to include a variety of formats and a variety of activities from a baby's chiming in on Patty-cake to a scholar's poring over a document. We know that reading begins almost at birth and is a lifelong activity. We know that what reading means to an individual reader changes over the course of a reading life, as more books and stories and materials make up the reader's repertoire. We also know that it's never too late to start reading for pleasure. Although many, perhaps the majority, of avid readers come from reading families, some others come late to reading, often introduced to the pleasure of the text by a reading mentor. The gift of reading can best be given by another reader, who models what it is like to get pleasure from reading.

This new research on reading is reassuring for librarians, parents, and teachers alike. For librarians, it legitimates what you are doing to support reading for pleasure as a central function of a public library. You can stop feeling apologetic when it turns out that the biggest use of your collection is by readers who borrow popular fiction. For parents, the research confirms that you have unrecognized expertise and naturally do the things that research has shown to be critical: reading stories aloud in a context where stories are treats to be savored and prolonged at bedtime and not tests to be evaluated. You can also stop worrying over those series books that your child is consuming voraciously, one after the other; they are teaching him or her crucial lessons in reading. For many beginning readers, series books are an important part of their apprenticeship in reading. For community members, the research confirms that the activities that booklovers do naturally all the time anyway—giving books as gift, borrowing books from the library for other family members, talking about books with friends—are important in keeping others among the community of readers. For teachers, the research confirms the importance of making time for voluntary free reading, by which we mean giving readers the chance to *choose* what they want to read. It also confirms the value of reading aloud, not just in the early years of elementary school but right on into high school.

For the avid reader, reflecting on reading is a pleasure in itself—which explains the mini-boom in books by readers who report on their reading experiences, book clubs, book recommendations, and the like. We hope our readers find this book useful in their own reflections on reading and why they find reading such a lifelong source of pleasure.

References

Department of Canadian Heritage. 2005. *Reading and Buying Books for Pleasure: 2005 National Survey.* Final Report (CH44-51/2005E). Available at http://www.canadianheritage.gc.ca/study/pdf/study.pdf (accessed July 12, 2005).

National Endowment for the Arts. 2004. *Reading at Risk: A Survey of Literary Reading in America.* Research Division Report #46. Washington, DC. Available at http://www.nea.gov/news/news04/ReadingAtRisk.html. (Accessed June 16, 2005).

Name and Subject Index

Title Index

This index lists titles of books cited in *Reading Matters*, along with author and date of publication. These are indexed to the pages on which the book or its findings are discussed, and one page on which a full citation can be found. Article titles are not indexed.

About the Authors

CATHERINE SHELDRICK ROSS, Professor and Dean of the school of Library and Information Studies, University of Western Ontario, teaches a course in readers' advisory, and is involved in ongoing research on reading for pleasure.

LYNNE (E. F.) MCKECHNIE, Associate Professor at the school of Library and Information Studies, University of Western Ontario, is conducting a longitudinal study of the role of the public library in the lives of 30 children.

PAULETTE M. ROTHBAUER, Assistant Professor, University of Toronto, has done extensive research on adolescent readers and the role of pleasure-reading in the discovery of identity. She is the winner of the Eugene Garfield Dissertation Competition.